The Reformation

PROBLEMS IN EUROPEAN CIVILIZATION

Under the editorial direction of
John Ratté
Amherst College

The Reformation

Basic Interpretations

Second Edition

Edited and with an introduction by

Lewis W. Spitz
Stanford University

D. C. HEATH AND COMPANY
Lexington, Massachusetts   Toronto   London

Published simultaneously in Canada.

Printed in the United States of America.

International Standard Book Number: 0-669-81620-5

Library of Congress Catalog Card Number: 72-2273

CONTENTS

                                                                v

INTRODUCTION

It was a historian of the Reformation, Lord Acton, who pronounced the dictum that history should concentrate on problems and not on periods. The question of the essential nature of the Reformation and how it came to be what it was seems as obvious a historical problem as the decline of the Roman Empire or the inevitability of the American Civil War. Like them and all other historical events of first magnitude, however, it proves upon closer examination to be protean and elusive, difficult to grasp even with all the aids of technical history. It twists in our hands and we find ourselves examining its parts, the cultural, economic, political, social, intellectual, or religious aspects, without comprehending the phenomenon itself in either its totality or its inner meaning. This fact caused the distinguished Cambridge historian Herbert Butterfield to wonder whether technical history can claim to give us the mirror of life any more than modern physics provides us with an actual picture of the universe, especially since almost by the rules of the game so much of the spiritual life of man seems to be left to evaporate. It is paradoxical, in fact, that nature seems to be more unambiguously susceptible to human understanding and control than is history which man makes and in which he is personally and intimately involved.

The interpretation of the Reformation is particularly challenging to the historian. It was clearly the most decisive event of the sixteenth century, the first major movement of the post-Gutenberg era. Mountains of material are available for the study of almost all its phases, and the leading protagonist, Luther, was himself an open and accessible personality. Moreover, as a religious movement in the first instance with ramifications for all areas of life, it is a particularly useful case study of the relative significance of the spiritual and material forces in history. Because so many of the religious questions involved touch upon conscience, deep emotion, and firm conviction, the professional historian feels a special challenge to achieve objectivity and impartiality. Leopold von Ranke, the father of modern critical history, was, in fact, moved to write both a history of the Reformation and a history of the popes in order to demonstrate his transcendence over partisan polemics. Since his day historical scholarship has made tremendous advances, but challenging basic problems still remain, among them the analysis of the Reformation in terms of its material and spiritual causes and components. In the first selection Roland Bainton, a leading authority in the field, outlines some of the main currents in the historiography of the Reformation and identifies the positions of various historians on problems of interpretation.

One of the most complex and perplexing questions is that of ordering the Reformation within the total historical development from medieval to modern times. The vast literature on the Renaissance in historical thought is almost all relevant, at least conversely, to the interpretation of the Reformation. The classic debate on the relationship of the Reformation to the Renaissance and the significance of each for the decisive emergence of the modern world was that between Wilhelm Dilthey and Ernst Troeltsch early in the present century as to whether or not the Reformation was the religious expression of the Renaissance. Many of the older authorities had tended to assimilate the Reformation to the Renaissance, seeing it simply as the German expression of the same cultural phenomenon. Another view saw both as parallel national movements, differing in character, but each making its special contribution to the modern world. Dilthey, one of the great intellectual historians of modern times, saw both as parts of a general European struggle for intellectual liberty. He traced their common origins to the ascendancy of urban life, the progress of industry and commerce, the rise of the bourgeoisie, and the formation of modern states. In Germany, he held, this rediscovery of the world and of man took the form of a demand for ecclesiastical reform and a new inwardness in religion. The Reformation freed man from ecclesiastical domination; gave man an inner liberty also against the power of external environment;

directed his moral energy toward work in secular life; and thus, breaking decisively with the medieval world, contributed together with the Renaissance to the rise of modernity.

Dilthey's critic, Ernst Troeltsch, theologian and pioneer in the sociology of religion, became the central figure in the controversy which has continued beyond his death down to the present time. In a number of essays, one of which is represented here, he argued that the Reformation produced essentially an authoritarian ecclesiastical culture analogous to that of the Middle Ages. In its most important aspects, he held, it was more medieval than modern, more religious than secular, more supernaturalist and transcendent than this-worldly and immanent, more spiritual than material. He believed that the Reformation was fundamentally opposed to the Renaissance and that it contributed in no important way to the rise of the modern world. It is obvious that the extent to which Jacob Burckhardt's conception of the Renaissance or that of the revisionists is accepted is of vital importance also for the interpretation of the Reformation. Conversely, the understanding of the nature and relative importance of the religious forces or material factors at play in the Reformation movement is of critical importance in defining its position in the whole historical development.

The magisterial reformers, Luther, Zwingli, and Calvin, owed much to Renaissance humanism, as did some of the Anabaptist leaders and Catholic reformers. Without the philological achievements of the humanists in reviving the knowledge of Greek and Hebrew, the reformers could not have worked with the Bible in the original languages. Luther spoke of humanism as a kind of John the Baptist heralding the coming of the Gospel. Erasmus, through his criticism of abuses and his editorial work on the New Testament and the patristic writers, had made such an important contribution to church renewal that his critics declared he had laid the egg that Luther hatched. Once the Reformation was underway the humanists served as the major carriers of Luther's evangelical revival during the first critical years from 1517 to 1521. The humanist sodalities, for example, had Luther's Ninety-five Theses printed in several cities of the empire within weeks after they were first posted. Within the whole question of how Renaissance humanism and the Reformation geared in with each other, the role of the generations is exceedingly fascinating. While the older humanists for the most part, at a certain point, turned away from the Reformation, the younger humanists became increasingly committed to the evangelical movement. Those humanists provide a concrete case study of how the Renaissance and Reformation movements related to each other in a generational context.

One bright undergraduate is fond of referring to his university's history department as the "cause and effect" department. Indeed, beyond the level of "innocent" descriptive narrative history, analytical history necessarily works with the concept of cause and effect. The nature of the effect, it is presumed, can be understood much more precisely if the factors which help explain why an event happened are known and understood. Very few historians would be so thoroughly historicist or developmentalist as to agree with Henri Bergson that the present contains nothing more than the past and that what is found in the effect was already in the cause. Everything is not merely the outcome of something preceding. In each historical event there is, after all, much that is creative, unique, and ephemeral rather than predetermined, repetitive, or permanent. Nevertheless, much can be learned about such a great conglomerate historical movement as the Reformation, made up of a multiplicity of particular events, from the study of its causal nexus. So challenging is the problem of causation that the German historian Georg von Below ventured the opinion that the literature on the antecedents of the Reformation is more extensive than on the Reformation itself. This approach avoids the common fallacy of overemphasizing the immediate occasion at the expense of long-time and deep-lying causes. It should also lend a measure of insight into the multilateral rather than unilateral causation at work in historical happenings.

With the advance of secularism and materialism in western culture, as well as with the development of economic history as a discipline, increasing emphasis has been placed by some historians upon economic causation—until for some, religion and the spiritual appear to be nothing more than cloaks disguising economic change. The selection from P. C. Gordon Walker, British economic theorist much under Marxian influence, makes the case for economic determinism. The author sees drastic economic change, particularly the highly inflationary price rise, as primarily responsible for the Reformation in its two successive phases. Consistent dialectical materialism presupposes also the inevitability of historical events, thus raising a further problem of the philosophy of history. Hajo Holborn, renowned historian of the Reformation, on the other hand, argues that the homeland of the movement had not undergone significant economic and attendant social changes, so that the economic factor could hardly have been the critical determinant.

Most of northern Europe could not experience a Renaissance of the same kind as Italy enjoyed in its golden age. There could be a true Renaissance only in the homeland of classical Latin culture and of the Roman empire. The Renaissance could be a genuine revival only where classical culture had flourished in ancient times, where remnants of classical architecture and sculpture could serve as a direct inspiration to modern artists. But literary culture is as mobile as books, manuscripts, and letters can make it, so that Renaissance humanism was diffused much more naturally from South to North. There it fused with indigenous intellectual elements to form a somewhat different but still inherently related cultural pattern. The humanists were all concerned with the *humaniora*, those humane studies best designed to perfect and ornament man. Humanism was a cultural movement rooted in a desire for the rebirth of classical antiquity. Like the Italians, the northern humanists, too, were concerned with the humane content of antique letters and their relevance for life, not merely with their admirable style or outward form. Northern humanism, however, retained more of a literary–philological character than that of Italy. It gave expression to a kind of cultural nationalism in rivalry with the Italians who had not infrequently been demeaning toward the English, French, and German barbarians. It developed an ever increasing concern for religious enlightenment and ecclesiastical reform.

One of the most revolutionary and dynamic developments in Western history, the Reformation burst the bonds of the old theology and ecclesiastical institutions. As a historical event of first magnitude, moreover, it involved also social, political, and economic forces from the very outset and effected basic changes in many aspects of society. The political and social situation in the homeland of the Reformation was exceedingly complex. Through the repeated selection by the seven electors of Hapsburg emperors, the Holy Roman Empire became involved in their international dynastic schemes and in their wars against the French and the Turks. Internally the empire was subdivided into over three hundred lesser states ranging from larger territorial states such as Bavaria, the Palatinate, Saxony, Bohemia, Brandenburg, or Württemberg, to small dukedoms, margravates, or free cities. Within these many states the structure of government varied considerably and traditional law codes were rivaled now by the introduction of Roman law. Traditional class structures were being challenged as well. In the prospering cities, especially along the Rhine and Danube, the newly rich families contended with older patrician families for power on the city councils. Larger numbers of workers were now employed in the newly expanding enterprises such as mining, textiles, and printing, dwarfing some of the older crafts and smaller guilds. The territorial princes and the cities equipped their troops with new armaments and powerful cannons which rendered the feudal knights and their strongholds obsolete. The status of the peasants had improved considerably, thus stimulating a desire for still further improvements and fear of regression. In such a complex situation undergoing persistent and increasingly rapid change, social forces were bound to play an important role in a major historical development such as the Reformation movement. Much Luther research in recent decades has transformed Reformation studies into a special adjunct to systematic theology. On the other hand, the Marxists and equally naive nonideological determinists have elevated the economic factor to a position of absolute importance as the critical determinant in the causal nexus. An appreciation of the complexity and variety of the social forces at work contributes in an essential way to a sophisticated historical analysis of the event. Harold J. Grimm and his students have pioneered in exploring the social forces operative in the Reformation, directing their research to the concrete situation in such cities as Nuremberg.

Before the advent of the "new history" which has given more attention to social, cultural, intellectual, and religious factors, historians concerned themselves primarily and often exclusively with political history. The Reformation, too, has been interpreted by some largely in terms of the political exigencies of the time. Particularly the conditions within the Holy Roman Empire are credited not merely with making the Reformation possible, but with actually precipitating it and determining the course of its development. This view emphasizes the weakness of the emperor, the particularism and aggressiveness of the princes, the political involvement of the church, the rise of cultural nationalism, and similar considerations. H. C. Lea, famed as the historian of the Inquisition, in his influential contribution to the *Cambridge Modern History*, stressed the decisive role of these external social and political factors.

Other contemporary historians have come to see the Reformation as basically theological and religious, not merely a reaction against abuses but in the first instance a positive movement for theological and ecclesiastical renewal responding to a great popular increase in religious fervor. The two historians in this volume representing the effort to understand the positive and negative spiritual elements involved are interesting also for another reason. Through the years partisans of the Catholic or Protestant points of view have frequently written the history of the Reformation in black and white as a conflict between right and wrong. Catholic historiography following in the tradition of Cochlaeus, a dedicated defamer of Luther, has all too often attacked the reformer's character and motives, attributing his rebellion to ego, lust, or demonic possession. Joseph Lortz, distinguished Catholic church historian, has broken decisively with this tradition represented even in this century by Heinrich Denifle and Hartmann Grisar. Passionately dedicated to ecumenicity and the restoration of the unity of the *una sancta ecclesia*, Lortz has undertaken a reappraisal of the causes underlying the Reformation as well as of the event itself. Lortz seeks to assess the religious together with the political and cultural currents. While criticizing Luther for "religious subjectivity," he neither impugns his integrity nor deprecates his spiritual creativity. Protestant historiography has frequently responded to the charge that "Luther did it" with the assertion that the "church was hopelessly corrupt." The famous Protestant historian Gerhard Ritter, in answering the question of why the Reformation occurred in Germany, looks more deeply into the problem and sounds out also its religious depths. Neither of these two historians jettisons his private views and personal valuations, so that the measure of their agreement may be a significant indication of the changing mood within Christendom, as well as a triumph for academic historical discipline.

The most profound religious assessment of the Reformation, however, has come not from the church historians but from a theologian who was the spokesman for the most vigorous theological movement of the twentieth century. The Swiss Reformed pastor and later professor of systematic theology, Karl Barth, with his *Commentary on Romans*, published shortly after the first World War, rang a church bell which awakened Christendom to a renewed earnestness about the Gospel. His message came to be known as neoorthodoxy, dialectical theology, or theology of crisis, a word to a world in crisis. He criticized the cultural accommodations of liberal theology, its psychologizing, historicizing, anthropologizing. Idealism no less than materialism lets man play God. God is not to be captured in an ontological system or understood by analogy, for there is an infinite qualitative difference between God and man. God is "wholly other." The gospel of Christ presents religion itself with a crisis, for in religion as such man still seeks himself and not God; but the gospel requires a complete 180-degree turn about, a conversion. The crisis of all crises confronts sinful man when he stands in the presence of the holy God. This crisis can be resolved only by the divine initiative, not through man's efforts. Theology has to do not with divinizing man but with the God who became incarnate in Christ and through him offers redemption. This theology is dialectical not in a philosophical sense, but because it recognizes that the truth of God can be expressed, not in simple propositions, but only in a dialogue of sentence and counter-sentence, the only method adequate for faith. This theology is in the strictest sense a theology of the Word. *Deus dixit!*

Barth dropped a bombshell on the playground of the theologians! Theology, he declared, is not to present the individual's opinions, it is not philosophical speculation, not history, not a description of pious feelings, not an account of subjective religious experiences, not a system; it is an exposition of the Word. It does not live by the "law of the hour," but on commission from God. This twentieth-century theology was directed against the religious tendencies which from the Enlightenment on had tended to proceed in various forms from the consciousness of man. Barth drove back over the entire nineteenth and eighteenth centuries to the way the magisterial reformers, Luther and Calvin, did theology. The result was a new understanding of Reformation theology, immediate, existential, dynamic, urgent. From Barth's concern with the content of the Word grew his twelve-volume *Church Dogmatics*, a theological monument that could hardly have been anticipated in this century of ours.

Those mysterious abstractions like economic man, social forces, statistical evidence, or political trends, which are the stock in trade of most historians, all too often become disembodied concepts which conceal the fact that history is human history and that it is made by men. The individual, Veronica Wedgwood reminds us, is at once infinitesimal dust and the cause of all things, a stupendous and beautiful paradox. The great medievalist Marc Bloch felt that in the final analysis the basic element in history is psychic. Properly understood, history may be viewed as the product of human nature in action, a projection of individual human nature on to the collective plane. The importance of biography as an indispensable adjunct to general history is today receiving new recognition. There is also a rising interest in the contributions of psychology and psychiatry to historical understanding. Luther, the first reformer, is a particularly valuable subject for this type of inquiry. He wore his heart on his sleeve and revealed his whole personality with an openness which is rare among the outsize men of history. His cause, moreover, must be counted as an instance where the spiritual in the sense of the religious was the primary concern. In this context the problem of the material or spiritual nature of the Reformation takes the form of an inquiry into the relative significance of theological considerations or psychological motivations in determining the reformer's career, a delicate problem indeed.

An account of Luther's early years from the reformer himself would naturally be invaluable for either a psychological analysis or a theological inquiry into his development. Luther provided precisely such a precious document in the preface to the complete edition of his Latin writings, 1545, the year before his death. In this unique personal testimony the aged reformer reviews his road to reformation, the indulgence controversy, Cajetan, Eck, Caraccioli, Miltitz, the Leipzig debate, and above all his inner struggle and his discovery of the true meaning of the phrase "the righteousness of God" in Romans 1:17. Luther seeks to avoid the charge that he had recklessly precipitated the disturbance in the church. He asks the reader of his early writings to bear in mind that he was then a pious papist and a monk who became involved in the controversy by accident and

FIGURE 1. *Luther in 1520.* Copper plate etching by Lucas Cranach the elder, called from Vienna in 1505 to serve as court painter for Prince Frederick the Wise in Wittenberg. The inscription reads: "Luther himself has shown the immortal image of his spirit,/But the wax of Lucas shows his mortal features." From Peter Meinhold, *Reformation im Bild* (Berlin and Hamburg: Lutherisches Verlagshaus, 1967), no. 34. Used by permission of Staatsbibliothek Bildarchiv, Berlin.

not by design. His evangelical convictions grew, he recalls, the more deeply he searched the Scriptures. This reminiscing apologetic, done with a detectable touch of irony, provides some firsthand psychological and theological insights into both the young and the old Luther and serves as a good point of departure for the two selections which follow.

In his widely heralded book on the young man Luther, an excerpt of which is included among the readings, Erik Erikson, one of the country's leading figures in the *rapprochement* of psychoanalysis and the social sciences, analyzes Luther's psychological make-up, his identity crisis in young manhood, his ideological conflicts, and seeks to explain how he came to be the reformer who shook the Western world. The brilliant theologian and church historian Roland Bainton, the author of the leading biography of Luther, is critical of the presuppositions which Erikson brings to bear upon the interpretation of the facts. He believes that the facts about the young Luther which are definitely established are not the kind of thing we need to know for a successful psychoanalytical treatment. Although Erikson very carefully avoids a judgment on the reality and quality of the theological questions and answers involved in Luther's conflict, Bainton feels that the materialistic presuppositions of many Freudians prevent an adequate appreciation of the spiritual realm and a serious treatment of theological problems as such. In his article on Luther's struggle for faith, Bainton, while taking cognizance of emotional and psychological considerations, stresses the theological nature of Luther's problem and solution, allowing to the spiritual realm its real though not entirely independent existence.

The serious student keeps meeting himself in history. Goethe, who with light cynicism pronounced history a "web of nonsense to the higher thinker," also penned these memorable lines:

> *What you the spirit of the ages call*
> *Is nothing but the spirit of you all*
> *Wherein the ages are reflected.*

In his encounter with history the student perceives on a wide space–time screen problems which he confronts in a different shape and on a reduced scale in his own private life. It may be hoped that probing into the material and spiritual aspects of the Reformation movement in an era so portentous for our own will improve the student's understanding and judgment both of history and of his own world. *Historia vitae magistra!*

Conflict of Opinion

[Ranke's] hope that history might be written with utter objectivity, just as it happened, proved to be illusory. In order to bring the record of the past into manageable compass, the historian must perforce select his sources, and that selection can be highly subjective. . . .

The liberal Protestants of the late nineteenth and early twentieth centuries associated the Renaissance and the Reformation as conjoint phases of a movement of emancipation away from the authority of the church. . . . Then in the early twentienth century Ernst Troeltsch approached the question from the point of view of the interconnection of religion and culture. . . .

Some historians, here as elsewhere, offer an economic explanation. . . . Other interpreters stress political factors. . . . Contemporary histories of the Reformation tend to be misleading because the religious understanding of the Reformation is subordinated to the exigencies of teaching. . . . During the last quarter of a century several new approaches to the Reformation have emerged. The first is the application of psychiatry to history. . . . There are, however, grave difficulties in psychoanalyzing the dead.

ROLAND H. BAINTON

I. Was the Reformation the religious expression of the Renaissance?

Among the Germanic peoples in the north of Europe the reformatory movement now came forward, slowly, tenaciously, laying hold of the nations in their ultimate depth, a movement which by bringing freedom from the Roman hierarchy created the external conditions for an independent scientific movement. . . . Thus it happened that in the German-speaking lands the spiritual movement which in Europe transplanted itself from country to country received a religious expression.

WILHELM DILTHEY

If one understands both movements the way they worked out in their historical development, then they appear very clearly as the schism of European culture into its main components, the separation of the Christian, supernatural, ascetic element from the antique, inner-worldly human element.

ERNST TROELTSCH

Within the framework of the great debate exemplified best by Wilhelm Dilthey and Ernst Troeltsch as to the modern or medieval nature of the Reformation, progress can be made only in terms of specifics, through an examination of the precise circumstances within which the Reformation developed. The juxtaposition of humanism and the Reformation, of humanists and reformers, may provide more concrete evidences than the general assertions with which the arguments on both sides of the question are usually promoted.

LEWIS W. SPITZ

II. Was the economic factor the critical determinant?

The Reformation was a movement divided into two chronological phases, corresponding to the two phases of the Price Revolution. . . . The inescapable conclusion is . . . that the Reformation was the reaction to a force external to itself. . . . The Reformation was not the cause of capitalism; rather it was the result of needs created by capitalist advance at a particular place and time. . . .

P. C. GORDON WALKER

It is doubtful whether the rise of early capitalism in Germany actually revolutionized German society as a whole. We observe the growth of finance and large-scale trade and new forms of industrial organization chiefly in upper Germany, whereas middle and north Germany preserved the traditional habits of agrarian society. . . . Nothing sensational was to happen for a long time to come.

HAJO HOLBORN

There should be no doubt concerning the priority of theology in the minds of the reformers, for all attempts to attribute to them economic and other motives have failed. On the other hand, it is equally futile to attribute the spread of the Reformation solely to religious motives.

HAROLD J. GRIMM

III. Was a deeper religious drive decisive?

There has been a natural tendency to regard the Reformation as solely a religious movement; but this is an error. . . . The motives, both remote and proximate, which led to the Lutheran revolt were largely secular rather than spiritual. So far, indeed, as concerns our present purpose we may dismiss the religious changes incident to the Reformation with the remark that they were not the object sought but the means for attaining that object.

HENRY CHARLES LEA

The Reformation arose out of the dissolution of the basic medieval principles. . . . It has to do with a displacement of powers which takes place in the *heart of the church*. Long before the Reformation, things "reformatory" existed in Western Christendom and in the Roman church.

JOSEPH LORTZ

In retrospect we see both currents of church opposition at work simultaneously though at first independently. The one struggles against manifest abuses and insists on reforms. . . . The other current is less concerned with the outward appearance of the church, but instead touches on the substance of religion and the spiritual roots of church life. . . . In the figure of Martin Luther the two currents combine for the first time.

GERHARD RITTER

One certainly came much closer to the truth of the matter when in previous centuries one simply perceived the merit and greatness of the Reformers in the fact that they again proclaimed certain Christian truths, forgotten or half-forgotten in the church, and thereby restored the church: the glory and authority of the Bible, the lordly majesty of God the Creator, the significance of Jesus Christ as the reconciler of sinful man, the power of faith in this Christ, the freedom of the Christian in the world, the necessary humility and the necessary courage of the true church.

KARL BARTH

IV. Was Luther's impulse to reform primarily psychological or theological?

I pursued the matter with all seriousness, as one who, in dread of the last day, nevertheless from the depth of my heart wanted to be saved. . . . At first I was all alone and certainly very inept and unskilled in conducting such great affairs. For I got into these turmoils by accident and not by will or intention. I call upon God himself as witness.

MARTIN LUTHER

The characteristics of Luther's theological advance can be compared to certain steps in psychological maturation which every man must take.

ERIK H. ERIKSON

[Luther] was always concerned with real problems. . . . He began with the religion and theology on which he had been reared and discovered there genuine difficulties to which others were not properly sensitive.

ROLAND H. BAINTON

The Reformation

Roland H. Bainton

INTERPRETATIONS OF THE REFORMATION

Roland H. Bainton, born in England in 1894, is the Titus Street Professor of Ecclesiastical History emeritus at Yale University. He is the author of many articles and of more than a dozen books in the area of Reformation history. His most recent work is Women of the Reformation in Germany and Italy.

Ranke did a great service to Reformation history by discarding the philosophical presuppositions of the idealistic school and insisting that the history of the sixteenth-century religious upheaval should be written only after a fresh and full confrontation with the sources. But his hope that history might be written with utter objectivity, just as it happened, proved to be illusory. In order to bring the record of the past into manageable compass, the historian must perforce select his sources, and that selection can be highly subjective. Witness for example Janssen's *History of the German People*, which by judicious inclusion and omission of sources contrived to present the Protestant Reformation in ugly colors. Or again Döllinger's *History of the Reformation*, which filled three volumes with direct quotations from the despondent utterances of the Protestant reformers, who lamented that their achievements fell short of their hopes. Then Wilhelm Walther countered with a solid body of statistical evidence. Here were sources fighting against sources.

The modern historian is aware of all this and seeks to fortify himself by declaring his prejudices in advance. Then he strains in the opposite direction as a corrective and ends by being nonobjective in the very effort to be objective. But a deeper difficulty is that we are not even aware of our prejudices because frequently they are those which we share with our age. If we are to recognize that they are prejudices, we must engage in a comparison between the point of view of our time and those of previous times. Thus we invoke history to disclose to us our presuppositions in the approach to history. Hence today the vogue of historiography.

In the field of the Renaissance it has produced the admirable work

From Roland H. Bainton, "Interpretations of the Reformation," *The American Historical Review* 66 (1960): 74–84. Used by permission of the editor of *The American Historical Review*.

of Wallace K. Ferguson. For the Reformation there is nothing comparable. We do, though, have studies of how individual leaders of the Reformation have been treated throughout the succeeding centuries: Erasmus, Zwingli, Luther, and Castellio. The historiography of the Reformation as a whole, however, still awaits treatment.

The main lines for such a study may be indicated. The age of the Reformation itself was polemical and documentary. The *Magdeburg Centuries* on the Protestant side and Baronius' *Annals* on the Catholic marshaled sources in support of confessional claims. The eighteenth century tried to achieve impartiality. This was done in either of two ways: by the historian's dissociating equally from all parties and movements or by projecting himself into them all with equal sympathy. The rationalists of the Enlightenment were inclined to the first. It is interesting that in this period we have the first effort at an objective account of Michael Servetus by Johann Lorenz von Mosheim. Pietism took the other method and responded with equal warmth to every vital religious movement of the past whether orthodox or heretical, Catholic or Protestant. The great exponent of this viewpoint was Gottfried Arnold. This is not to say of course that he was sympathetic toward everything. He commended piety and condemned institutionalism and arid speculation. But his line cut through all of the confessions, and it split Luther down the middle. The earlier Luther was regarded as a warm evangelical, the later as an encrusted institutionalist.

Under the impact of idealistic philosophy the nineteenth century sought to surmount the disjointedness of all previous treatments and to discover connections, motifs, and laws. Hegel saw in the Reformation a movement toward the emancipation of the *Weltgeist* to be valued in terms of its cultural effects, but none of the idealists produced a history of the Reformation. In the meantime the romantics disparaged the Reformation for disrupting the medieval heritage.

Ranke swept away philosophical theorizing with his demand for a thorough and extensive examination of the sources. But he, too, had a philosophy—that of divine providence in history, evidenced in order, necessity, and cohesion. The discontinuities of the Reformation were, therefore, minimized and the conservative side of Luther was exalted.

The liberal Protestants of the late nineteenth and early twentieth centuries associated the Renaissance and the Reformation as conjoint phases of a movement of emancipation away from the authority of the church. The German nationalists saw in Luther's religion an expression of the profundity of the German *Geist* and in the Reformation a stirring toward the emancipation of the German people. Then in the early twentieth century Ernst Troeltsch approached the question from the point of view of the interconnection of religion and culture. Christianity, if it is to influence a culture, must to a large degree identify itself with that culture. Protestantism, he held, was that form of Christianity which corresponded to sixteenth-century cultural needs. But these needs, he felt, were still largely those of the Middle Ages, and for that reason he stressed the medieval character of the Reformation alike in theology and ecclesiology. To his mind the great dividing line between the medieval and the modern period was to be found not in the Reformation but in the Enlightenment, though to be sure the Reformation created a situation out of which the later emancipation could arise. The Reformation itself, however, was addicted to dogma, intolerance, and constraint.

The most radical break with all of these positions was inaugurated by the essay of Karl Holl in 1917, "What Did Luther Mean by Religion?" Holl rediscovered the core of Luther's piety, his overpowering sense of moral obligation, his feeling of utter impotence before the demands of God, his terror of the divine wrath justly impending, his unshakable clinging to God's Word and promises. Luther was afflicted with the *malaise de l'univers* and found surcease only through a new view of God and the Scriptures. Neither philosophy, sociology, nationalism, nor economics can explain Luther. Only religion can provide the explanation.

From this analysis, which inaugurated the Luther renaissance, we may take our departure. The question immediately arises, if this be a true picture of Luther, what then of the Reformation? Why did he gain a following? Did his disciples really understand him or did they rally for the wrong reasons? Were they convinced that indulgences were blasphemy because they are based on the contention that the saints have earned merits which can be presented as a claim upon God, or did the populace respond in order to rid themselves of financial exploitation?

There are those who say that this or some other extraneous consideration must have been determinative because, as a matter of fact, Luther's religious affirmations were in no sense novel and when previously made had had no such effect. Luther happened to emerge amid a set of circumstances peculiarly auspicious. Without such a stage and without concomitants both economic and political the Reformation would never have taken hold.

As for the claim that Luther was in no sense original, there is no better reply than that to be found in the recent work of Erich Hassinger, who finds Luther's contribution to have been his rediscovery of the historical core of Christianity. The claim of the Christian religion is that God did something unique in history. In the year that Caesar Augustus ordered all the world to be taxed the Word became flesh. The incarnation, the crucifixion, and the resurrection constituted a unique self-disclosure of God in Christ. To Him the ages lead up and from Him the centuries lead out. By faith in His redeeming work man is forgiven and remade. The assertion of the unique historical role of Christ is an offense because it assumes unevenness in the work of God, who, if this be true, declared Himself more manifestly to the men of the first century than to those in any other. There are various ways of escaping from the historical singularity of Christ. One is mysticism: God is accessible at all times equally to the waiting heart. Another is moralism: man is saved by his own good deeds done and now. And still another is institutionalism: the church is the custodian and continuator of the revelation once and for all given. Luther asserted unequivocally the historical uniqueness of the work of God in Christ. Its continuance in the present is mediated through Scripture, which is the record of the event. And though it must be interpreted by the Spirit, yet the Spirit can never be dissociated from the outward Word. This position divided Luther from Catholics on the one side and from Protestant sectaries on the other.

But if it be granted that Luther was original as to religion, the question still remains whether men were stirred by his religion or merely by his revolt. Some historians, here as elsewhere, offer an economic explanation. This of itself is by no means novel. The charge arose almost at once that the princes supported Luther in order to expropriate the goods of the church, that the peasants at first rallied to him in the hope that the freedom of the Gospel would mean freedom from serfdom, that the masses espoused the Gospel in order to throw off tithes, fees, and indulgences. To such an explanation there are several replies. The most decisive is that in short order the populace and the princes risked their goods and their lives by adherence to the new faith. At the Diet of the Empire in 1530, the German princes presented the Augsburg Confession, fully aware that the emperor might in consequence deprive them of their titles, lands, and lives. In the 1540s the emperor came with Spanish troops to crush Protestantism, but neither princes nor people would yield. Had their concern been only economic, one cannot understand such intrepidity. One may note also that some simple laymen like Hans Sachs did grasp what Luther meant in the very core of his theology. Perhaps one reason why they did and could understand his message was that the way had been in some measure prepared by the German mystics who had stressed not outward good works but inward attitudes of humility and love.

The economic explanation for the movement's success in Germany is more plausible if it is compared with the failure in Italy. Some writers have suggested that the Protestant reform did not take hold there because the gold flowed from over the Alps into Italy. That may have been a partial factor, but there are other possibilities. One historian suggests that Protestantism failed because Catholicism is ingrained in the very fiber of the Italian people. But that simply is not true. No European land had seen so many revolts not only against the church but also against the faith from the late twelfth to the sixteenth century as had Italy. The peninsula pullulated with sects. One by one they were plucked by the Inquisition. Italy was tired. Heresy was played out. That may be one explanation. Another is the adroitness of Rome in capturing and utilizing the movements of vitality. Had there been a great revolt against the papacy in Italy in the sixteenth century, it could probably have come only from the Capuchins, imbued as they were with the ideals of the spiritual Franciscans. If the popes had rejected the first Capuchins, they might easily have become rebels and heretics. Discretion made of them apostles and saints. A still further explanation is the nature of the preparation. The preaching in Italy in the fifteenth and sixteenth centuries was highly moralistic, directed against specific sins: usury, prostitution, luxury, extortion, tyranny, feuding, and the wearing of vanities. Lyrical raptures over the wounds of Christ ended in appeals to imitate his sufferings. The inference was that penitence and amendment of life would win God's pardon. But this was just the point that Luther denied. He could denounce sins with all the vehemence of a Savonarola, but his point was that divine forgiveness is a sheer act of God's grace and in no way contingent upon anything that man can do. Amendment of life flows from the assurance of pardon. The German mystics had come closer to this than ever did the Italian friars, and the difference in the religious preparation may have had more to do with the outcome than had economics.

Other interpreters stress political factors, contending that the Reformation could have begun in no other country than Germany because of the political decentralization. The point is that in a great monarchical state an obscure professor would have had little chance to persuade a monarch like Francis, Henry, or Charles to embrace his religious ideas. And if the monarch were not at least neutral, the advocate of new religious ideas would be promptly snuffed out. Saxony was small enough and the relations sufficiently personal that a teacher at the University of Wittenberg, supported by his colleagues, could gain the support of a little prince like Frederick the Wise, who was sufficiently independent to pursue a strategy of obstructionism over against the emperor. There is some point no doubt in this contention. Had Luther first appeared in the Netherlands he would have gone quickly to the stake, since here Charles ruled as a hereditary prince. But one cannot say that an academic reformer might not have converted a monarch. There is no inherent reason why John Colet in England or Jacques Lefèvre d'Étaples in France might not have converted the crown. As a matter of fact Henry VIII did introduce the Reformation into England without provoking a serious revolt, though to be sure it was not Luther's variety. Perhaps one may safely say that the Reformation took hold and survived only where it coincided with some sort of political interest, but the identification must not be too precise.

Contemporary histories of the Reformation tend to be misleading because the religious understanding of the Reformation is subordinated to the exigencies of teaching. Political history predominates in the works of Paul Joachimsen, Harold J. Grimm, Hajo Holborn, E. Harris Harbison, Erich Hassinger, and Gerhard Ritter. This is certainly not because they have failed to grasp the nature of Luther's religion and the sources of his critique of the Church. Ritter in particular has written a most penetrating book on Luther. The explanation may be that these works actually are not histories of the Reformation, but rather histories of Europe or of Germany during the period of the Reformation. The scope of the treatment is somewhat determined by the purpose for which the books are to be used, namely as texts in courses on European, German, or world history. The titles indicate the scope: *The Reformation Era, The Age of the Reformation, Die Neugestaltung Europas.* In these works politics and sociology play as much or even a greater part than religion. One suspects that the demands of university courses have determined the allocation of space.

But if the Reformation was primarily religious, what then of its relation to the Renaissance? The answer of course depends in part on the interpretation of the Renaissance. The diversities in that area are well illustrated by three recent works on Erasmus. The first of these, by Siro Attilio Nulli, depicts Erasmus as neither a Catholic nor a Christian. Nulli appreciates Erasmus' position because he holds the same beliefs. He is sorry only that Erasmus wasted so much time trying to prove that he was what he was not. Émile V. Telle presents an Erasmus who may have been a Christian, but was certainly not a Catholic since his attack on monasticism was earlier more virulent and persistent than that of Luther. But Louis Bouyer claims Erasmus to have been both a good Christian and a good Catholic. Several questions are involved here: What is a Christian? What is a Catholic? And what was Erasmus? The answers to these questions have an obvious bearing on judgments with regard to the Reformation.

A cleavage between the Reformation and the Renaissance certainly existed, but the tendency of late has been to accentuate it. The Renaissance was, as a matter of fact, a complex phenomenon, but certainly persons like Colet, Pico, Ficino, More, and Erasmus are not to be called frivolous or irreligious. Yet Renaissance religion was not Luther's religion. There was in it a strong ingredient of the Neoplatonic disparagement of the corporeal which when not restrained by the authority of the Church issued in iconoclasm, sacramentarianism, that is, the denial of the real presence, and even in a rejection of music. Tendencies in this direction were already present in Erasmus. At this point Luther was a good medieval Catholic. Another ingredient of Renaissance religion was tolerance toward other religions, a readiness to recognize that there is more than one way to God. And this was because the Renaissance minimized the historical uniqueness of Christianity. Luther, however, would have absolutely nothing to do with any such attenuation. Again the Renaissance shared with Catholicism a higher estimate of the capacity and worth of the natural man than Luther allowed. This was the core of his debate with Erasmus. Yet Luther enthusiastically appropriated and the Reformation adopted all of the philological tools and the historical critical method of the humanist.

During the last quarter of a century several new approaches to the Reformation have emerged. The first is the application of psychiatry to history. In his presidential address before the American Historical Association in 1957 William Langer held that the "next assignment" is to apply the insights of psychoanalysis to history. He is perfectly right in asserting that whatever illumines the present should be brought to bear upon the past, provided sufficient material of the right sort is available to implement this technique. There are, however, grave difficulties in psychoanalyzing the dead. In the case of Luther, we know much, and for some thirty years of his life we know something that he did on twenty days out of every month. What we know, however, is not what, for this purpose, we need to know. The result is that the psychiatrist fastens on three or four remarks of the aged Luther about his boyhood, remarks transmitted to us only at secondhand. Then on the basis of such sparse material the psychiatrist reconstructs all the turmoils of Luther's inner life. There is, however, a more serious difficulty in the case of all of the psychiatrists who have turned their hand to Luther thus far. They do not envisage the possibility that he could have been impelled by any motive except egocentricity. In any case, if one should succeed in psychoanalyzing a man there would still be the more elusive task of psychoanalyzing a movement.

Catholic historiography of the Protestant Reformation has advanced notably in recent years. Research has become much more objective, and the tendency is to pity the misguided rather than to rail at rebels. In Luther's own day he was traduced by Johannes Cochläus. Recently a German Catholic, Adolf Herte, has exposed Cochläus' misrepresentations and their baneful effect upon all Catholic historiography to our own day. Georges Tavard points out that in

Luther's day medieval Catholicism resembled a vase already shattered but with the pieces still in place. Luther's unhappy historical destiny was to come at the moment when a touch sufficed to make them fall apart. Joseph Lortz poses the question: How could Luther have persuaded his generation that Catholicism amounted to nothing more than purchasing heaven? A generation after Luther this might be explained as a Protestant legend, but not in the first decades of the Reformation. The only possible conclusion is that the behavior of the majority of Catholics lent itself to this interpretation. As for Luther's own religion, his trembling before the majesty of God and his demand for utter self-emptying are not to be brushed off lightly as exaggerations. And in the portrayal of sin, what terrific earnestness! At a number of points, nevertheless, Luther did exaggerate and therefore distorted.

With all such treatments a Protestant historian can come to grips. One of the Catholic historians' greatest contributions is their placing of Luther in the setting of late medieval Catholicism.

Another school of interpretation is that of the neoorthodox. The rebels against Protestant liberalism affirmed the depravity of man, the salvation of man solely through the grace of God, the utter transcendence of God, and the possibility of knowing God only through His self-disclosure in Christ. These theologians claimed that they were reviving the theology of the sixteenth-century reformers. In so doing they unquestionably called attention to points in Reformation theology entirely missed by the interpreters of the liberal school, who because of their presuppositions had not the eyes to see what was there. But by the same token the neoorthodox were tempted to impose their own meanings upon their reputed progenitors.

Their attempt to derive everything from Christ, including religious knowledge, salvation, and ethics, leads to exaggerations. First as to the knowledge of God: if knowledge is possible only through Christ then there is no room for natural theology. Peter Barth attempted to show that this was Calvin's view. But for all that Calvin said about the depravity of man's will and intellect he was to the end too deeply steeped in Stoicism ever to eliminate all natural religion.

Again, if Christ be the only source of ethics, what place is left for natural law, unless perchance for the non-Christian? The neoorthodox tend to exclude from Luther's thinking not only natural law but all law, claiming that his ethic was entirely spontaneous and unstructured. Incidentally this view is not a particular discovery of the neo-orthodox. Before them it was advanced by Karl Holl, who anticipated more than one of their contentions not by approaching Luther with their assumptions, but simply by steeping himself in Luther. At this point, however, one may suggest that they have all exaggerated. A Catholic author published a book on natural law in Luther in which he cited many passages that sound like Thomas Aquinas. To be sure, the theological framework in which natural law thinking was set differed for Aquinas and Luther, but it was, nevertheless, decidedly present in Luther.

Finally, if for the Christian everything proceeds from Christ, must not the Christian feel himself to be a stranger in the world, if not indeed an alien? No one would deny that Luther called upon the Christian to demean himself as a good citizen, but Heckel insists that this was not because the Christian belongs to the natural order but rather that out of love for his neighbor he should stoop himself to an alien yoke. The Christian, then, in his interior becomes a unified being. This view very sharply contrasts to that of Troeltsch who asserted that for Luther the Christian belongs to two realms and is governed by two codes, one might almost say two ethics, and must be torn by the duality of his role as a Christian and as a man in the world. Holl had already bridged the gap by insisting that in both areas the Christian is to be motivated by love. But Heckel makes the bridge unnecessary by eliminating the gap, and that I think is going rather too far.

The broader problems of the interpretation of any period depend for their verification and progress on documentary evidence. And progress in research means a constant quest for new materials and their dissemination in the original form or in modern critical editions. . . . Much work remains to be done.

Wilhelm Dilthey

THE INTERPRETATION AND ANALYSIS OF MAN IN THE 15th AND 16th CENTURIES

Wilhelm Dilthey, renowned German philosopher, was born in 1833. He taught at the universities of Basle, Kiel, Breslau, and, from 1882 to his death in 1911, at Berlin. Famous for his works on Schleiermacher, Hegel, and Leibniz, he made his major contribution in the systematic study of the intellectual-cultural disciplines, combatting positivism and the application of natural-scientific methods to the realm of the human spirit. The following selection is taken from his best-known essay on the interpretation of man.

The humanist movement in Italy belonged to the cities, the courts, and the upper estates. Its undisturbed development presupposed the character of the papacy of Alexander VI, Julius II, and Leo X. And the counterreformation proved that the humanist movement had not affected the depth and breadth of the nation. Among the Germanic peoples in the north of Europe the reformatory movement now came forward, slowly, tenaciously, laying hold of the nations in their ultimate depth, a movement which by bringing freedom from the Roman hierarchy created the external conditions for an independent scientific movement. It made the development of a critical theology possible by transferring the legal basis of dogmas into religious-ethical inwardness. And in its course it was to make the moral and religious autonomy of the person the basis of spiritual life in our land.

Germany, from where this movement went forth, was at that time undergoing an ascending development of its people's strength and of its wealth, of industry and of trade. Ever since Constantinople had ceased to be the point of departure for the major transportation routes to the north, commerce went from Italy over the Alpine passes now made practicable, then across Germany to the North Sea and the Baltic. Now the German cities blossomed out! A wealth of rare metals was being produced in the mines of the Erzgebirge and the Harz, which evoked the price revolutions in the second decade of the six-

Translated by Dr. Edna Spitz from Wilhelm Dilthey, *Auffassung und Analyse des Menschen im 15. und 16. Jahrhundert, Gesammelte Schriften,* II (Stuttgart, 1940), 39–42, 53–63. Used by permission of the publishers, B. G. Teubner Verlagsgesellschaft mbH, Stuttgart.

teenth century even more than did the imports from the American gold and silver mines. Added to this there was the continuation of relatively simple and frugal customs, a fact which Machiavelli in 1508 cited as the chief reason for the rising German wealth. "They don't build, they don't spend for clothes, they use nothing for household furniture. For them it is enough to have an abundance of bread and meat and a heated room." The German merchant now attended all markets. The international companies of Augsburg had their representatives in all big places. The exuberant power of the people pressed forth on all sides toward the outside world in colonization and in mercenary military services. Thus in this still decentralized people, which because of the opposition of cities, knights, princes, and kings was not capable of unified political action, there grew up independent centers of intellectual culture without number: a superabundance of surging spiritual powers was there. An influx of Italian art style and humanistic writings arose out of the increasing contact with Italy.

This entire country, however, was covered with a network of ecclesiastical power operations, which finally all had their center in Rome. The picture of a city of those days shows round about strong gates, moats, and fortifications. Within, however, there are domineering towers; portals with towering gables; and the extensive compounds of cathedrals, churches, and monasteries. Thus also the spiritual life of those people squeezed in there was governed by fixed ecclesiastical concepts. Man can redeem himself from sensual lust, sin, the devil, and eternal punishments only through the regulated help of the church, through the precisely ordered system of the sacraments, auricular confession, penances, and pious works. The religious duties of an individual's family to free him from purgatory extended even beyond his death. Into this gradual development of confession, sacrament, indulgence, sacrifice, and external works the complete profoundness of the mystics and the Franciscan *imitation of Christ* had poured themselves. Also, the scientific concepts of nature were still in a certain accord with this churchly discipline. The working of nature for the scientist was still ultimately composed of the working of spiritual powers within it. Magical powers were being accepted also by leading philosophers of nature. As the dark side of this concept of the world, the belief in the devil and in witches corresponded to the strong belief in prayer. Likewise, there was still no methodically founded historical criticism with regard to the sum total of ecclesiastical traditions. Among the people there occurred sudden outbreaks of fear of all these otherworldly forces, taking hold everywhere. In the churches there were blood-sweating hosts; in the sky bloody crosses and lances; in town and country an immeasurable number of pilgrims, flagellants, and prophets; miraculous images of the Virgin Mary, and preachers of repentance. One could not do enough, as far as the building of new churches and chapels and their decoration was concerned. All these influences of the ecclesiastical system were now, however, finally inserted into the constitution of the German Empire as if with iron clamps.

Thus it happened that in the German-speaking lands the spiritual movement which in Europe transplanted itself from country to country received a religious expression. And just because of this the ever-increasing, enormous religious tension, which existed for a long time in the whole Roman church and was growing steadily, led to an explosion here. The progress of civilization, inventions, discoveries, and of industry had during the fifteenth century worked together with nominalism, which was the grave digger of the old rational theology. The theological metaphysics of the Middle Ages disintegrated. Because of this very fact, however, within the ecclesiastical organization and its persons, the treatment of dogma as a legal system and the strengthening and utilization of the church apparatus, in short, curialism, was reinforced. This external pressure on the living religious forces had allowed the fire of the Hussite movement to flame up out of the sectarian faith secretly glowing under the surface. Also the ecclesiastical hierarchy had for its part, in vain, of course, taken up the battle with curialism in the three great councils of the fifteenth century and striven for a reform of the church in head and members. If according to this, the call for reform was a general thing, the kernel of the new was also germinating already. In the practical mystics the inner process became the central focus of religion and theology, through which the individual achieves inner peace from wrestling with his emotions and with his sufferings. From Bradwardin and the fourteenth century on, one had at the same time reached back to Augustinianism, which now for the second time was supposed to try to bring the metaphysical spectacle of trinity and incarnation closer to the human heart, so in need of peace. An expedient for a time! But the transfer of the religious interest from the cosmic drama to the personal relationship to the Christ with features full of suffering and to the God Father felt more intimately and more closely was definitive. This is seen also in the pictures of Giovanni Bellini and Perugino, of Rogier van der Weyden, and Memling, from the death dances and pictures at the stations of the cross of this fifteenth and beginning sixteenth century, as well as from the sermons. Indeed the curia was wisely exerting itself to utilize outwardly this shift of religious interest. But it was unable to satisfy it inwardly.

Under these conditions the movement in the lands of the German tongue turned to the religious and theological problems. We are not looking at the Reformation movement which began in this way from the point of view of church history or of the history of dogma. We are not pursuing the question of how new churches now organized them- selves and how changes in the stability of the Christian dogmas oc- curred. But we are attempting to interpret this movement as a highly important member in the concatenation of spiritual events of the six- teenth century. We would like to know how mankind out of the theo- logical metaphysics of the Middle Ages came forward to encounter the work of the seventeenth century, the founding of the rule of man over nature, the autonomy of the perceiving and acting man, the de- velopment of a natural system in the field of law and state, art, morals and theology. Here it is especially important to see how at the begin- ning of the sixteenth century a religious universal theism came vic- toriously to the fore; how Luther hurled himself against it; how this position, however, was taken up by Zwingli in certain limits; and how this position was continued by the sects, particularly by those of the reformed church. In most cases, then, the continued form of this posi- tion during the seventeenth century stands in a clearly recognizable historical connection with these sects and the reformed spirit. It is no less significant how a new ideal of life is formed by the changed con- dition of society, according to which the individual feels his inner, independent worth and joyfully seeks its development in activity within the concrete life relationships. Luther and Zwingli create space and freedom for this ideal of life in church life itself, even though also here the new struggles its way through only with difficulty against the old traditions. We would, then, like to understand how in the people of this Reformation era, different from the medieval heads and their theological metaphysics, there arose a new way of establishing and of confirming the higher convictions concerning the relationship of man to the invisible. We would like to comprehend in its origin the relationship of these ideas to society: a relationship by which all changes of European society were affected throughout the course of two centuries. Then one last thing. Here now lies also the beginning of a theology of a new character: freed from scholastic speculations, based on that which can be experienced, on the experienced religious event, and on Christian literature. For up to our day this new theology has had its foundations in inner experience and in the critical history of Christianity. Through it an insight into the moral autonomy of man, which takes all instances into consideration, has only gradually been achieved. . . .

Luther came.

In humanity there is not only a continuity of progressive learning, but also one of religious-moral development. Just as an individual exhausts his vital powers moving forward in the continuity of his life experiences, so also mankind itself. And indeed the great changes in the moral life are continually connected with those of the religious. Up to now history speaks nowhere for the ideal of a morality without religion. As far as we can see, new active powers of the will have always originated in connection with the ideas concerning the invisible. However, that which is fruitfully new in this area always originates in the historical context itself, on the basis of the religiosity of an expiring epoch, just as one condition of life proceeds from a former one. For the impulse and direction for the new is given only because on the basis of a changed condition of consciousness an insufficiency arises for the truly religious man precisely out of the most inner, deepest religio-ethical experience within the existing framework. It was that way also in Luther. He wanted to reform Catholicism; he wanted to renew the Gospel. As we today know Christian antiquity, Luther and his colleagues' moral concept of man goes one decisive step further on the way of religious-moral development, even beyond oldest Christendom. The task is to single out and to articulate this new element from the remainder of his ideas which are conditioned and burdened by tradition.

Luther has amassed in himself all the motives of the opposition.

He had an extraordinary talent for sensing the needs of the time and for unifying its active thoughts. At the same time he possessed in his religious genius a solitary and one-sided power, which drew contemporaries a stretch along the way or completely along with it as though with a higher force foreign to them. He was born to act and to rule. In his person there was something autocratic and sovereign. His invectives against Duke George as the apostle of the devil; against the King of England as the clown, whose writing against Protestantism he compared with the scolding of an angry public woman; the wild humor in the writing concerning the bull about the gluttonous Lord's Supper of the most holy lord, the pope, are the expression of a feeling of strength of a fearless person. He once comforts Melanchthon in his temptations with this: what more can the devil do than strangle him? Already in 1516 we find the Augustinian monk crowded round with work. He could have used two writers for his letters alone. His demonical eyes, which had already in the young man seemed so uncanny to the legate Cajetan, penetrated all realities of this German world. And his brave energy, his understanding of reality, his mastery of it rested upon the connection with the invisible world, which he was constantly conscious of. Let us feel with the Stoa or Luther, with Kant or Carlyle: here is the only foundation of heroic action and Voltaires without number would only get as far as the subjection of the wise to the dominion of raw force. To him was given a simple soul with all the exuberant creative ability and all the highly gifted abundance of spirit. There rules in his faith that which is peculiar to men of will power, that which goes from person to person. Out of this simple and yet rich nature he accomplished the reduction of the ecclesiastical chaos, comprehended the totality of man in faith, tore the nation away from Rome, and remained understanding and close to the largest part of the same, even then, when the hard one-sidedness of his conception of the religio-ethical process became more and more evident. He was master of the people of his time because they believed that they recognized in him their own self raised to a higher power. As the liberator of personal religiosity from the Roman rule of priests in a life and death struggle he had drawn the best men of his time to him. Luther burning the bull, then in Worms, at the Wartburg—that is the Luther which the nation will love, when the personal stamp of the religiosity, which had given him the heroic will for it, will long hence have made room for other forms of faith. Next to him was Zwingli in the pulpit of the cathedral in Zurich and on the battlefield of Kappel.

I wish to discuss that which allies Luther with the German mystics before him and with our transcendental idealism after him, that through which at the same time he was for his contemporaries the renovator of society on the deepest religious-moral foundations. It is contained in the three great writings of 1520: *On the Liberty of the Christian Man, Sermon on Good Works, Address to the Christian Nobility of the German Nation Concerning the Improvement of the Christian Estate.* But it has to be singled out from these works, for in them it is intermixed with constituent parts of a harder and coarser sort, the traditional dogma and the doctrine of sin and of justification. We must first of all speak of these constituent parts.

It is one of the laws of the history of religion that only in historical continuity and in the religious community does human faith have a strong life and continued development. Luther's power to form churches lay in the very fact that his reform corresponded to this law. If the first edict of Justinian's code, which established the results of the dogma-formulating councils up to that of Nicaea, still constituted in Luther's time the basis of public law, then Luther stood on this legal foundation. Also Zwingli, inwardly more liberal, in the Marburger discussion stood on this ground. Augustinianism was the spinal marrow of the medieval church. Its transformation, as the Augustinian monk accomplished it out of the need for inwardness, independence, and certainty of faith, changed the form and establishment of the dogmas decided upon at Nicaea through the change in the doctrine of the appropriation of salvation. The justification which the medieval individual experienced was an objective stream of powers, flowing downward out of the transcendental world through the Incarnation into the channels of the ecclesiastical institutions, ordination of the priests, sacraments, confession, and works to the believers. It was a supersensual regimental proceeding. The justification through the faith, which Luther experienced, was the personal experience of the believer standing in the continuity of the Christian community, who experienced in the personal event of faith the trust in the grace of God through the appropriation of the performance of Christ, brought about by the personal election of grace. If according to this a change in the conscious position toward dogma and in the establishment of faith in the same had to occur, still this change did not affect the substance of the old Christian dogma.

The content of Luther's faith insofar as it comes to terms with sacrament and the ecclesiastical association of the believers in the concepts of sin and grace, justification and atonement through the expiatory death of Christ, has recently, since Ritschl's significant presentation, been more clearly set forth than formerly. One must refer here to these presentations, particularly to the masterful one by Harnack. There is not the slightest doubt that in Luther, as in Zwingli, the energy of moral judgment, the certain conviction of the connection of man through his conscience with a highest Judge, the happy certainty, justified before him, to be allowed to work as his tool in the world, had found a deeper expression than at any time before. Precisely this content of faith, at one with the great tradition of the church, gave the reformers the heroic strength to shake off the apparatus and discipline of the curia and to be effective in forming churches. But at the same time there the matter must rest. This connection of religious concepts is not the exit of dogma, the "end of the old dogmatic Christianity" (if only one does not with this think of a system bound up in scientific demonstration). On the contrary, it has this dogma in all respects as its necessary presupposition. It stands and falls with the dogma. Indeed even the monastic, Franciscan religious ideal must be regarded as the hypothesis for the doctrine of sin and of the incapacity for good. In the measure in which the doctrine of original sin was detached from this dualistically motivated foundation it had to reach out to a completely indefensible representation of experiences concerning human nature. For Luther's doctrine of Christ and of justification through him makes Christ's "office and work which he has taken upon himself" the core of the dogma, to be sure, as opposed to the metaphysical definitions of existence. But precisely through this the concept of sacrifice, which for the moral sense is the most difficult part of the whole dogma, is placed even more decisively into the foreground. The limitation of temporal and eternal salvation to those vindicated and reconciled through the expiatory death by means of faith, a dogma which indeed reaches more mightily and more ominously into the feeling of individuals than any formed metaphysically, is held to by Luther more one-sidedly than ever before. And the necessary dogmatic-metaphysical hypothesis of this entire doctrine lies indeed in the nature of Christ, detached from the sinful context of all mankind. Finally, Luther's doctrine of Holy Communion preserved the entire metaphysical dogmatics of divine incarnation. All these dogmatic hypotheses have, to be sure, been placed into the service of a powerful, complete conviction of faith. Through this they become parts of a single vivid experience; they are removed from the reflection of reason. But they continue to stand firm. The doctrine of justification itself exists only so long as its dogmatic hypotheses are valid.

But now let us turn to what is new in Luther and Zwingli, that which reaches beyond their Paulinism and Augustinianism. We are seeking to lay hold of the inner progress of the framing and establishment of our higher convictions.

Greek Christianity remained in the metaphorical state of perceptual thinking. Its intelligible transcendent cosmos was the counterpart of the perceptually given cosmos. Its transcendence nowhere exceeded perceptual thinking. It lived in the supersensual drama of the trinity, of eternal generation, and of a world of divine powers. Roman Christianity was regimental. The Roman spirit could think of the religious process only as bound to a new spiritual imperium. The higher life flowed down from God upon the Christians only in the order and discipline regulated by this theocracy. The *Fides implicita* was the obedience of subjects. Only with the northern peoples did the religious process retreat into invisibility. It comprehends its complete difference from the perceptual thought processes, as they are operative in the formulas and proofs of the Greek dogma; and it detaches itself from the external apparatus of means, discipline, and works in a spiritual imperium demanding obedience, as this had been created by the Roman commanding spirit. In that Luther accomplishes this, the deepest movement of the Middle Ages, Franciscan Christianity and the mystics, completely culminates in him, and at the same time modern idealism begins in him. In the Franciscan and mystic movement the complete detachment of the religious event from all egoistic interest of man had taken place. This deeply true frame of mind, although containing only the one side of the religious-moral process, sometime had to be developed to its final consequences. Luther, the son of a miner; in the northern mountains; a monk in fogs, snow, and hardships of nature; without a shimmer of art in his soul; also without a stronger need for science, nothing but the uncertainty of everything higher around him—he for the first time detached the religious process completely from the metaphorical state of dogmatic thinking and of the regimental externality of the church.

For him life was the first thing. From life, from the moral-religious experiences gained in life, is derived all knowledge concerning our relationship to the invisible and remains bound to it. And thus the intellectual bond of the cosmos which ties the rational being to the world reason retires behind the moral connection.

And even if Luther continued to be negative towards religious universalistic theism, under the cover of his nominalistic hypotheses, as a progressive he attacked the ideal of life of the time all the more. Everywhere it surrounded him. He comprehended it in the highest sense: the inner occurrence of faith has its expression and sphere of activity in the formation of the entire external ordering of society. How this ideal later shriveled up for him!

On the basis of this position the treatise published in German and Latin in October 1520, *On the Liberty of the Christian Man,* developed the sum total of a Christian life, that is, the religious process, as it determined Luther's Christianity at that time. Man is free in the religious-moral process as the central point of his soul-life. With stoic energy Luther explains about the captivity of the body, of sickness and of pain. None "of these things reach to the soul, to free or to catch it." And with the idealism of a Carlyle or Fichte he characterizes holy garments, holy places, association with holy things as completely a matter of indifference. The religious process is in its essence a thing invisible, completely inaccessible to the intellect—faith. The presence of the Divine Word in the believing soul is a simple experience, the characteristic of which is trust in God. "The Word and faith alone rule in the soul. How the Word is, so also his soul becomes; just as the iron gets red-hot like the fire, out of the union with the fire." This writer, the most effective and most endowed with a ready command of language in our nation, was moreover at the same time also a poet. With a unique power of sincerity and of cordial poetry he clothes his religious experience in symbols. "Is that not a happy household, when the rich, noble, pious bridegroom, Christ, takes the poor scorned wicked soul in marriage?" "Who can think of

the honor and high place of a Christian person?" "Through his kingdom he is master of all things, through his priesthood he is master of
God." In this event there is contained in the first place that difficult
relationship of original sin to justification before God through faith by
means of the blood of Christ, which Luther found in Paul and the
Augustinianism around him and subordinated to his great fundamental thought of the autocracy of the believing person. At the same
time, however, it contains also the deeper and more primitive concept of a molding of the soul after God, which stems from the Gospels
and the mystics. From this follows the relationship of faith and work.
"Just as the trees have to exist before the fruits, and the fruits do not
make the trees either good or evil; on the contrary, the trees make the
fruits, thus man must beforehand be pious or evil in his character,
before he does good or bad works." "Therefore from faith flows the
love and desire for God, and from love flows a free, willing, happy
life, serving the neighbor freely."

The immediate consequence of this doctrine of the completely invisible and inner event of faith is the royal freedom of the Christian
individual and the universal priesthood. This freedom is not only the
external freedom from church discipline but also the inner one from
the complete power of the world, coinciding with the stoic concept of
freedom. "A Christian man through faith is so highly exalted above
all things that he, spiritual, becomes master of them, for not a thing
can harm him with respect to salvation. Yes, all has to be subject
unto him and help toward salvation." The freedom of the "inner man"
and his rule over all things consists in this, that everything becomes a
blessing for him and he doesn't even need any. The Christians are
consequently all independent through their faith. The priesthood is
universal. The spiritual office is only an office, a service, a "steward-
ship"; and the "worldly, external, splendid, terrible rule," which it has
become, must be condemned.

The *Sermon on Good Works* is regarded by Luther himself as belonging to that on *Liberty*. The relationship of faith to good works is
represented in this sermon as that of the health of the entire body to
the activity of the single members. "Life never rests." Human nature
is always action. Thus work must continually go forth out of faith.
The works originate, however, by themselves out of the content of
faith, since the believer therein "constitutes Christ in himself." The

work of faith alone reaches to God. And here we now encounter the formative principle of the social ethics of Luther. Out of faith follows as its expression "to do the work of God in the world." God "wants to accomplish his work in and through us." And now out of the richness of his inner experience, Luther conforming to the ten commandments, develops the formative endeavor of the believer in the world. Luther's power over the Germans rested upon the lively powers of transformation of the existing society, which grew out of his new way of interpreting Christianity. In a strong-willed, inventive, serious generation, which stood under new conditions and, in conformity with these, subjected the worn-out regulations to the criticism of the healthy intellect and finally wanted to set the constitution of the empire in order, he stood ahead of all. Above all his fearless stand toward the ruling forces more than anything else won for him all the better men. "It is easy to fight against the injustice which falls to popes, kings, princes, bishops, and other big-wigs. Here each one wants to be the most pious one." "Where, however, something happens to a poor and humble person, there the false eye does not find much pleasure, but it sees indeed the disfavor of the mighty ones. Therefore he probably lets the poor person remain unaided." "See, there many good works would exist, to be sure. For the greater part of the mighty, the rich and friends act wrongly and exercise authority against the poor, the humble and adversaries—and the bigger, the worse."

But here now for all practical purposes the most powerful writing of Luther takes hold in the continuity like a new link in a chain: *Address to the Christian Nobility of the German Nation, Concerning the Improvement of the Christian Estate,* 1520. It treats of the bearer of the transformation of German society and of the chief measures for such a transformation. The bearer of a social endeavor, such as follows from the deepened religious morality, is given in the political organization of the society. The "inner individual," the invisibility of the religious process in him, his freedom, contain in themselves no relationships of power and obedience in an ecclesiastical whole. Only the political alliance makes possible the organization of the social endeavor. Thus this alliance becomes the seat of all activity for the work of God in the world. The sphere of the works of faith is the secular society and the ordering of it. With this statement the complete dissolution of every thought of ecclesiastical activity has been accomplished for the first time. In it Luther's hard struggle against the "official boys"; against "the holy hypocrites"; against the pomp, might, and mass of good works; against all the "holy garments" first comes to a close. With it one of the greatest organizing thoughts which a person has ever had enters history. How unfortunate that Luther did not succeed in carrying it out in its purity! In opposition to the medieval doctrine of the two kingdoms, the secular and the spiritual, the Reformation sentence now appears: "Christ does not have two or two kinds of bodies, one secular and the other spiritual. He is one head and he has one body." The secular power is "baptized right away with us," that is, it is likewise practiced by Christian people, it is consequently likewise "a spiritual estate." Since in accord with divine regulation it is now endowed with force, through it the Christian society of the German people receives its organization. This includes all social activities, "shoemaker, smith, farmer, each has the office and work of his trade, with this each shall be useful to and serve the other. In a community, therefore, many kinds of work are done to benefit body and soul—just as the limbs of the body all serve one another. Now just such an office and work for the whole also all those commissioned to ecclesiastical acts perform, from the mendicant friar to the pope. And the state authority rules equally over all offices and all works. Thus one shall let their office go free, unhindered, through the whole body of Christendom." But since it is now filled with the new ideas, which are related to the entire change of the European spirit, the state must become the bearer and the voice of reforms in the ecclesiastical as well as the secular realm. In the name of the new Christian spirit Luther demands a transformation of German society in its secular and ecclesiastical arrangements. This was the time in which the words of this most German man resounded in almost every German breast, and all that the nation longed for in the empire and its government seemed in agreement with Luther's reform. Papal power, cardinals, canon law, annates, earnest-money for the pallium were condemned by Luther—in general, the carrying off of so much German money to Rome. Whoever came from Rome to let himself be assigned an endowed position ought to be thrown into the water. No confirmation of a spiritual office ought to be obtained from Rome. The pope should only superintend over the bishops in matters of faith. Everywhere the sharpest control of the financial power of the curia ought to take place. To remain in the monastery or to leave it was a matter of every monk's choice, to marry of every priest's. In the secular realm Luther demanded laws against the extravagance in clothes, against the enormous importing of foreign spices, the interest-buying, the big commercial businesses, the old German vice of enormous eating and drinking, the brothels—then general concern for the teaching of the youth. He refers to his words concerning the legal system: the spiderweb catches the little flies but the millstones fall through. Next to war the greatest evil seemed to him to be the wicked beasts—lions, wolves, snakes, dragons—those are the wicked rulers.

These were Luther's ideas of 1520. With them a new day seemed to be dawning over Germany. They arose out of a situation in which a reformed, national church under the pope still seemed possible. Luther at that time no longer expected the accomplishment of this reform through a general council, but rather from the German Empire, from the emperor, princes, nobility, and cities. When Charles V at that time, in October 1520, came to Germany for the coronation and the Diet, Hutten called out to him: "Day and night I shall serve you without pay. I want to awaken for you many a proud hero. You shall be the captain, the initiator, and the achiever, only your command is wanting!" Thus there existed in the spiritual life of the nation a close connection between the striving for a strong national government of the estates, an inner animation of the government through the pure gospel, and an ordering of the new faith into it. The memorandum from the bosom of the Diet at Worms concerning papal mismanagement and ecclesiastical abuses did in the final analysis stand on common ground with Luther's writing to the nobility and with Hutten's pamphlets. Would a realization of these ideas of Luther have been possible? To our misfortune our ecclesiastical imperial politics was conditioned by the foreign relationships between the emperor, the French king, and the pope.

Ernst Troeltsch
RENAISSANCE AND REFORMATION

Ernst Troeltsch, theologian and sociologist, was born in 1865. He taught at the universities of Bonn, Heidelberg, and Berlin. He died in 1923. Under the influence of Max Weber he applied sociological-historical methods to the investigation of religious subjects such as the social teachings of the Christian churches. A pioneer in his field, he was also much preoccupied with the problems of historicism.

Renaissance and Reformation constitute the end of the Catholic-ecclesiastical culture of the West, which one usually refers to as the Middle Ages. This position of the two movements in universal history and their contemporaneousness has caused many authors to take them for two different yet inwardly related and complementary instances of one and the same great common movement. Having once recognized, with Jacob Burckhardt, the Renaissance as the discovery of the individual and having found modern individualism with respect to its aesthetic and philosophical side essentially developed from it, it was easy to see in the Reformation the breakthrough of this very same individualistic principle with respect to the religious side. One could add to this that the destruction of the old bonds at the same time meant liberation for the concrete fullness of life. Thus one recognized in both movements a turning toward the world and this present life, in the Renaissance with the full emancipation of secular culture and in the Reformation with a new religious consecration and sanctification of life in the world. Thus both movements taken together could be viewed as the genitor of the modern spirit and depending upon the personal cultural conception of the author could be portrayed either as permanently determinative for each other or at least as the molding powers of modern culture temporarily promoting each other. F. C. Baur, the pioneer of scientific research on the history of Christianity, already spoke in this sense: "The Reformation can only be viewed as the product of a time involved in the greatest progress. Nothing is better established than the assertion that from

Translated by Lewis W. Spitz from Ernst Troeltsch, *Renaissance und Reformation, Gesammelte Schriften*, IV (Tübingen, 1925), 261–296. Used by permission of the publishers, J. C. B. Mohr (Paul Siebeck) Verlag, Tübingen.

the point of view of a time in which the general enlightenment and culture had made such progress and had pressed so deeply into the life of the people, the condition of a church which still carried the whole stamp of the Middle Ages upon it could not remain what it was up to then. Also here the revolution demanded by the spirit of the time had to follow, and the greater the importance everything related to religion and Christianity had, the more thorough and consequential the change had to be once it took place." But it was not only the pupils of Hegel who judged in this manner, which can be easily understood in terms of Hegel's philosophy of history. Also a modern presentation of the history of philosophy, proceeding from entirely different premises, but also distinguished by a keen understanding of general relationships appertaining to the history of civilization, namely, Windelband's *History of Modern Philosophy,* holds:

> *What one customarily designates as the religious Reformation or simply as the Reformation is a partial aspect of the general Renaissance, which indeed holds an important place in it, but by no means constitutes, as it has every now and again been portrayed, its most important and compelling motive. It has merely gained this appearance, because the rebellion against the church common to all the movements of the new mode of thought had to come to its simplest and clearest articulation in it. . . . And so one came upon the idea that the individual might possibly find the comfort and blessing of religion in himself and the wish for an unmediated independent religiosity powerfully forced its way through. This wish was nourished by the unbroken tradition of mystical teachings—they actually contain the spiritual kernel of the religious Renaissance.*

Both assertions yield approximately this formula: in the movement leading from the Middle Ages to the modern spirit the Renaissance and Reformation are related to each other as secular and religious Renaissance. This formula would not be a thing of indifference, or of no concern, to the accurate historian. For it would lay down, if for the most part correct, a very important conception of the development of European culture and of the essence of the modern world, which would also have to give the accurate historian direction in many ways in his conception of the facts. It is, therefore, very much worthwhile to ask to what extent and in what sense such a formula is justified.

Now it is not to be denied that various considerations and observations seem to speak for the correctness of the formula. Above all it is perfectly clear that in reality the dissolution of the medieval world brought with it the feeling of great universal total changes, that the religious, political, and cultural reform efforts in all of Europe in the fourteenth and fifteenth centuries flowed inseparably together, that the possibility of success was for both movements based on this general feeling, and that thereby in both the individual came to the fore in a very important way. It is furthermore indisputable and established through the total historical effect that as a result of both movements the position of man toward the world and this life became essentially different from what it was in medieval culture. In its total effect Protestantism benefited the rendering independent of the political, social, and economic life; and after the shattering of its first dogmatic hardening it also opened up a fruitful field for modern learning. The Renaissance for its part at least established the modern absolute and secular state as well as artistic and intellectual culture completely dependent upon itself and thereby gave the first stimuli to the development of the modern world of ideas. Above and beyond this general total direction the particular means and establishments of both movements also seem to be closely related and in intimate association. In both cases one returned to the oldest bases of European culture; purified it of scholastic distortions; and endeavored to renew life from these genuine, revived authorities. The call *ad fontes* and the feeling of rebirth, of *renascens pietas,* and of *renascentes litterae,* are common to both. They feel themselves to be a rejuvenation of the European spirit from its sources and are actually just that, even though, to be sure, they brought forth from these sources something new which had not previously been there. And it is possible to go farther. The two movements are not only in content and form closely related quantities within the total movement, but they affect and interpenetrate one another in many ways. They are not divided roughly between North and South Europe, so that they correspond to the folk-characteristics and general relationships of North and South and thereby could almost appear to be the nationally different inflections of the total movement, which, however, are indifferent to each other. Rather, the Italian Renaissance produces a mystical, Platonizing Paulinism, the results of which flow into the northern Reformation and the individual representatives of which could pass for parallels to the religious movement of the North, as they then indeed adopted for themselves in many ways the teachings of the northern reformers. Conversely, in the North humanism imported from Italy was the forerunner of the Reformation and through the actions of Lefèvre, Erasmus, and Melanchthon it frequently amalgamated with it. Yes, the humanist theology of the Sozzinis, of Servetus, and of Hugo Grotius actually signified a combination of both movements. Finally when after the close of the age of confessional battles Protestantism under the leadership of Locke and Leibniz appropriated the whole learned culture of modernity and the new Protestantism of the Enlightenment arose allied with modern philosophy and natural science, then Reformation and Renaissance appeared as the great modern achievements which had at last found each other and united for the founding of a new ethical-religious and at the same time learned and humanistically minded Christianity. Out of this total situation come the utterances of the older Goethe which are often cited as the basis for such a view: "It is not to be denied that the spirit tried to free itself through the Reformation. The enlightenment about Greek and Roman antiquity brought forth the wish, the longing for a freer, more respectable and more elegant life. It was favored not a little thereby that the heart (with the Reformation) strove to return to a certain simple natural condition and to flee from the power of imagination." The other expression is better known which likewise is an interpretation of the Reformation with the help of the humanist spirit of the Renaissance: "We do not know at all what all we have to thank Luther and the Reformation for in general. We have been freed from the fetters of spiritual narrow-mindedness; as a consequence of our growing culture we have become capable of returning to the sources and of grasping Christianity in its purity. We once again have the courage to stand with firm feet on God's earth and to perceive ourselves in our God-given human nature." [Goethe]

These observations and expressions show us, to be sure, that a certain elective affinity and possibility for contact indeed exist. But the question is, whether it is precisely this side of the matter from which the essence of both phenomena and their position and effect in universal history is to be grasped above all or whether, much more the other way around, this significance is not due to precisely the differences and contrasts suppressed and blurred in such judgments. The frame of mind in which Goethe passed his judgment is for us today, now that we have experienced Schopenhauer and Nietzsche, no longer so self-evident. In the feeling of the tensions and contrasts of our time the contrast between Renaissance and Reformation comes to our consciousness more than their mutual complement. Above all, we have available today for both phenomena and for the Middle Ages out of which they grew much more deeply penetrating researches which show us the relationship of the facts in a much different light. Dilthey summarized and furthered the condition of present-day research in his famous treatise on the "Interpretation and Analysis of Man in the Fifteenth and Sixteenth Centuries," as well as in various other large treatises on the seventeenth century. But also here the Renaissance and Reformation are brought too close to each other and are viewed too much as common presuppositions of the "natural system of the Enlightenment," in which the system of theologically transcendent metaphysics, dissolved by both of them together, was replaced by a new rationalistically immanent system. For him the Middle Ages is the vital expression of theological metaphysics, whereas the Renaissance and Reformation are for him the dissolution of the same through an individualistic subjectivism and an autonomous retreat to one's own self. For him the natural system follows from this as the last great European expression and domination of life by metaphysics, which (proceeding from a deepening into the subject incorporates in its autonomy an unmetaphysical transcendental thought, but which thereupon still—essentially under the influence of the Stoa—would have become metaphysics again, but) today has been subdued by an unmetaphysical relativism and psychologism of historical appreciation. But also this construction is too much under predominantly philosophical points of view, (yes, even under epistemological theoretical viewpoints, searching for the theory of historical and intellectual sciences). We must rather allow both movements to speak more for themselves and above all try to grasp uniformly as much as possible in each one its spirit and import. Only then can the further questions follow about the derivative conception of the European total development.

The spirit of the Renaissance at any rate with the expression "the discovery of modern individualism" is not accurate for the total compass of the movement and is not exhaustive for the high point designated thereby, namely, the high Renaissance. For on the one hand this individualism flowed into European life already, out of late antiquity and Christianity and, precisely, in the first stages of the Renaissance, the mystical reformatory movements, and revolutions of the late Middle Ages; it was already exceptionally strongly pronounced in a mixture of Augustinian, Neoplatonic, sectarian, and political-social motifs. On the other hand the specifically modern individualism with its rationalistic and ethical autonomy, its natural law and competitive principle, has completely different presuppositions and goals for the creation of a closed rational and organized cultural whole. The peculiarity of the Renaissance lies not in unfettered individualism as such, but in the change in the direction of interests, whereby the increasing loosening from the hereafter and from the church as the institution of grace and the monkish ideal on the whole first resulted. Indeed, this was accomplished by a development which was very diverse and full of tensions. The motifs which changed the direction of interests are of very different kinds. Only in the final results of the high Renaissance is the opposition against the medieval and ecclesiastical-Christian world worked out, which from that point on is viewed as characteristic for the Renaissance as such and which in reality indicates its universal historical effect. But wherein does this change in the direction of interests consist, which established the difference as against the medieval spirit and which in the end effected the break with the old authorities, constraints, and collective unities, that is, the rendering independent of scientific aesthetic humanity?

Taken as a whole the Renaissance is the entrance of Italy into general history, the contrast of an Italian culture against the French theological and chivalric world of ideas which previously ruled the Middle Ages. In this cooperation of the political and economic elevation of the Italian states and cities and of the reawakening antique traditions of Italy this Italian spirit came into being, which discovered itself as a rejuvenation of itself and through the increasing secularization of its cultural ideas withdrew from the great late medieval program of the reform of church and empire. . . .

The spirit of the Renaissance, therefore, is not at all to be formulated too uniformly and above all is not simply to be equated with modern ideas, whether those of Goethe or of Nietzsche. It can be formulated only in the most general, more formal basic directions: it is the independent individualism of the universal and autonomous unfolding of the self and the freeing of the image of things from the shadows and depreciations interposed from the supernatural. Only in this sense is Burckhardt's formula justified that it was the discovery of man and of the world. . . .

The final intellectual result, the spirit of the Renaissance, is first expressed in Renaissance philosophy proper, that group of philosophers who stand between the Aristotelian church philosophy and medieval nominalism on the one side and the modern natural-scientific mechanical orientation of philosophy on the other side. Their leaders are Giordano Bruno and Michel Montaigne. Here we encounter the meaning of the Renaissance philosophically conceived, and the whole world agrees that thereby precisely here the great anticipations of modern thought were really accomplished. What we find here are the conceptions familiar to us which are merely reformulated and expressed more scientifically in the whole modern philosophy. These are: the doubt about an absolute, which Descartes then built up into a basic principle of an autonomous philosophy; the proceeding from the conscious or from the microcosm as the mirror of the macrocosm, from which Leibniz's monadology created a central conception of modern speculation; the optimistic-aesthetic total view of the universe, which in Shaftesbury and Herder became the formula of the universe; the Copernican universe and infinity, from which derived the infinity of the spiritual worlds and the dissolution of anthropocentrism and anthropomorphism; the idea of progress and development, which allows the divinity which is so intensely comprehended in the microcosm to expand itself in the genesis and growth of souls; the comparative psychological relativism, which everywhere dissolves conventionalities and makes the absolute a problem; the pressing back of the absolute into the depths of the subject, whereby its splendor spreads out again over all that is sensual and real; the realism free from illusions, which seeks the laws of the soul and of history and then again in them honors Reason; the feeling of aloneness, that maintains the principal homogeneity of the universe and of that which occurs in all reaches of space and struggles with the irrationality of the individual. Briefly, macrocosm and microcosm appear in a new light, and from the latter's self-understanding arises all knowledge and from its pure self-representation all art arises.

From this vantage point the question of the relationship to the Reformation may be raised. The moral weaknesses of the Renaissance can remain out of consideration here. It is undeniable that such a way of thinking psychologically offers a narrower footing and more confused impulses for moral force than does the concentrated and established Christian world of ideas which precisely on this point is so very effective. Nor is it necessary first to refer to the innumerable causes of Italian corruption, which were not given with this spirit itself. In mere theory the Renaissance, too, is not without a lofty moral impetus, as far as its Stoic and Platonic ideals come into consideration. On the other hand also in the case of the Reformation the ethical ideal was only very conditionally realized and showed many shadowy sides in practice, which Luther and the reformers bitterly complained about, as is well known. But such a pure historical point of view is not at all concerned with a moral judgment, but rather with the recognition of the relationships of facts. It is not immorality here and morality there that makes the historically effective difference, but the inner contradiction of the spirit on both sides.

To be sure the spirit of the Reformation is also not to be formulated so simply and is far from being correctly comprehended in the usual theological dogmatic formulas. The formula of the formal principle of the Bible as sole authority and of the material principle of the doctrine of justification is an entirely dogmatic and, in addition, a very late schematization. But also the formula of religious individualism and of the sanctifying of life in the world through the individual assurance of salvation living itself out in vocation is completely unclear and useless. For Protestantism is individualistic only in comparison with Catholic authority. To be sure, it allows religious certainty to come into being only in individual personal experience and to that extent differentiates itself fundamentally from Catholic certainty, which depends upon the hierarchical institution, the supernatural authority of dogma and canon law, finally, on the miracle of the healing and forgiving sacrament, and overcomes all variations of subjective feeling through the divine institution which hedges it in and directs it. But the certainty of the Protestant is individual only insofar as it is an inner, intellectual, spiritual reassurance and there-

FIGURE 2. *The Four Horsemen of the Apocalypse,* by Albrecht Dürer (1471–1528). First published in 1498, this illustration refers to Rev. 6: 1–8 and reflects the somber mood of the time. From Kenneth A. Strand, *Woodcuts to the Apocalypse in Dürer's Time* (Ann Arbor: Ann Arbor Publishers, 1968), no. 4, p. 15. Used by permission of the author.

fore can be achieved only individually and personally. But the object by which it is won, the Bible, the proclamation of salvation of the reconciling work of the God-man and the sacramental reassurance of this salvation, is still also in its case something completely supernatural, given, authoritative. As far as spiritual certainty is concerned it also is only an intellectual object to be accepted in faith. Therefore this religious individualism is based nowhere directly on God and his presence in the soul, but always on the Bible and on the Word of the forgiveness of sins in Christ. Communication with God is always objectively mediated, only that the mediation does not exist in a hierarchical sacramental salvation-apparatus, but in the Bible and in its central teaching. For that reason real Protestantism also passionately rejected as enthusiasts the representatives of an immediate contemporary revelation of God in the spirit. Therefore also with this objective means of certainty, of the Scriptures and of the Word, it reconstructed the institution of salvation of the church, as an institution based on the objective Word and the sacrament and recognizable through them. Or, rather, it purified the Catholic church concept of priesthood, divine right of the priest, and magian sacramental magic and in its place built up a church based on pure doctrine and rendered too firm through its safeguarding of the doctrine. And this church, as a result of the inner logic of its thought as well as through practical necessity, became just as authoritative and coercive a church, tied to state power, as the Catholic.

But precisely here lie the great differences from the individualism of the Renaissance. This is really free of authority with the full autonomy of the subject, fully, freely flexible in its artistic view and bound in intellectual work only by the rules of logic. The tie to the authority of antiquity is a carry-over of the Middle Ages and a sign of the childhood of modern thought, but at the same time it was a new interpretation of antiquity, a radical critique of the pseudo-antiquity of the Middle Ages and in the end yielded completely, when the new natural scientific method had given the thinkers an independent and fruitful new principle. But for this very reason the Renaissance is sociologically completely unproductive. It is anarchistic and aristocratic in its innermost circles and moreover it leans with complete dependence upon the existent powers in state and church. It creates sociologically the aristocracy of culture and the salon and for the rest pays homage to might and power. In contrast, the individualism of the Reformation is only a deepening and spiritualizing of purely objective, supernatural binding realities, but in no way an unconditional religious autonomy. But for this very reason the sociological energy of the Reformation is most extraordinary. It creates the territorial churches of Lutheranism and Calvinism, which gave to developing absolutism a religious consecration. It increases the religious cohesion of the masses, in that every single member is made interested and responsible. And against governments of a different faith it battles for popular rights and religious freedom. Those are very extraordinary differences going into the innermost structure of the spirit of each.

But the contrast is even greater, when we turn to the ethics of world affirmation, which for Protestantism results from the putting aside of monasticism and of extrameritorious works and to that extent follows from the spirituality valid for all believers and from the inwardness of faith. If religious achievement consists alone in the trusting personal yielding to conviction in God's Word and if this demand is completely the same for all, there can be no extrameritorious works and no religious exceptional positions. But if these do not exist, all men are assigned in the same way to trial in secular life and this must be viewed as the natural and God-ordained room for the activity of the Christian. Thereby the world and secular life indeed assume a place of honor as the material and form of faith's activity, and at this point Protestant pathos could very well tie up with the new secular tone of the late Middle Ages, with the national alienation from Rome, with the political and social needs for emancipation from the ecclesiastical and monastic order of life, with all sorts of economic and civic needs of the masses. Only this Protestant affirmation of the world is still in its inner essence something completely different from the dissolution of Christian asceticism and otherworldliness by the Renaissance. It remains on the foundation of the strongest conception of sin and of the most convinced otherworldliness. Original sin or the complete lost condition and condemnation of all non-Christians and nonbelievers is even more significant for it than for Catholicism and the conception of life as a place of testing, sorrow, and trial for the heavenly beyond is, if possible, even more emphasized. The belief in the devil and demons is stressed more sharply than before. Under these circumstances the Protestant affirmation of the world could only occasionally mean the recognition of the divine glory of creation, as it is expressed inwardly and piously in Paul Gerhardt's hymns, but it was never failing also in Catholicism. Christian sin-pessimism, Christian otherworldliness, and Christian belief in the devil increased in the Reformation; and these elements belong very particularly to those points at which the Reformation renewed antique Christianity in contrast to the medieval Catholic secularization. It is only the basic Christian optimism of creation shining through these dark clouds, when in the fine arts and good gifts of God the divine character is also for once acknowledged in nature. In particular all secular social orders, the family, the state, private property, commerce, society divided into estates are for it the expression of reason and nature, to be sure, but exactly as in the case of Catholicism, the expression of a nature which has become sinful, in which the rational capacity reacts against the selfishness of original sin through the establishment of secular orders and discipline under God's permission and dispensation. As in the case of Augustine all of these things are also for the Reformation establishments of sin, that is, of reason under the condition of sin, punishment, and remedy against sin. This way of looking at it is here increased rather than made paler. Under these circumstances the Reformation affirmation and sanctification of the world appears to be a special kind of thing. It limits itself basically to the freeing of the secular life from the priestly-hierarchical government and control, in that it leaves it to itself and to its relative rational capacity as well as to the conscience bound to God's word. With that a freer and less restricted development was given to it, which finally burst the Reformation limitations, but no new meaning.

As far as a new meaning is given to it at all it is in the concept of vocation. The callings meant for the Middle Ages already the system of division of labor, in which in different forms and local administrative unions, the cultural achievements of procreation and education, of government and administration, of food production, of industrial labor, and exchange of goods are accomplished. A view of society which is estate, corporate, and traditionalist lies behind this conception of vocation as its foundation. For the Middle Ages, however, this system of vocations was merely the rational-natural order of the profane natural relationships of life, above which the priesthood and ascetic estate elevated itself as the higher and actual Christian order. But insofar as the latter was omitted for Protestantism, the vocations or the natural estate system of the division of labor became the natural material and room for Christian activity, which was now no longer to rise up over these in the region of the transcendent-supra-sensual, but was to pour out its loving disposition, free of the world and reconciled to God, into these natural forms of life. They were closely tied in with the sinful world, to be sure, but signified within its hypotheses the means to a wholesome self-discipline and to a furthering of human society and thereby of the neighbor. Thus the secular callings are everywhere only the forms and means for the activity of a loving disposition free of the world and of a wholesome discipline of life. It itself and the secular life involved in it are never ends in themselves and contain nothing of an immediate divinity of the world and of creative human power. They are merely the God-given traditional forms in which the transcending of the world of a strong and self-controlled heart as well as the passion of love of a religious brotherly love should be invested. The most sublime disposition, beyond the world, in the everyday worldly forms, the drawing in of the system of vocation out of the merely natural order into the self-activation of religious ethics itself: that is the essence of this Reformation affirmation of the world. Thereby the system of vocation should and must naturally be held on a level on which it becomes only form and means and nowhere a secular end in itself, on the level of an estate-incorporated order which assures the modest satisfaction of needs. This is in reality a new reconciliation of the world and the supernatural, an inner contraction of Christian asceticism and secular work, such as Catholicism had known it only as a concession to the world, but not as an immediate and essential basic truth and power of the Christian ethos. It is no wonder that Protestantism in this way promoted secular work and secular interests. But this revision of the world was in truth and in its real meaning actually a crude Christian idealism and a Christian Utopia which had to learn by experience that the sanctification of the world is a dangerous and two-sided thing which is easily more favorable to the world than to sanctification. And especially art and learning were not advanced in this way, for they really do not lend themselves as concerns of a

Christian vocation and Protestantism always permitted them merely for the use or ornamentation of the state and church. Its Christian purism recognized an end in itself in both cases much less even than Catholicism had. It appropriated humanism and Renaissance only in the sense of utility or of the permissible ornamentation of speech, of edifices, of festivals, of the conduct of life, of the church and of the court. The powerful cultural effects of the old and genuine Protestantism therefore lay only in the areas where loyalty to vocation, earnestness, sternness, industry, the sense of duty in office, and the freedom of conscience in belief could have an effect. Thus it strengthened the absolute princely dominion and bureaucracy, produced popular freedom together with freedom of belief, generated the modern disposition toward business management and labor, and organized half the world through freedom from Rome into a new political system. These are all extraordinary cultural achievements and affirmations of the world, through which a very thin borderline indeed runs between the Protestant Christian animation of this secular labor and the secularization of state, economy, and society which is no longer Protestant. To be sure a Protestant art did exist, and art on its own soil and with clear evidence of the influence of its spirit. Everyone will immediately think of Johann Sebastian Bach and the Netherlands. But that the artistic spirit should arise also in this sphere and then show the evidence of the spirit ruling here is only self-evident. But the "spirit of Protestantism," its ethics and its theory had for these things only the category of vocation and even today has nothing else for them. But that is merely an indication that it has no room for the metaphysical and ethical content of art. Art is a good gift of God like the beauty of nature. It offers an opportunity for useful callings and adapts itself to God's honor and man's pleasure and recreation in the system of Christian life in the world.

How different by way of contrast is the Renaissance affirmation of the world! It is in no way bound to the concept of vocation which in Protestantism became the synthesis of the world and of asceticism. Yes, it does not even know the concept of vocation and just the other way around signifies the emancipation of artistically free culture, of free research, of personal self-exhibition and self-culture from all the bonds of a bourgeois scheme of vocation. Its ideal is the man without vocation who receives freedom for self-development and self-achievement in the universality of his strength and talents through joining the ruling powers, through annuities, or through his own exploitation of government. Its goal is the *uomo universale,* the gallant, the man of spiritual freedom and of culture, the precise opposite of the man of vocation and the specialist. The Renaissance man admits also religious idealism only as an ingredient of rich and full human nature in the harmony of his being, not that he conversely completes an essentially religious way of life through cultivation of good ethics also in the realm of the natural. In this difference there is found not just a single instance of distinction, but the whole principal contrast of the position vis-à-vis the world. The affirmation of the world in both instances is basically different. In the case of the Reformation it is the surrender and submission of the otherworldly man to the present God-given orders of life and livelihood with the greatest faithfulness in labor but with inner independence. In the case of the Renaissance it is the working out of the microcosm within the divine macrocosm, with which it is basically identical and whose divinity lives precisely in the fullness of his natural essential instinct. To be sure a changed position of the total life toward the world is contained also in that Reformation doctrine of vocation and in the decidedly relative affirmation of the world expressed through it. But here again it is in a new sense subjected to Christian asceticism. In contrast, the world affirmation of the Renaissance succeeds in the sign of the universal man of culture and of the optimistic master of nature, who sees the divine essence of man realizing itself, where anything of this essence matters to him at all, in the immanent working out of self.

If one now stresses these contrasts in proportion to their actual meaning, then a fundamental difference appears between both movements in spite of all the possibilities for contact. The unanimous condemnation of Copernicus by all the reformers; the picture of the lonely and foreign Giordano Bruno wandering through the narrow streets of Wittenberg, Marburg, and Geneva; the funeral pyre of Servetus—all that sheds glaring light on the inner essential difference. The one is a rejuvenated Christianity which has taken up within itself the Catholic idea of the church, of Christian secular culture, and of mystical inwardness as well as a large part of the late medieval secular bourgeois interests. The other is rejuvenated antiquity, which has incorporated within itself the Copernican universe, Christian depth of soul, practical rule over nature, universality of culture, and all sorts of specifically modern interests and thereby has become a new comprehensive modern principle of life. . . .

If one understands both movements the way they worked out in their historical development, then they appear very clearly as the schism of European culture into its main components, the separation of the Christian-supernatural-ascetic element from the antique, inner-worldly human element. In both cases the special shape and form in which each of these elements shows itself is naturally determined in a characteristic and new way by the context of circumstances. The northern Germanic Reformation is connected with the late medieval bourgeoisie and with the condition of the empire; the Italian Renaissance is connected with the Italian republics, courts, and financial aristocracies. It is not merely a matter of working out abstract contrasts which they did not observe and recognize as such in their own time. But this contrast came to light in its universal historical effect—and indeed it revealed a cultural and intellectual-historical point of view in the meaning of such a separation on principle. It is the moment of greatest distance in the mutual movement of the two stars which continually attract and repel each other. . . .

That this is the true relationship is shown finally by the further course of development of each.

First of all, the religious renewal or the Reformation was by far the stronger principle. It won back interest in the religious goal of life, rekindled religious passions, knotted them together with all possible material interests, and transformed Europe. Meanwhile the old church also followed the reform drive in its way for two centuries in an inflexible armed power struggle of confessional battles in which also the secular interests had to allow themselves to be religiously motivated. The coercive ecclesiastical system set up everywhere again, the unification of political and ecclesiastical power, the resurrection of scholasticism and of scholastic Aristotelianism in all the churches, the tying of spiritual life to the confessions and clerical points of view—all that seemed to mean the return in threefold multiplication of the Middle Ages, which had long since been overcome. . . .

In contrast, the base of the Renaissance in rudimentary human instincts was much narrower and especially the sociological cultural drive and the formative power in this thin aristocratic-individualistic cultural stratum was much too weak. It needed union with the great ruling powers in which the popular instincts were ordered and bound together and from which the virtuosos of the intellectual and artistic life received their means of existence. State offices, ecclesiastical prebendaries, annuities and pensions, the good deeds of great Maecenases or of public authorities were the material foundation of the entire spring of culture. For that reason these people everywhere clung firmly to the old or new church and hung on to the political authorities. . . .

Under these circumstances there was nothing left for the Renaissance to do but to attach itself to the great powers of the day, to the church and to the absolute princedom. And here, then, its attachment to Catholicism and the Catholic powers is infinitely stronger, more inward, and more productive. That is easy to understand from the essence of Catholicism. It had always viewed the natural sphere as a relatively independent substructure of the kingdom of grace and save for the readiness to be submissive had granted to natural life a very ample freedom of movement. Moreover, it, i.e., the natural life, could indeed at any time be led through the institution of confession and penance and its excesses could thereby always be atoned for. On the other hand, indeed, the Stoicism and Platonism of the Renaissance had also asserted the old elective affinity of these ideas to the Catholic Church to a largo oxtont. It io thoroforo no wondor that tho Renaissance first found its great universal historical success and extension in this amalgamation with the Catholicism of the counterreformation. . . .

It follows from this that the next strongest adoption and amalgamation of the Renaissance took place in that Protestant state and church which remained the closest to the Catholic, that is, in the Anglican absolutism of the Tudors and Stuarts. . . .

All the rest of Protestantism is much more reserved toward the Renaissance. To be sure everything more specific must first be established by monographic research, which up to now has not been accustomed to such viewpoints as these. One can say, however, on the basis of a general impression that Calvinism still always advanced to meet it halfway more than did Lutheranism. . . .

On the whole, Christendom—the church and especially Protestantism—therefore appears first of all for two centuries vis-à-vis the Renaissance as the much stronger power. To be sure this power is in no way a purely contrary and destructive one, but means an assimilating transformation, only that the latter is much more reserved and averse in Protestantism than in Catholicism. But it was precisely in this weakening, refraction, and assimilation that the Renaissance became a world culture and permeated all the pores of high society. It is no wonder, therefore, when in the eighteenth century the page was turned and the Renaissance, strengthened in that manner, made itself independent in turn and overcame the old opponent, in Catholic territory through radical anti-Christianity, in Protestant territory through the inner conquest and penetration of Protestant Christianity itself. To be sure that is no longer the old Renaissance, but the Enlightenment. The Enlightenment, however, is not merely the continuation, strengthening, and rendering independent of the Renaissance, but a most complicated new principle, the essence and origin of which is also only now being made the object of really penetrating research. . . .

But as far as the past is concerned and the changes in the relationship of the two great movements upon which this essay has thrown light, it teaches us to recognize something typical in this single case of the contrast between German Reformation and Italian Renaissance at any rate. It is the original contrast of European life, which returns in ever new forms and is never set aside in all emerging of great new problems of life. It is the original contrast of the double origin of our European world out of the prophetic, Christian religious world and out of the spiritual culture of antiquity. The contrast is not mutually exclusive. At all times, from the first amalgamation on, lines of relationship led back and forth from the one to the other. But the contrariety is by far most predominant. Both elements postulate in their tension greatness and wealth, variation and sudden change of our spiritual development, and together with the tension associated with them will be our fate as long as our culture still possesses a living spirit at all. Christian asceticism always builds anew its kingdom of the supernatural and thereby subordinates all natural excellence and self-strength to a higher world of earnestness and of austerity, in order to attain which everything else must be sacrificed as for the precious pearl in the Gospel. On the other hand, against this the needs and drives of nature, the aesthetic feeling for the world, the creative consciousness of power, the antique tradition and universal thought which questions everything always rebel anew. From that spring up then again and again the results of a more artistic than moral ethics and the metaphysical identity systems of the most different types. But insofar as the souls also here nowhere find rest, asceticism once again raises its head and directs attention to the great otherworld beyond nature, sometimes more in a Christian or sometimes more in an Indian form which is today more fashionable. A witness for this is that the same scholar who created for us the picture of the Renaissance which is today the dominant one and who thereby presented to the phantasy of countless numbers the dreamland of an artistically ennobled naturalism, Jacob Burckhardt, in a more comprehensive reflection on the totality of history [*Reflections on History*] concludes a remarkable chapter on "historical crises" with these words: "The whole major decision can only proceed from the inner depth of mankind. Will the optimism, expressed as sense of power and sense of might, continue and for how long? Or will, as the pessimistic philosophy of this present time might possibly indicate, a general change in the way of thinking set in as in the third and fourth centuries?" These centuries to which Burckhardt refers are the centuries of asceticism.

Lewis W. Spitz

THE THIRD GENERATION OF GERMAN RENAISSANCE HUMANISTS

Lewis W. Spitz is professor of history at Stanford University. He has taught at Harvard, University of Missouri, and Duke, and was Fulbright Professor at the Institute for European History of the University of Mainz in 1960–1961. He has published extensively on the Renaissance and the Reformation move-ments and is the American managing editor of the Archive for Reformation History, *the official journal of the American Society for Reformation Research and the* Verein für Reformationsgeschichte.

After a full century of scholarly research, we are much better in-formed about the relationship of the Renaissance to the Middle Ages, much better informed than we are about its relationship to the period which followed. Similarly, we have learned a good deal more about the relationship of that cultural movement which we call humanism to its medieval sources of origin, to its scholastic prede-cessors, to its Byzantine inheritance, to its classical fountainhead than we have about its relationship to that movement which followed it, the Reformation. This paper is concerned with one facet of this relationship. Within the framework of the great debate on the medi-eval or the modern nature of the Reformation, exemplified best by Wilhelm Dilthey and Ernst Troeltsch, progress can be made only in terms of specifics, through an examination of the precise circum-stances within which the Reformation developed. The juxtaposition of humanism and the Reformation, of humanists and reformers, may provide more concrete evidences than the general assertions with which the arguments on both sides of the question are usually pro-moted. The present problem was posed for historians by Luther himself, a man not insignificant in the events of his day, who, per-ceiving quite early that the Gospel made very little headway among the older men, wondered why. The Reformation was revolutionary, cutting deeper than had humanism, and breaking more decisively

Lewis W. Spitz, "The Third Generation of German Renaissance Humanists," in *Aspects of the Renaissance: A Symposium,* edited by Archibald R. Lewis (Austin and London: University of Texas Press, 1967), pp. 105–121. Used by permission of the University of Texas Press.

with the past. A young man's movement, it was in large part the work of the third generation of humanists in the North.

The Christian humanism of the North reflected the pattern of development familiar from the Italian Renaissance. A literary-philological phase was in many areas followed by a Platonic metaphysical phase. To a greater extent than has heretofore been realized humanism also invaded the courts and chancelleries of the secular and ecclesiastical princes as well as the councils of the city-states in the empire and played a formative role through Roman law and classical letters. In the case of each of the major countries of the North it is possible to distinguish three generations of humanists: a pioneering generation, exhausting much of its energy in the acquisition of new classical learning and confronting some of the normative issues raised by the classical world view; a second generation, marking the highest achievement of renowned humanists; and a third and younger generation setting out upon a course of action to change that society which their elders merely criticized.

Thus in England the pioneers in classical studies such as Grocyn and Linacre were followed by the high generation of Oxford reformers, More, Colet, and Erasmus. These, in turn, were superseded by the young activists such as Starkey and Morison, who became the founders and expediters of Tudor policy in statecraft; or Tyndale, Roger Ascham, and others, who became leaders in the religious and educational reform movement. In France the early pioneers such as Fichet, Standonck, and Gaguin were followed by the high generation of French humanism such as Budé and Lefèvre d'Étaples. Then came the young humanists, such men as Jean Calvin, who were no longer satisfied with criticism, but, following upon the impetus of conversion in many cases, were bent upon changing the world, The special vocation which this generation felt can be detected in Guillaume Farel's account of his dramatic interview with the aged Lefèvre. "That pious old man, Jacques Faber, whom you know," wrote Farel, "having taken my hand there forty years ago, said to me: 'It is necessary for the world to be changed and you will see it'."

In German humanism such pioneers as Rudolph Agricola were followed by such great names as Mutian, Reuchlin, Celtis, Pirckheimer, Wimpheling, Erasmus, and Peutinger. The younger humanists of the third generation were impatient for change and became the men who, with Luther, made the Reformation. Bernd Moeller at Göttingen University asserts with epigrammatic force: Without the humanists there would have been no Reformation. With the singular exception of Luther himself, the leaders of the Reformation in the German cultural area moved from humanism into the Reformation. Major figures such as Zwingli, Melanchthon, Oecolampadius, Bucer, or Vadian come immediately to mind. Scholarship has come increasingly to appreciate the importance of humanist learning also in the case of the radical reformers: Anabaptist leaders such as Balthasar Hubmaier, or the evangelical rationalists, or spiritualists such as Servetus or Sebastian Franck. But the historian must not stay with the major figures, leaping from peak to peak, for, like the alpinist, he must traverse also the valleys and lesser plateaus or foothills between the heights. A host of less well-known men were Christian humanists in their formative years and became local leaders of the evangelical movement. Hubmaier once commented that almost all the learned were Lutherans. "Young men," observed Francis Bacon in his *Of Youth and Age,* "are fitter to invent than to judge; fitter for execution than for counsel; and fitter for new projects than for settled business."

A list of lesser men who fall into this category might prove to be at least statistically reassuring. Johann Forster, a favorite pupil of Reuchlin, worked with Luther as a Hebraist in translating the Scriptures and was later a close friend of Melanchthon. Kaspar Peucer, mathematician and astronomer, was a son-in-law of Melanchthon and the electoral physician. Paul Eber as a philologist, historian, and natural scientist became a student and friend of Melanchthon. Friedrich Taubmann became professor of poetry at Wittenberg. The list might be extended almost indefinitely to include Aesticampianus, teacher of Hutten, who ended his days in Wittenberg; Franz Fritz (Irenicus); Johannes Brenz; Theobald Dillichanus; Heinrich von Eppendorf; Bartholomaeus Bernhardi; Hieronymus Schurff; Johann Rivius, educational reformer in Saxony; Michael Neander, rector of Ilfeld and textbook writer; or Johannes Zwick, the reformer of Constance; and many others.

During the decade of 1510 to 1520 a change is discernible in the atmosphere of the humanist microcosm. No longer satisfied with enjoying intellectually the stimulation of the classics, the humanists seek ways of applying their philosophy to life. The sharp criticism of abuse with its long ancestry back into the late medieval period is coupled now with a determined effort to effect the changes necessary to realize their ethical ideals. The *libido sciendi* is transformed into a wish to shape and form life. The interest in medicine becomes an insatiable desire to control nature. The scholarly pursuit of legal studies is transformed into a new preoccupation with jurisprudence and with entry into the political life of the empire. In the humanistic sodalities the humanistic scholars and the political administrators, secretaries and bishops alike, reinforced their common interest in change. In some men, such as Conrad Peutinger, the *vita studiosa* and *vita activa* blended harmoniously. Konstanze Peutinger, in a charming letter addressed to her father, who was representing the city of Augsburg at the Diet of Worms, writes that he should hurry back, for his books are longing for his return. In religious life the criticism of abuses and the desire for religious enlightenment merged into a universal readiness for reform and an eagerness to get on with it.

Luther once commented that his Ninety-five Theses had been carried within fourteen days throughout the length and breadth of Germany. The humanists were the chief agents for their distribution. Thus Christoph Scheurl in Nuremberg sent them to Peutinger in Augsburg, and they were quickly reprinted in Leipzig, Basel, and possibly Nuremberg. In 1520 Luther was the most read author in Germany, and Ulrich von Hutten the second most. There were strikingly few pamphlets and tracts or popular preachers active in those first years. Humanist support was comprehensive and universal. Without it Luther would not have succeeded. Almost all of the humanists of the older generation gave him a friendly word and at least provisional approval. And the younger humanists pledged him their loyalty and enthusiastic support. On May 1, 1518, Bucer wrote about the Heidelberg disputation to Beatus Rhenanus: "He [Luther] agrees with Erasmus in everything, except on one point he seems to excel him, for what he [Erasmus] merely insinuates, he [Luther] teaches openly and freely." Even some theologians such as Fabri and Cochlaeus, who were soon to become his fierce enemies, at first were kindly disposed to Luther. Eck himself reacted in a not unfriendly fashion, however fleetingly. To Crotus, Luther was like a god come to bring justice. His virtue and erudition were everywhere praised. Bernhard Adelmann in Augsburg identified *doctus* and *Lutherus*. "I see the whole world reviving!" exclaimed Beatus Rhenanus. The canon at Constance, Johann von Botzheim, an Erasmian, praised Luther as "the man who, after all the other disciplines have been renewed, is now renewing theology itself."

Specifically, the humanists approved of Luther's uncompromising assault on scholasticism and his return to the pristine sources of Christianity, the Scriptures. Mosellanus in his description of the Leipzig debate wrote, "Ille [Lutherus] Philosophiam Aristotelicam . . . ex theologorum theatro explodit!" Melanchthon described the debate as a battle of primitive Christianity with Aristotle. Only a few, such as the keen-minded Oecolampadius, perceived that Luther's objection to scholasticism was less to its barbarous dialectic than to its *theologia gloriae* and that his drive *ad fontes* was less a preoccupation with antiquity than a thirst for the content, for the gospel itself. The general humanist reaction to Luther's acts proved to be productive misunderstanding and without just this kind of *felix culpa* history would not move forward! But from 1520 on, the Reformation derailed humanism. The humanists had been attracted more by Luther's constructive educational and devotional writings than by his polemical treatises. His *On the Babylonian Captivity of the Church* seems to have opened the eyes of many of the humanists to the real thrust of his reform. Precisely this treatise which offended some of the older humanists inspired some of the younger to join Luther's movement. Many of the mature humanists now discovered that in their heart of hearts they were Catholic and had to stay with the old church. Others, like Mutian, were shocked at the revolutionary *lapidatores* and shrank away from the boisterous reformers. Many of the younger humanists became Evangelicals. Almost all of the Evangelicals were young, although not all of the young became Evangelicals.

I blush to suggest that what the social scientists refer to as a "generations problem" is apparent here. Sigmund Freud candidly conceded that the poets had anticipated many of his seminal insights. Social scientists must likewise confess that the *literati* first pointed up the conflict of the generations. The theme is time-honored and even biblical, suggested in the mocking of the sons of Noah and given classic form in the story of David and Absalom. Literary historians from Herodotus to Voltaire have been aware of the generation factor. In the second book of his *Histories* Herodotus observed that for the Egyptians three hundred generations in the male line represented ten thousand years, for three generations made up a hundred years. Voltaire conjured with the notion of generation in his *Siècle de Louis XIV.* In modern letters this theme is the main burden of Turgenev's *Fathers and Sons,* Dostoevsky's *The Possessed,* or Thomas Wolfe's *You Can't Go Home Again,* and is prominent in Simone de Beauvoir's *Mémoires d'une Jeune Fille Rangée,* not to mention the unmentionable, John Osborne's *Luther.* Social scientists have undertaken to define, structure, and systematize this factor and make it useful to historians.

The most masterful description of the problem of generations is clearly that of Karl Mannheim, who has described the two approaches as "positivist" and "romantic-historical." The different ways in which the two schools approach the problem reflect the contrast in their basically antagonistic attitudes toward reality. The methodological ideal of the positivists naturally is that of reducing all problems, including the generations problem, to quantitative terms, attempting to establish a quantitative formulation of factors which ultimately determine the forms of human existence and the movement of human history. The second approach may be characterized as qualitative, shying away from the clear daylight of mathematics, introverting the whole problem. The intellectual ancestry of the positivist approach can be traced back to David Hume and Auguste Comte. Hume translated the principle of political continuity into terms of the biological continuity of generations. Comte, whose six-volume *Cours de philosophie,* which appeared between 1830 and 1842, linking sociology closely to biology, thought that man's span of life and the average generation period of thirty years were necessary correlatives of the human organism. The discussion of the length of a generation continues today, with some theorists such as Ortega y Gasset setting the limits dogmatically at fifteen years, others arguing that a generation diminishes rapidly in length as the tempo of social change accelerates.

A man whose importance for historical thought in the twentieth century is enormous and whose influence upon historical methodology has increased tremendously in recent years, Wilhelm Dilthey, in his essays on the *Geisteswissenschaften* gave to the generations problem a peculiarly Germanic romantic-historical turn. He shifted away from the positivistic quantitative approach to an interiorized qualitative method. Possibly taking his cue from St. Augustine—and no Reformation research paper, as Santayana once remarked of sermons, is complete without at least one reference to St. Augustine—Dilthey saw the phenomenon of generations as the problem of the existence of an interior time that cannot be measured but only experienced in purely qualitative terms. Dilthey was concerned with the generations problem primarily because the adoption of the generation as a temporal unit in the history of intellectual development makes it possible to replace purely external chronological units with a concept of measuring qualitatively from within (*eine von innen abmessende Vorstellung*). Dilthey held that the use of generations as interiorized units makes it possible to appraise intellectual movements by an intuitive process of reenactment.

A second proposition which Dilthey advanced in connection with the generations problem is that the coexistence of a generation in many individuals is of more than mere chronological significance. Not only is the succession of one generation after another important, but the fact that the same dominant influences deriving from the prevailing political, social, religious, and intellectual circumstances are experienced by contemporary individuals, both in their early formative and in their later years, is of great significance to the interior, qualitative measurement of intellectual or cultural evolution or devolution, as the case may be. Individuals are contemporaries and constitute a single generation precisely because they are subject to common influences. Wilhelm Pinder referred to this phenomenon as the "noncontemporaneity of the contemporaneous." The generation is thus conceived of as a collective of mentality which tends to become the basis for social groups. From the point of view of intellectual history, contemporaneity, then, means not merely something chronological, but a state of being subjected to similar influences and a state of collectively escaping other influences. This formulation of the concept shifts the discussion, while complicating it, from a level on which it ran the risk of degenerating into a kind of Pythagorean number mysticism to the sphere of interior time which can be appreciated and at least partially comprehended by intuitive understanding. A survey of the extensive literature in the field reveals that a commonly accepted formula for a quantitative/ qualitative correlation or even a uniform approach to the problem does not exist today among social scientists (such as Eisenstadt, Mentré, Pinder, Rintala, Berger, or Heberle). Nevertheless, as genial eclectic Renaissance dilettantes we shall make bold to apply some of the social-scientific techniques in a most humanely humanistic fashion.

The quantitative or statistical analysis of the positivists when applied like a census taking to the men around Luther yields interesting if not deeply satisfying results. In that fateful year 1517 Luther was thirty-four years old, a man who was moving out of his youth toward maturity. It is intriguing to discover that nearly all of Luther's followers at Wittenberg and abroad were younger than Luther, most of them thirty years old or younger, and that nearly all of Luther's major opponents (except Eck) were older than Luther, most of them fifty years old, or older.

At the calculated risk of trying the reader's patience, we shall now quantify. The younger Wittenberg faculty members were among the earliest of Luther's followers. Amsdorf was born on December 3, 1483, less than a month after Luther (November 10, 1483). Bartholomäus Bernhardi von Feldkirch was born in 1489. Melanchthon was born in 1497; August Schurff in 1495; Heinrich Stockmann in 1495; Stephan Wild in 1495; Tilemann Plettner in 1490; Paul Knod in 1490; Johannes Eisermann in 1490. Outside of the university and even beyond Wittenberg, Luther's first adherents were younger, with the exception of Link and Lang, who were approximately the same age as Luther and had shared common experiences with him. Bugenhagen was born in 1485; Stiefel in 1486; Jakob Propst in 1486; Heinrich von Zütphen in 1488; Mykonius in 1488; Bucer in 1491; Billican in 1491; Justus Jonas in 1493; Pfeffinger in 1493; Agricola in 1494; Schnepf in 1495; Brenz in 1499; Cruciger in 1504. Oecolampadius was just a few months older than Luther, and Kaspar Güttel, Eberlin von Günzburg, and Aesticampianus were the chief exceptions in the long list of Luther's supporters.

Conversely, the older men at Wittenberg and elsewhere for the most part turned against Luther. Staupitz, as is well known, could

not stay with him. At the University, Henning Goede, seventy, the
first ordinarius in canon law, could not grasp Luther's theology.
Peter Burchard in medicine split with Luther on questions of university discipline and returned to his home university at Ingolstadt,
in 1523, signing the University's condemnation of Luther. Johannes
Dölsch, a canon at All Saints, was only slowly convinced and then
later broke with Luther on the question of the Mass. Christian Bayer,
second professor for the Pandects, opposed Luther for minimizing
the importance of canon law, and Luther often complained of Bayer's
legalism. Three older canons at the famous Castle Church, Beskau,
Elner, and Volmar, put up a stiff resistance and only when the students broke in Beskau's windows did he see the light. They resisted
until 1524. Otto Beckmann continued to read Masses until he was
released in 1523. Sebastian Küchemeister remained a convinced
Scotist and finally in 1522 left the heretical city for Ducal Saxony.
Johann Rochals was fifteen years older than Luther and remained
his opponent. Ulrich Dinstedt, born before 1460, undertook no
changes in his parish at Eisfeld. The dean of the Castle Church,
born sometime before 1450, was a stubborn opponent of Luther. In
1518 Johann Böschenstein was appointed to the chair of Hebrew.
He was forty-six years old, or twenty-five years older than Melanchthon. When he did not work out he was replaced after an interval by
Arrogallus, who was thirty and who lived until 1543.

Luther's opponents in the larger arena were also older men.
Cochlaeus was born in 1479; Berthold von Chiemsee in 1465; Wim-
pina around 1460. Emser was six years older; Dungersheim was
eighteen years older; the famous Hochstraten of Cologne was twenty-
three years older; and Erasmus, the "flitting Dutchman," as E.
Gordon Rupp has dubbed him, was, of course, forty-eight or nearly
fifty in 1517. The same age differential exists between Luther and his
opponents at Louvain and Paris. Nothing can be gained by multiplying instances. "To live beyond forty," comments Dostoevsky's
underground diarist, "is bad taste."

At this point one might be tempted to conclude that we have arrived
at the perfectly obvious. Social scientists, after all, are quite often the
apostles of the obvious. It is a clearcut case of the conservative nature
of the old and the liberal propensities of the young. In that case we

would have advanced very little beyond Pope's lines in his *Essay on Criticism:*

> *We think our fathers fools, so wise we grow;*
> *Our wiser sons, no doubt, will think us so.*

Socialization and progressivism tend to decelerate with age, we are told. Such a conclusion would indeed be prosaic to the point of being banal. The reader would justifiably be tempted to quote the lines of Oliver Wendell Holmes' *Apostrophe to a Katydid:* "Thou sayest an undisputed thing in such a solemn way." But complications remain. The generations problem cannot be merely the time-honored or dishonored father-son conflict at work, for in that case the young humanists might have revolted against their humanist mentors. Moreover, not all of the young humanists turned reformer. Not all of the young whom we have surveyed above were humanists. Romantic-historical techniques must be adduced to describe and analyze the qualitative differences of those for whom quantification provides no key. Psychoanalysis will not help, for we do not have the information needed for this approach to a whole generation. As Roland Bainton once expressed the problem, there are grave difficulties in psychoanalyzing the dead. More can be gained by a cultural analysis of their "common" humanist experience in order to improve our understanding of why the young humanist reformers reacted as they did, and by an examination of the nonhumanist young reformers in order to underline the "noncontemporaneity of the contemporaneous" or the polyphonous cultural pattern of the epoch, each voice sounding out the *verbum evangelii vocale* in its own way and at its own time.

The young humanists who joined the Reformation did indeed have common experiences which qualify them for collective generational identification. These intellectual coevals played the *sonata appassionata* of their lives upon fundamentally the same keyboard of environment. They were witnesses of the same events, they read the same books, they were all university men. They had all encountered classical culture, posing alternatives to traditional values. They showed an openness to new ideas, they observed the same deficiencies in society, they concurred in the chorus of criticism against abuse. They reacted negatively to scholastic philosophy, many of the younger escaping the study of scholastic theology altogether. They were deeply concerned with the search for religious enlightenment. They were captivated by the evangelical appeal, either from Luther, or, in surprisingly many cases, from the Scriptures themselves. Between 1518 and 1523 most of them changed their callings, many from law, for the preaching office. A certain dynamic in humanism and a set of attitudes with latent implications simply required time and an interiorized appropriation to begin operating in a collective way. For the Germanies, that time began in the 1510s and 1520s with the third generation of humanists.

This pattern is evident in the life of Justus Jonas (1493–1555), who was typical in almost every respect. Precisely because he is less well known, he may be of special interest here. Jonas enrolled at the University of Erfurt when only thirteen years old. He first studied law, then theology. At Erfurt he was a friend of Johannes Lang, a man of humanistic interests and a friend of Luther. Jonas became an enthusiastic follower of Erasmus and other leading humanists. He made a pilgrimage to Basel in order to visit the most famous scholar of the day and returned to Erfurt with such prestige for his Erasmian friendship that he was elected rector. This was in 1519, the year in which Luther wrote a postscript to Lang which reads: "P.S. Especially remember me to our Jonas, and tell him that I like him" (April 13, 1519). Jonas was drawn to Luther and accompanied him to the Diet at Worms for his ordeal. On April 17, 1521, the day of Luther's first appearance before the Diet, Hutten wrote to Jonas: "And so you have followed the preacher of the Gospel to be in his garden! O piety worthy of love! Truly, Justus, I loved you before, but on this account I love you a hundred times more." On May 10, 1521, Erasmus wrote from Louvain:

> *There has been a persistent rumor here, dear Jonas, that you were with Martin Luther at Worms; nor do I doubt that your piety has done what I would have done had I been present, to assuage the tragedy with moderate counsels, so that it would not in the future burst forth with greater damage to the world.*

But Jonas went all the way with the Evangelicals. Some time later Luther wrote: "Dr. Jonas has all the virtues which a preacher should have, but he clears his throat too often." The circuit was completed.

The pattern is similar among most of the other Wittenbergers in the inner circle, Georg Spalatin, Caspar Cruciger, Johannes Bugenhagen, and Philipp Melanchthon. They changed the frontier city in the sandbox of the empire into a "little Athens on the Elbe." Spalatin (1484–1545) had belonged to the most outspokenly critical circle of humanists at Erfurt under the leadership of the intellectual canon of Gotha, Mutianus Rufus. Mutian once posed for Spalatin the question loaded with universalist implications: "If Christ is the way, the truth, and the life, how then were people saved before the birth of Christ." At no point in Spalatin's development, however, did he ever deviate from basically Christian presuppositions. Since he had never studied theology on the university level, he was never encumbered with a load of scholastic learning. Even Hutten had freed himself only gradually from scholastic dialectic acquired on the arts level, but Spalatin approached biblical studies unencumbered, thanks to his early and sustained humanist interest. He followed Erasmus' counsel to approach the Scriptures directly and with benefit of guidance from patristic literature. Luther's exegesis of the Scriptures captivated him and he became a devoted follower of the reformer. Luther's forces were divided between the radicals pressing for a strong confessional stand and the Melanchthonian moderates favoring accommodation and a search for common ground. It is typical that Spalatin, the young humanist turned reformer, belonged to the moderates both at Augsburg in 1530 and thereafter.

The youngest and most precocious of the Wittenberg circle of Luther's associates was Caspar Cruciger (1504–1548), the most regular professor of theology at the University, which was crippled by the frequent absences of its key professors. Cruciger was twenty years younger than Luther and seven years younger than Melanchthon. Instructed as a child by the humanists Georg Helt and Caspar Borner, he enrolled at the University of Leipzig at the age of nine. As a teen-ager he was present at the famous Leipzig debate between Eck and Luther. Though in the opinion of the majority of those present Eck carried the day, Luther convinced young Cruciger, who followed him to Wittenberg in order to study theology. At twenty he was appointed rector of the City School in Magdeburg, but four years later returned to Wittenberg for life. Cruciger was quiet and unassuming, a mediating spirit. In 1529 he accompanied Luther to Marburg. After

Zwingli's death he and Melanchthon persuaded the Swiss to come to Saxony for discussions in May 1536. The Wittenberg Concord was the result. Luther, who had called Cruciger his Elisha "who will teach theology after my death," sent him with Melanchthon to the Colloquies at Worms and Regensburg in 1540 and 1541, the last attempt before Trent to reunite the church. During the period of the Schmalkald War, Cruciger as rector stayed in Wittenberg and saved the University. Together with Melanchthon he drew up, shortly before his death, the Leipzig Interim, a compromise document, held by the orthodox to be a compromising document.

A third figure among Luther's intimate friends illustrating the pattern emerging from the bewildering number of humanist reformers is Dr. Bugenhagen. On September 20, 1522, Luther directed Spalatin to do some academic wirepulling: "It remains for you to accept the task of securing from the Elector for John Bugenhagen one of those stipends that have heretofore been thrown away on the sophists. For next to Philipp [Melanchthon] he is the best professor of theology in the world." Bugenhagen (1484–1558) was the son of a city councilor in Wollin. He studied at the University of Greifswald and became a teacher at Treptow in 1503. He is an instance of the subtle influence of humanism upon a not very subtle personality. A practical, not particularly creative, type, he is perhaps representative of a large body of clergy who helped effect the Reformation on the parish level. Although the sources are not adequate for the study of his early intellectual development, every indication is that his theology was colored by Erasmian humanism. Even before 1517 he was interested in the reform of the church on that level. He wished to combine classical learning with a practical Erasmian piety. The humanist Murmellius recommended to Bugenhagen readings in such modern theologians as Pico, Lefèvre, Bouillus, Reuchlin, and Erasmus. His history of Pomerania was in many ways a typical humanist production. But in 1520 upon reading Luther's *On the Babylonian Captivity* he wrote to Luther declaring for the Reformation. The next year he moved to Wittenberg, where he became a professor and preacher. But for the remainder of his life, whenever he was not immediately under Luther's influence, he habitually reverted to a moralistic emphasis not unlike Erasmus' *philosophia Christi.* He seemed to be almost blissfully oblivious to the radical Copernican (Son-centered) revolution Luther had launched in theology.

The story of Melanchthon is so common that, to turn a phrase from Chaucer, every wit that hath discretion knows all or part of it. He remains the true archetype of the young humanist turned reformer. A student of his, Johann Agricola, tagged with the nickname "Magister Eisleben," was his pale shadow. Agricola (1492– or 1494–1566) studied the arts at Leipzig, escaped any training in scholastic theology, and came to Wittenberg, where he was overwhelmed by the personality of Luther. He studied philology with Melanchthon and theology with Luther. He was embroiled in the antinomian controversy, eventually helped to frame the Leipzig Interim with Melanchthon, and outlived his major opponents. Of the two dozen leaders at the time of the Diet of Augsburg in 1530 all except Luther and Nicholas von Amsdorf (1483–1565) had come to the Reformation from humanism. Very possibly the lack of a humanist experience led Amsdorf in later years to exaggerate the effects of original sin upon man in the loss of the image of God and to caricature Luther's theology, holding to such extreme statements as that good works are harmful. He held to his positions with an inflexibility which can most charitably be described as singlemindedness. He sided with Flacius Illyricus against Melanchthon.

In the other centers of Protestantism the humanist reformers also assumed the leadership. Strassburg had Martin Bucer, Wolfgang Capito, Nicholas Gerbelius, Caspar Hedio, and Jakob Sturm. It was Sturm who wrote to his humanist uncle, Jakob Wimpheling, "If I am a heretic you have made me one!" The Swiss reformers in this pattern included Zwingli; Oecolampadius; Pellicanus; Vadian; Myconius; and preeminently, Calvin. Where the dynamic of humanism was still in process the Reformation took especially creative forms. The leadership of the Reformation was in the hands of the young men with a humanist experience.

Many of the young men who turned reformer did not enjoy a humanist education or even a vicarious experience of humanism. Hajo Holborn has pointed to the fact that at least during the first phase of the Reformation period nearly all of the reformers were recruited from the ranks of disaffected priests and monks. The roster of students at the University of Wittenberg indicates a major flow of such men who came to Wittenberg for education or reeducation. Their encounter with humanism was through the biblical humanist curriculum adopted in 1518. It followed rather than preceded their turn to the Evangelical faith. These men did not provide the intellectual or organizational leadership of the movement, but, representing great numerical strength, they responded loyally to the confessional stand of Protestantism and became the bulwark of orthodox conservatism in subsequent decades.

The young humanists who either remained loyal to the Catholic confession or reverted to it shortly, such as George Witzel, born in 1501, are difficult to categorize, and complicate the problem of generations a great deal. Very preliminary studies indicate in some cases a thorough and unreserved commitment to an Erasmian *philosophia Christi* theology which outlasted any evangelical experience. The importance of the humanist ingredient in both confessions during subsequent religious history is a story which carries us well beyond our theme and even more hopelessly beyond our space limitation. You will bestow upon me Spalatin's nickname, "Loquax," for that prolix humanist chancellor wrote over eight hundred letters to Luther alone.

Perhaps the factor of the generation in the historical context of humanism and the Reformation will find its place side by side with such generalized concepts as the growth of bourgeois optimism and self-confidence, the birth of the lay spirit, the rising tide of religious expectations, or the well-worn notion of a new individualism. At that time it was at most only one of many factors at play in the great historical drama. Moreover, only at certain widely separated junctures in history has the generation element been an important contributing cause to historical events. It is not possible to generalize the generation factor into a universally applicable formula. The modest assertion of this paper is simply that the generation factor played a significant though minor part in the genesis and development of the Lutheran Reformation. We must, of course, beware of scientizing and bedeviling the world of history with impersonal abstractions and invisible powers or mysterious entelechies. If the idea of generation, understood in a qualitative even more than in a quantitative sense, as one of the mutually interdependent variables in the etiological syndrome of Reformation history is to be of value, it must be given substance from the realities of history itself. This is the difficult task of the historian. Humanists engaged upon such an undertaking can find solace in Plato's words:

Chalepa ta Chala
The good is always difficult!

P. C. Gordon Walker
CAPITALISM AND THE REFORMATION

Patrick Chrestien Gordon Walker, born in England in 1907, has had a unique career as a scholar and public servant. He was a student and tutor in history at Christ Church, Oxford University, from 1931 to 1940. He has published an outline of man's history and a volume on the sixteenth and seventeenth centuries. He has been a member of Parliament (Labor Party) and has served variously with the British Broadcasting Corporation, as chairman of the British Film Institute, and as Secretary of State for Commonwealth Relations.

Until the early twentieth century the relationship between the Reformation and capitalism was really no problem at all. Almost as old as Protestantism itself was the truism that "among the Reformed the greater their zeal, the greater their inclination to trade and industry, as holding idleness unlawful." There was virtual agreement on the facts; Protestants and Catholics were only concerned to draw different consolation from the common observation that "usury was the brat of heresy." Marshall may be taken as typical of these views, which prevailed down to our own day.

The bombshell was dropped by Max Weber at the beginning of this century in a brilliant development of an idea suggested to him by W. Sombart in his 1902 edition of *Der Moderne Kapitalismus.* Sombart here proclaimed as the guiding force in the evolution of capitalism and the modern world the "spirit of capitalism," which consisted in the pursuit by the individual of gain for its own sake, in exact calculation, and the rigorous rationalization of every department of life. Max Weber in his *Protestant Ethic and the Spirit of Capitalism* (1904–1905) found a personal vehicle for this capitalist spirit in the Calvinist and the Puritan and demonstrated with ingenuity the causal connection between the doctrine of Calvinism and the inculcation into its adherents of the capitalist spirit.

It was at once felt that both Protestantism and capitalism had been gravely impugned by Weber's thesis and he was attacked on

From P. C. Gordon Walker, "Capitalism and the Reformation," in *Economic History Review* 8 (1937): 1–19. Reprinted by permission of the editors of *Economic History Review.*

all sides. The main arguments used against him were (a) that capitalism was much older than Protestantism, and (b) that many other factors had played a much larger part than Protestantism in the evolution of modern capitalism. . . .

This controversy has troubled the world long enough and I do not intend to join in the subtleties into which it has now largely degenerated. My purpose is to show that Weber has led the whole body of historians, both adherents and opponents, down the wrong path in the study of one of the most important problems of modern European history; that the methods of inquiry used by both sides in the controversy *must* lead to false results; and finally that the only solution is to take a new method and a new point of departure.

Weber created a special method of inquiry and argument for the purposes of his study of Protestantism. This method has been tacitly taken over by his main assailants, who have not attempted to destroy it but rather to turn it against its creator. Critics like Tawney and Sée have suggested only minor modifications and cautions. The consequence has been that the problem of the Reformation as a sociological phenomenon has been colored and, in my opinion, vitiated by a method which has been so easily accepted that its implications and assumptions have been hardly realized.

The most striking aspect of the Weber method is the use of an abstract definition of capitalism. The particular definition was arrived at as follows. It was assumed, after Sombart, that there was an eternally valid quality of mind, abstracted from, and independent of, any particular period or place of history, which was called the "capitalistic spirit"; and that a society was capitalist in so far as this spirit could be found in it. In order to give this spirit authentic letters of credit it was related to human nature. Brentano considered it as equivalent to human nature; Weber, as a development triumphing over its earlier form; Sombart, as at the same time a subjugation of human nature, over whose departure he romantically lingered, and as identical with human nature. Such an assumption was bound to be arbitrary and external to problems of past history; in this case, it reflected faithfully nineteenth-century laissez-faire. The result was a concentration upon the individual and upon emancipation. Attention was focused upon the emancipated individual, upon economic individualism, as the sole and eternal need of capitalist society at all periods, as the sole and eternal test of whether a society was capitalist or not.

This particular definition of capitalism in terms of the emancipation of the individual (in common with all such abstract definitions) springs from a very serious misconception concerning the vital historical distinction between changes in quantity and changes in quality. The Weber method has silently concentrated search upon the discovery of changes in quality, in kind; of a new and distinct attitude of mind in individuals, unlike any preceding attitude. Once this attitude can be isolated and pinned down, we are told, then we have the beginning of the spirit of capitalism and hence the origins of capitalism itself.

This is a gravely misleading method of approach. The distinction between changes in quality and changes in quantity is an unreal one. If historians looked for changes in quantity, in degree, they would find that "changes in quality" only in fact result from changes in quantity. This holds good both for changes in ideas and social outlook, as well as for changes in economic organization (without for the moment postulating any connection between the two).

Let me put it like this. Social outlook can only be changed, e.g., from feudal to bourgeois, by a sufficiently powerful bourgeois *bloc* in the society, not by the mere presence of individual capitalists. The simple discovery of a feudal or a bourgeois outlook in an individual can mean nothing by itself; for ideas the same in kind must produce very different results according to their social context. They may be isolated and socially insignificant, or they may be dominant and color and control their whole society. Somewhere between these two stages will come a period of time in which the outlook of the society will be altered in kind; but the alteration will have been brought about by simple changes in the relative social importance of the ideas in question, that is to say in the numbers and strength of the people holding the ideas. In the same way, changes in economic organization will occur gradually but will, if they continue, reach a point at which they are strong enough to necessitate a radical alteration of the whole economic organization of the society in which they occur. Qualitative changes in society, thus, can only result from preceding changes in quantity; changes of quality are nothing else but a certain stage of intensity reached by preceding changes in quantity. The absolute distinction between the two is misleading. . . .

If we penetrate behind the rigid distinction drawn between changes of quality and quantity we come upon the heart of the matter and find the explanation why Weber used the method he did and why he is unable to escape from abstract definitions and qualitative categories. The whole apparatus of the method results from an approach which Franz Borkenau has called "isolierendkausal" and which Henri Sée perhaps sought to indicate when he said that Weber's method was "unilatéral." What is meant is the simplification of the enquiry down to the tracing of the effects of *one* isolated historical factor upon some historical development. . . .

The major defect, however, is the inevitable failure to discover or even enquire into the historical causes of the factors whose influence the method is used to investigate. The question of the cause of the Reformation has hardly been broached at all in the whole Weber controversy. And this is no accident. Weber set out to disprove the materialist conception of history; and, within its own limits, the unilateral method can easily, indeed inevitably, be made to do this. Weber in effect asks, Did the Calvinist ethic and attitude toward work precede and largely influence the application of this ethic in the capitalist world? Weber, for all his critics, showed the answer to be substantially Yes. The conclusion must be that ideas that came to birth in the mind effected economic and material developments and not vice versa.

Such conclusions are inevitable from the way the question is put; for if Weber starts with Protestantism as a datum and has merely to examine its development and its social repercussions, he cannot, within the framework of his enquiry, go behind this datum. His type of argument can throw no light at all upon the validity of the materialist conception of history, because it is debarred from facing the vital problem of the origin of the ideas whose reaction upon the material world it is engaged in discovering. Some of Weber's critics have sidetracked the issue by finding sufficient material explanations for the evolution of capitalism, without bringing in the Reformation at all; but they find that they are forced to dismiss the Reformation as an historical accident without causes. Others have found an alternative "spiritual" cause for capitalism, either in Catholicism or in some secular spirit of mind; but these, like Weber, do not find a cause for their spiritual factor. Others still, like Sombart or Robertson, do both these things, and find mixed spiritual and material causes for capitalism. As far as the problem of the Reformation is concerned, all of them treat it in the same way, either directly or invertedly. This is the fundamental reason why Weber's method has been productive of some important discoveries but cannot be used to solve the whole problem of the cause and effects of the Reformation. . . .

Another significant fruit of the method is the way in which it has concentrated upon the seventeenth and subsequent centuries. This is the first moment at which Protestantism begins to show any significant signs of behaving in the way Weber wanted; in consequence he coolly left out the vital first century during which the Reformation established itself and caused the most stir. Other historians have equally concentrated on some special period, pre-sixteenth century if they are against Weber, post-sixteenth century if they incline his way. The curious result has been that a controversy about Protestantism has hardly touched the Reformation in the first great century of its establishment. Similarly, the theory has found no place for Luther. Although Weber found some of his deepest ideas best illustrated in Luther, although Calvin looked to Luther as his master, Weber was prepared to agree with his enemies that Luther was part of the Middle Ages and therefore outside the world with which he was dealing.

Clearly a new method of approach is needed. What is it to be? The method I propose to follow is simple; I shall abandon all abstract, cast-iron definitions, and get away from the psychology of the isolated individual, and from the obsession that all that the capitalist individual ever needed was emancipation, escape from discipline. Instead, I shall approach the problem as a social one; ask what were the social and economic needs of society at the time of the Reformation; and then examine how far the Reformation (amongst other factors) was a response to these needs.

In spite of my strictures on abstract definitions I have already used the word "capitalism"; it is too useful as a shorthand symbol to forego. Wherever I use it, it is not as a *definition* of the psychology of individuals but as a description of a type of social organization. I shall use "capitalist" to describe a society which is preponderantly a money economy, in which workers labor for wages and in which employers own and control the means of production and decide to what use they shall be put by a calculus of profits. Anything that makes for the spread and establishment of such an economy out of preexisting, feudal conditions, I shall describe as advancing capitalism.

There is one immediate obstacle to be cleared away, which was a stumbling block to Weber; namely the existence of capitalism in fifteenth-century Europe before the occurrence of the Reformation. It is no use trying to define this capitalism out of existence by dismissing its leaders, as Weber does, as mere unscrupulous money makers; or as exceptions, as Sombart does of Jacob Fugger and his saying "Let me earn as long as I am able." Even by Weber's own psychological standards the way of life of north Italy, as described by Sombart (who, as usual, is on both sides of the controversy) and Brentano, was capitalist; L. B. Alberti with his "Holy Economy" and his saying "Whoso loses no time can accomplish almost everything" and Lorenzo da Vinci with his list of Sins are exact counterparts of Franklin, on whose "Little Book" and "Time is money" Weber builds so great a superstructure. Nor was this capitalism confined to north Italy; it stretched across the Alps into the mining areas of south Germany and the manufacturing districts of northwest Europe and into the cities along the Rhine and the Danube.

The nonoccurrence of a Reformation in these circumstances throws light on the problem of the Reformation when it did occur. Capitalism in the late fifteenth century could by no means be made compatible with contemporary Catholicism, which was intertwined with the law, thought, needs, and property of feudalism; and which must inevitably go down if the social basis and presuppositions on which it had built were destroyed by capitalism. But there were factors which made a working compromise possible. . . .

The real thing [came] at last at the other end of Europe. The intruding factor was the Price Revolution, the effects of which were enormous. It speeded up the economic development of Europe into an Industrial Revolution (of which all subsequent have been in the family). The sixteenth century became the age of water power; cranes, pulleys, pumps, coal for heating, gunpowder, and innumerable inventions in particular industries transformed the productive capacity of Europe. The driving force behind this industrial expansion was the profit inflation caused by prices rising faster than wages, which then formed a very high part of the costs of production. Europe was introduced to the age of manufacture (in the strict sense as opposed to mechanofacture). These improvements hastened the displacement of north Italy by the northwest of Europe as the commercial and manufacturing center of the continent. Therewith the position of Rome as against capitalism was reversed; the area for which Catholicism was socially necessary became less important than the area dominated by capitalism; Rome was suddenly put upon the defensive.

But this was not all. The Industrial Revolution brought with it the displacement of the class system on which the Roman Church was based by another class system that grew out of the first. The bourgeoisie, which had been a middle class under feudalism, had to break forth from its social and political subordination and from its self-imposed restrictions (the guilds) and become a ruling class. This involved the transfer of blocks of feudal property to the bourgeoisie for exploitation by capitalist instead of feudal methods of production; the destruction or conversion to new ends of feudal law and ideology; the absorption or ruin of the feudal upper classes; and, finally, the supplanting of the feudal working class by a class of wage earners.

Above all, the Price Revolution meant that all these problems needed urgent and immediate solution over large parts of Europe which had received insufficient slow and gradual preparation for them.

I have to show how these circumstances gave rise to the Reformation.

It has often been pointed out that the Reformation was a great ascetic movement within Catholic Christianity. Weber's description of the Reformation as intramundane asceticism, as a taking of the Catholic ascetic outside the monastery walls into the world, has been generally accepted. It is important to see how far this description provides an explanation of the origin of the Reformation. . . .

It can therefore be said that the Reformation, being an ascetic movement, was bound to disrupt the church and rend its theology. But this does not wholly solve (as is implied by Troeltsch or K. E.

Kirk) the problem of the cause of the Reformation. It does not explain why an ascetic movement occurred at this moment; nor why a movement *within* Christianity came about; nor why just these elements in the Catholic tradition and none of its other ideas were so developed; it does not explain why such a development occurred at just this moment and in some places, but not in others.

The attempts to explain the origin of the Reformation in terms of the inner logic of Christianity, as if Christianity were bound from the beginning to develop just as it did and just at the right moment, are so far from successful that they force one to the conclusion that there must have been another factor at work, external to Christianity, which impinged upon it and brought out of it results that were, sure enough, conditioned by the Christian tradition, but could not have been caused by it. When Europe at the time of the Reformation is surveyed the only force capable of working such results seems *prima facie* to have been the pressures of the social needs suddenly posed by the Price Revolution. The Price Revolution brought these problems upon Europe with a speed that was totally unexpected, and with an urgency for which there had been no gradual preparation.

To prove this assumption it is necessary to examine the Reformation in detail and to go further into the nature of the social problems facing parts of Europe at this time. So far I have taken the Reformation as a single, undifferentiated movement; and there is a sense in which such a treatment is justified. There was an underlying similarity running through all the parts of the Reformation, just as there was a basic similarity in the problems set by the Price Revolution, wherever it transformed the European economy. On the other hand, within this basic similarity lay a great variety of appurtenant but not identical lesser movements. There are amongst others three factors, without which it seems to me impossible to account for these known subdivisions within the Reformation:

1. The social problem, presented by the Price Revolution, was really a problem with two parts. The first need was primary accumulation, that is to say the accumulation of capital into sufficiently large units to permit of the new methods of production by means of water power, pumping, and enclosure; all of which were beyond the capacity of the previous scale of capital accumulation. In conditions like those of Colbert's France it

would be possible for the state to make capital available; but, in the early stages of capitalist advance, the better and perhaps the only way was by an extension of the methods and mentality of the bourgeois merchant. That meant by private enterprise; which again meant a large-scale transfer of feudal capital into the private hands of the advancing bourgeoisie. The second, subsequent, and really basic need was the acclimatization of the classes of capitalist society into the new positions made necessary by the results of primary accumulation. The proportions in which these needs were present would affect the nature of the responses to the social needs of the time, amongst which I am claiming the Reformation as one of the most important.

2. The dual problem that was posed by the Price Revolution was partly a political one; that was especially true of the problem of primary accumulation. The Reformation with its development of the ascetic to the point of heresy would naturally join any state that wished to transfer feudal property, for "ecclesiastical property had been the bulwark of the traditional system of landownership"; and the state, for its part, would join forces with a movement aimed at the heart of the Roman system. The problem of the acclimatization of the new classes was also, but to a less extent, a political one. The form of the Reformation would, thus, be affected by the particular forms of government and local political problems in different countries. Without organization into nations, Europe would not have reached her actual degree of economic development; the Reformation, therefore, had to occur in and accommodate itself to a system of nations. The relationship between Reformation and state would also partly depend on whether the concrete problem of primary accumulation or the ideological problem of class acclimatization was the more pressing.

3. The pressure exerted by the Price Revolution, moreover, was not equal throughout its course. The Price Revolution occurred in two phases. The first, lasting from about 1520–1540/50, was relatively mild and was limited to two areas: (a) Germany with the Netherlands, under the influence of the expansion of production in Saxony, Austria, and the Tyrol: (b) Spain, particularly Andalusia, under the influence of the first imports from America. From 1521–1540 Mexico sent no more silver to Europe than the product of the single mining district of Schwarz, Tyrol; and there was little if any reexport from Spain into the rest of

FIGURE 3. *Miners on a Treadmill*. This plate from Georg Agricola's *Vom Bergwerck XII Bücher* (Basle, 1557) illustrates a major industry in which many workers formed a new proletariat. Reproduced from the Dr. Leon Kolb collection of the Division of Special Collections, Stanford University Libraries. Used by permission.

Europe. Prices in these two areas seem to have risen by about 20 percent. The second phase of the Price Revolution was introduced by the discovery of Potosi (1545), Zacatecas (1548), and Guanaruato (1558), and by the application of the mercury amalgamation process, invented in 1557. American silver poured into Europe; the production of German mines fell off; the silver spread from Spain to the manufacturing centers in the northwest. This import and the consequent rise of prices lasted for about a century, varying in different countries. But each successive increment of silver was a smaller percentage of the total circulating stock and the major shock of the inflow was limited to the first years, i.e., between the years 1545–1580 (rather later in England).

These two phases controlled the economic importance of various parts of Europe. From 1520–1540 the leading areas were Spain (which inherited no strong middle class from the Middle Ages) and Germany (which had a strong feudal bourgeoisie). From 1545–1580, both Spain and Germany fell away, and the lead was taken by England, the Netherlands, and parts of France and Scotland. The parallelism between these areas and the areas of the Reformation is striking; as also the parallelism in time between the first phase of the Price Revolution and Luther (both about 1520–1540); and between the second phase and Calvin (both about 1545–1580).

If it can be shown that the actual Reformation can only be explained in the light of these factors, it will go a long way towards establishing that the Reformation was rooted in the material conditions of the time and examination of the various parts of the Reformation will also explain (what we have not yet ascertained) why the Reformation was an ascetic movement.

We may call the two phases of the Reformation Lutheran and Calvinist, though neither phase was entirely represented by the man after whom it is convenient to name it.

The concrete results of the Lutheran phase, including the violent period of Anabaptism, were destruction of the Catholic hold upon the middle and lower classes, and sanction for the seizure of Catholic and feudal property. On the whole, the religious movement was subordinate to the state, except in Germany, where the absence of a political head who could give expression to national feeling allowed religion at first to give the lead to the secular powers.

The second stage of the Price Revolution meant that Germany could not lead the capitalist revolution. The initiative passed to England, the Netherlands, the industrial parts of Scotland, France, and Switzerland; the very parts where the second, Calvinist, phase of the Reformation took root. The problem of primary accumulation was already partly solved and the chief problem became class acclimatization. This problem was very urgent; the bourgeoisie had to exchange its subservience for the will to govern, it had grave economic and political tasks ahead; the working class had to exchange its loose, extensive labor for disciplined, regular, and organized work. These great changes in mental outlook had to be solved quickly enough to keep pace with the Industrial Revolution.

It is here that the Weber method leads most astray. Weber saw enough of the truth to force him into a contradictory position. He could describe the Reformation as an ascetic movement, as one that made the piece-wage system workable; yet he could also conceive of it primarily as a movement bringing nothing but economic liberation from all restraint. Clearly capitalist society was individualist as opposed to feudalism; it was based on private enterprise; it needed individualism to cloak the class structure of society, which was nearer the surface than in feudalism; it thought mechanistically in terms of quantities rather than a priori in terms of qualities, both of matter and of mankind. In the same way capitalism could only come into existence if it broke through the feudal ideas, which had become restrictions upon it as a system of society. Hence, if the Reformation was a chief ideological expression of capitalist society at this stage, it must be shown to have been both individualist and emancipating. But this does not imply that it must preach license from all restriction for each separate individual. The pressing need was the opposite; the *disciplining* of individuals to the ends of a new society, which was breaking forth out of feudalism and basically individualist in its social outlook. The urgent need was a restatement of the ascetic that was deeply embedded in the Christian tradition; an ascetic so interpreted that it would inculcate by discipline the necessary social attitudes. Both the bourgeoisie and the wage workers must be submitted to this ascetic according to the ends each had to serve.

It was natural that Calvin should stress the ascetic, that he should erect into first principles the Original Sin and Predestination which Luther had kept increasingly in the background. The chief results achieved by Calvin were (1) the rigid division into Elect and Reprobate (which also had been latent in Luther) and the Sovereignty of the State (which Hobbes later deduced from the same premises). And (2) the need for incessant goodness; if a Calvinist sinned, he could not recover by the magical aid of the priest; a single sin was sufficient sign that he had been damned from eternity. It was to achieve this second result, which was in fact the setting out of a single standard of morality in place of the Catholic double standard, that Calvin had to make his main theological innovations. It was because this change was involved that men disputed so bitterly on points of academic dogma. The effect of these doctrines in social terms was that the capitalist class structure was both justified (from eternity) and obscured by the stress upon the individual's spiritual behavior as the sole criterion of social division; and that the correct social ethic and methods for its enforcement were ready made for self-imposition amongst the Elect, and, if necessary, coercive imposition upon the Reprobate.

The Calvinist system thus provided for the lower class; but in some parts (notably Holland and later England) the lower class was powerful enough to play its own part. By now it had lost its early Anabaptist hope of violent emancipation; capitalism was firmly enough established to make labor within the system the only road. The result was that Menno Simon, the complementary contemporary of Calvin, was able to win the Anabaptists back to their earlier nonresistance. He preached an ethic suitable for the working class and therefore similar to that which Calvin preached for the Reprobates; but the Anabaptist retained his silent protest of withdrawal from the affairs of a wicked world; he lacked the Calvinist's interest in politics, his belief in a strong state and his desire to have that state as his servant. From the amalgam of Calvinist and Anabaptist resulted Puritanism, a vague attitude of mind covering every gradation from the obscure sect to the prosperous Calvinist; and with no fixed internal boundaries; for the Protestant ethic led to worldly success and so, often, to the progress of the successful Protestant up the rungs of the social ladder of Puritanism.

Such was the real spirit of capitalism needed by capitalist society and inculcated by the Reformation. Had the Reformation really produced the libertine "spirit of capitalism" it would have endangered, not advanced, capitalism.

Puritanism was clearly an influential factor: the magic mirror described by Tawney, reflecting back the narrow, arid qualities that led the Puritan to success in this world. It set men striving after new virtues, that yesterday had been vices, rather than their actual achievement. But such a superhuman struggle necessarily left a real impress; apart from moral attitudes, Puritan society saved money and developed novel notions of interest; it developed a special attitude towards colonization; and naturally evolved the Puritan Sunday as the only way of securing regular intervals of rest in peoples avidly devoted to work as the highest end.

But, though Puritanism was thus bound up with capitalism in the sixteenth century, the relationship between Protestantism and capitalism is not eternal and absolute. The Reformation was the product of peculiar circumstances; it could occur only against the background of Christendom, in a civilization of nations, and under the stress of the special and urgent problems posed by the Price Revolution. From the beginning of the seventeenth century, Protestantism began to lose its special functions and therewith its spiritual position. Two sets of factors brought this about. First, as the class acclimatization which was the highest task of the Reformation was gradually accomplished, Protestantism had to yield ground to other activities which became more important; above all, it had to give place to the secular state and to science.

Secondly, Protestant societies had no monopoly of the advance of capitalism. The Reformation was necessary for the vital first advance in the sixteenth century; but once this advance had been safely made, other countries could follow in the tracks and "step over the Reformation." In such circumstances, certain social devices became important, especially the military-bureaucratic state (e.g., Colbert's France), that were closed to Protestantism, with its depreciation of state and court service. Protestantism ceased to have a monopoly of world capitalist advance and this lowered the prestige it was already losing in its homes; wide concessions were made to the state and to the individual businessman, which Protestantism would have scorned to make in its heyday. Protestantism, of course, has retained considerable social importance; in Protestant countries it is bound up with the achievement and the thought texture of capitalism. But it is noteworthy that the Reformation was the culminating ascetic revival of Christendom; all subsequent revivals have been Protestant, but of steadily decreasing social significance.

To draw the arguments together. The Reformation was a movement divided into two chronological phases, corresponding to the two phases of the Price Revolution; it was also divided laterally throughout its course into Church and Sect; the emphasis shifted from the problem of primary accumulation to the problem of class acclimatization; and there were the expected relations to the state. The movement was diverse and blind, but wonderfully related in its parts; innumerable leaders, Calvin, Menno Simon, Luther, Melanchthon, Martyr, Melchior Hoffman, Bucer, Olivetan, and a host of others, each played his part, though his only guide was his private conscience; behind these was a mass of anonymous followers, each in his own eyes choosing his adherence according to the logic and reasonableness of his particular leader. The inescapable conclusion is the same that we drew from an examination of the inner logic of Christianity, namely that the Reformation was the reaction to a force external to itself. The genius of leaders, the devotion of followers, even apparent accidents, were not so much independent forces controlling the destinies of the Reformation as factors that were present or called into being and made use of by a force greater than themselves. The Reformation corresponded in its various parts so closely to the social needs created by the Industrial Revolution, its effects (if properly conceived) were so apt, that in my submission we are entitled to say that our *prima facie* supposition that the Industrial Revolution was the external force we were looking for is now proven.

The Reformation was not the cause of capitalism; rather it was the result of needs created by capitalist advance at a particular place and time. *For this reason,* once it was in existence and throughout its various stages and forms, the Reformation played an indispensable part, amongst other factors, in the triumph of European capitalism over difficulties that had threatened to overwhelm it.

Hajo Holborn

THE SOCIAL BASIS OF THE GERMAN REFORMATION

Hajo Holborn, the late Sterling Professor of History at Yale University, began his career as a lecturer at Heidelberg University in 1926. He became Carnegie Professor of International History at the School of Politics in Berlin in 1931. Forbidden to teach by the Nazi regime, he emigrated to the United States in 1933. Professor at Yale from 1934 on, he also taught at Stanford, Columbia, Harvard, and as a Fulbright Professor at the University of Vienna. Although he wrote extensively in more recent European history, he is best known in the area of Reformation history for an edition of Erasmus' works, a biography of Hutten, and a history of the Reformation in Germany.

One of the intrinsic weaknesses of our historical studies is that we can understand the past only by utilizing analogies to our age. What we comprehend of past events or personalities most readily are the features which they seem to have in common with our own forms of life, and it is from these associations that we take our cue in exploring the past. We know how fallacious this method can be, since a closer study of the historical landscape possibly reveals that what we regarded as a landmark had actually little significance in its own age and what we believed a resemblant factor was nothing but a superficial similarity. So we have very often to burn the bridges over which we entered into the territory of the past.

This applies particularly to sociological methods in history. They are delusive if used as an absolute criterion or without historical sense, that is, by not making allowance for the differences of historical societies. And if we look at the studies of social life in the sixteenth century, we shall find that the gulf that separates the social life of the nineteenth and twentieth centuries from that of the sixteenth has often been too easily bridged over (cf. for example Roy Pascal, *The Social Basis of the German Reformation,* London, 1933). A great deal of work will have to be spent on reexamining our general conceptions and on a new reading and uncovering of source material

Hajo Holborn, "The Social Basis of the German Reformation," *Church History* 5 (1936): 330–339. Used by permission of the editors of *Church History.*

before we shall obtain an adequate picture of the social situation of Germany at the beginning of the sixteenth century. That is a prerequisite for a true evaluation of the influence which social conditions had on the Reformation.

We stand on firm ground as far as the knowledge of economic history is concerned. The work of the last two or three generations of economists and historians has endowed us with a knowledge of the history of German trade, commerce, and industry in the later Middle Ages and in early modern times which enables us to follow the great changes in that sphere with little difficulty. Even the study of agrarian conditions, which for a time did not keep pace with the research done on capitalism, has advanced and produced more definite and reliable results. But in estimating the impact of these economic factors upon the structure of society we are still in an exploratory stage. Two points especially should be given more careful attention.

First, the scholars—and a great number of most able ones made the economic and social changes of the sixteenth century the field of their study—approached their subject largely with a view to inquiring into the origins of modern capitalism. Consequently, they were more interested in the advent of fresh changes as such than in the average conditions of that particular age. They treated the economic history of the sixteenth century as a prelude to the present-day system of economy and hence were prone to overemphasize all that seemed to indicate a breaking away from the older economic system. Yet it is doubtful whether the rise of early capitalism in Germany actually revolutionized German society as a whole. We observe the growth of finance and large-scale trade and new forms of industrial organization chiefly in upper Germany, whereas middle and north Germany preserved the traditional habits of agrarian society. For the bulk of Germany the sixteenth century did not bring forth a considerable change in economic conditions, the revolution of prices perhaps being the only experience in which the nation as a whole participated. With this single, though of course important, exception we may say that northern Germany, the birthplace of Lutheranism and future stronghold of Protestantism, was not witnessing a considerable transformation of economic life during the sixteenth century. The economic constitution of these sections of Germany had been established considerably earlier and nothing sensational was to happen for a long time to come. The south of Germany was going through an age of profound transformation of its economic status, but the period of bold achievements and successful enterprises was superseded by an epoch of deterioration and contraction. In space as well as in time the rise of capitalism in Germany is distinctly limited. The era of the Fuggers marks a new departure in the general economic history of Europe, but in German history little more than a glamorous episode.

But if it is true that the influence of the new capitalistic enterprises on the general life of the people should not be overrated, it becomes even more urgent to differentiate German society of the sixteenth century from modern society. That leads us to a second aspect of principal significance. We are too much accustomed to such convenient class divisions as feudal, upper, middle, and lower classes and to conceiving the social relationship of these groups in analogy to the structure of modern society. Recent sociological studies have taught us that these classifications do not suffice to understand social actions and reactions in our society; they are, moreover, even less appropriately applied to the social life of the sixteenth century. There was a greater variety of social groups than the three or four classes into which we usually divide society today. More essential, however, is the discrepancy of the underlying social principles. The terms upper, middle, and lower classes are taken from the stratification of an acquisitive society, a type of human society in which property and income confer a definite social rank upon its members.

Medieval society, however, was built on different principles. The order of feudal ranks was in theory constructed not on the pattern of income and property but according to functional duties. We know, to be sure, that the authority which was wielded for the good of society was endowed with material wealth, particularly with income from ground rents. But since ground rents could not be accumulated, a kind of social superiority developed which was very different from what we see in modern society. In the sixteenth century this system of medieval feudalism was in decay; landed property had become convertible into capital wealth and vice versa. But a great importance was still attached to landed property, which still bestowed on its holders certain political prerogatives, and the new rich were therefore very eager to join the ranks of the landed aristocracy.

Medieval society, furthermore, was not only feudal but religious in a way that made itself felt in the social structure. Again, we are aware that the church fell victim to feudalism, but the fact nevertheless remains that it possessed a sense of social honor and distinction quite at variance with feudal classification. The struggle between church and state, emperor and pope had forced the church to become a political power, and it was this development which forced the church to approve of and to participate in feudal organization. Yet though the church's servants and its head became feudal lords and in the later Middle Ages capitalists, the church showed itself able to call into existence a group of people who took their stand outside a society organized on the lines of rich and poor.

Again and again the demand had been renewed which Christ made upon his followers to live in poverty and to seclude themselves from the temptations of the world. The church preached this belief and, on the other hand, made use of it for political purposes. In order to have at its disposal a body of true servants and independent officials, it tried to separate its priests from the rest of the flock not by giving them social advantages but by taking away social rights. All these attempts, like forcing celibacy upon the clergy and asking for abstention from property, succeeded only for a time. But they were not fruitless. If we compare the endeavors of the secular lords to build up a corps of state officials with the parallel attempts of the church, it is quite obvious that the church reaped a better harvest. The majority of the clergy failed in their duties; yet there were not only individual saints but a large group of priests and monks who conceived their task not as a private occupation but as a functional commission.

But what did this mean for the structure of society? The priests and monks were socially disenfranchised in order to gain at once higher social dignity. To take up the humble life of a monk was meritorious in itself. However paradoxical to attach social dignity to a renunciation of society, such holy conduct could not be divested of social significance. It was always uncertain what place priests and monks would exactly claim in the scale of social ranks. Little doubt, however, was voiced that they deserved a high station. Thus, in addition to the importance of landed property, a second principle became valid which is opposed to the life of modern society, or at least to what modern economists mostly describe as such. Within a society which was not originally founded on property and income, though already in a state of transformation toward such an organization, there still existed groups which derived their social distinction from their social detachment, from the idea of service to the whole.

It was very important that during the later Middle Ages this idea of service underwent a change. Service to the church was the aim in the beginning; now it became service to the community of which the clergyman happened to be a member. Church and state came closer together in the fourteenth and fifteenth centuries, the state gaining control over many departments of church life. The clergy, on the other hand, obtained a new hold over the life of the larger classes. Besides many deplorable results as revealed in the abundance of superstitious miracles and similar phenomena, we find that what was best in the thought and practice of the clergy and monasteries kindled the flame of true Christian enthusiasm among the laity. The "brotherhoods of common life" stand out as an example of how the realization of Christian principles among the clergymen and monks awakened the laymen to emulate them and partake in their works of prayer and love and in their renunciation of outward distinction.

The influence of these movements of reform in the fourteenth and fifteenth centuries was varying. These centuries were full of reform movements within and without the church. We see that in many cases the movements result in putting at the disposal of the Roman church a group of people who saw their task in mere zeal for the pope. I mention the Dominicans and their role in building up the Inquisition. And again in spite of all the examples of stupidity and brutality of which we know, I cannot find that the revival of this ardor can be traced merely to selfishness and economic interests. The work done in more recent years, chiefly by Catholic scholars in Germany, has convinced me that the old church still commanded a great number of irreproachable and able preachers and theologians.

But there was a second group of reformers who did not join the struggle for the restoration of papal authority, but instead began to apply the ideal of apostolic poverty to the church itself, demanding that not a single class but the church as a whole live in poverty. This view appealed to many people as early as the beginning of the Franciscan movement, and the church had generally a hard task to reconcile the tendencies of the mendicant orders with its own compromising attitude towards social problems. The church never quite succeeded. The ideal of apostolic poverty most forcefully preached by St. Francis, the son of a rich merchant, resounded throughout Christendom. It was carried on in the monasteries and among laymen, and it was eventually supported by the rising states which wanted to exclude the church from all secular affairs. Thus the religious ideal became a political claim as well. The conflict between church and state, now renewed on a different level, gave new opportunities to the clergy. Henceforth we meet more often in history with the undesirable type of theologians who proved themselves submissive to all demands of secular government. But there were others who used the tension which existed between state and church in order to assert the Christian ideals in criticizing both forces. They received support from their bishops or from the princes and magistrates or whoever might show himself readiest to lend assistance to the priest who wanted to fulfill his task within his assigned community.

The tension between state and church, as it appeared in the fifteenth and at the beginning of the sixteenth centuries, gave the clergy an opportunity to play a more independent part in society. In countries like England and France, where the state had already been centralized to a comparatively high degree and the authority of the central government could make itself felt throughout the nation, even a reformed clergy could not assume command of affairs, since the government was able to remove the tension by bargaining with or fighting against the papacy. In both countries it was more a change of institutions than of faith that took place in the first half of the sixteenth century. The religious reformation of these countries began in the course of later social and political upheavals, a development that was to connote an episode in French and an epoch in English history.

The situation in Germany was unique. The pressure of the decadent Roman church bore heavily on the whole people, for no other country had so many just grievances against the Roman See. On the other hand, not only was Germany divided into many territories, but the governmental authority of the territorial states was comparatively weak. No territorial prince could hope to carry through a thorough reformation of the church. He necessarily feared his neighbors and his subjects who were still bound to the Roman church. Since the way of political reform of the empire was blocked, only a religious principle could open the way into the future. A principle, however, was of little use unless it was made vital by a group of people who enjoyed the confidence of various classes because of their devotion to a higher cause than the pursuit of economic interests. An earnest preacher who lived up to the ideals which he proclaimed was still exercising an enormous authority in Germany. He was remote from the daily struggle for social hegemony, his office was functional and reflected a higher unity of human relations for which people most ardently longed.

If we consider what channels of influencing society were at the disposal of the clergy, we can understand the responsibility which the clerical office carried with it. Theologians were the only men who knew Latin, except for the small though increasing groups of educated people like jurists and humanists, and they were the people who had to read pamphlets and books before the laity, even when the publication of books in the vernacular had become a common feature. In the fifteenth and early sixteenth centuries the clergy were holding an almost absolute monopoly of information, and there is little doubt that the agitation of the common people before and after the appearance of Luther was effected chiefly through clerics.

Now we come to the problem of Luther. I do not see the slightest possibility of ascribing the origins of Luther's reformation to a particular social class in the sense that his theology was a rationalization of existing class interests. His father was of peasant stock and had become a miner and ultimately made a moderate fortune. The son could look forward to attaining a higher social status by studying law, when his sudden conversion to monkish life led him far away from all thoughts of a social career. It seems to me absurd to read any social feeling into the development of Luther's religious experiences and conception. Like all great religious prophecies they came to maturity in a mind ready to withdraw from the life of the world and not bent on world dominance.

But at least medieval society had given room to these searchers for truth and grace, and monasticism had become an acknowledged institution. It is very important that Luther attained his new religious insight as a monk and not as an outsider to the church. His earnest strife for attaining the highest ideals of the church gave him the strength to set up a higher goal. And being a member of the church, he was seeking reform of the church and not a revolt against her tradition.

But the special structure of society in the fifteenth century was auspicious for what was going to happen. The University of Wittenberg, like most of the German universities of that age, enjoyed comparatively more freedom of teaching than the old church universities. Founded in the capital of a territory by a secular prince, the University of Wittenberg was not so closely under the control of the church authorities. It was here that Luther as professor of the Holy Scriptures began to lecture on his new conception of Christian faith. Most probably he was not aware of his audacity; it seemed but natural to him that professors should not simply expound the law of the church but contribute by their work and thinking to its reformation. A new conception of academic office revealed itself here which can be fully explained only by reverting to the particular situation of society. To conceive of the professors as the living conscience of the church, instead of as simply executing its rulings, was an unthinkable idea in the heyday of the Middle Ages. It shows that these reforming clerics conceived of their functional authority in a much wider sense than before. They had originally derived their authority from the church for the good of the church. But now they applied it to the church itself, to a church which had become hopelessly entangled in worldly affairs, while they had kept a certain aloofness from secular life.

Perhaps, on the other hand, they knew the life of the laity better than the church government, although certainly not the political or business life. They alone were aware of the deep desire of individuals of all ranks to embrace the Christian life and obtain inward peace.

They had brought the Gospel to the rising classes, they had kept the fire in all divisions of society. But now they got into a serious conflict between their prior mandate and the confidence that their congregations had thrust upon them. Luther started his controversy over indulgences which was to drag him into the world-wide arena in the course of the difficulties which had arisen within his congregation. He became the Protestant reformer because he wanted to maintain the dignity of the clerical office. That added fresh power to his strength in those moments of weakness when an inner voice was warning him that a single man could not pretend to be wiser than the *consensus saeculorum.*

Thus the realization of functional authority as accomplished by the Roman church proved of great importance even in the inner life of the man who was to abolish monasticism and priesthood. But even greater was the significance for the first expansion of Lutheran ideas. We have no book on Protestantism comparable to the scope of Harnack's *History of the Mission and Expansion of the Christian Church in the First Three Centuries.* But toward such an analysis, it may be said at least that it forms an outstanding characteristic of the first phase of the Reformation period that from Luther to Thomas Müntzer all church reformers who entered the battle came from the ranks of monks or priests.

In the light of what has been said, this phenomenon can be more easily expounded. These reformers lived in the same conflict of duty to the church and to the people as did Luther. They were therefore prepared to follow the path that Luther showed, and so they made public the new truth to all the classes of the people. It was they who awakened overnight the enthusiasm of the people and from that great achievement we may learn how strong was their authority over the masses. This authority was not due to the conformity of the clergy to the existing social stratification but to its independence. Since they derived their social honor not from feudal or property privileges, they appeared as more objective and reliable leaders as the best-fitted intermediaries between the classes of society. Whether this clerical group, which was a small minority within a much wider class, lived up to the expectations of the people, I do not wish to discuss. That question belongs to the history of the period in which the Protestant churches constituted themselves as new social units.

It is, however, obvious that the Protestant reformers were in a position to form their original social program without much consideration of special class interests.

I have attempted to demonstrate three things. First, a problem of the method of approach: the stratification of our modern society should not be expected to offer much help for the understanding of other ages. The directing principles on which the society of the later Middle Ages was founded are at variance with those of our age. Second, a closer study of the society of the fifteenth and sixteenth centuries shows that the idea of the monk's calling was still a potent force which was embodied in a number of powerful personalities. Third, it was this minority that used the opportunity to assert its unifying religious ideas against and amidst conflicting economic interests. To this cause the strength and the rapid spread of the German Reformation in its first years can be largely traced. There was no one-sided social basis of the origins of the German Reformation, but there was a particular constellation of social groups and social factors which was auspicious for the cause of reform. The most fortunate result was the fact that Protestantism as a religious idea was not from its very inception bound up with a distinct class interest.

Harold J. Grimm

SOCIAL FORCES IN THE GERMAN REFORMATION

Harold J. Grimm, one of America's foremost Reformation scholars, was born in 1901. He took his A.B. degree at Capital University, his Ph.D. degree at Ohio State University, and studied also at the Evangelical Theological Seminary, and at the universities of Leipzig and Hamburg. He has taught at Capital University, Freiburg University, Indiana University, and Ohio State University, where he served as chairman of the history department for many years. He has been president of the American Society of Church History and of the American Society for Reformation Research. He has published extensively on Luther and the Reformation era, especially stressing in his research the play of social forces in history.

The period of the Reformation touches the interests of most people in one way or another and consequently receives attention from historians with a great variety of interests, running the gamut from dialectic materialism to theology. Much of this concern stems from our preoccupation with the strong revival of religion subsequent to the first World War and evinced in neo-scholasticism, Barthian evangelicalism, neoorthodoxy, the Luther renaissance, the ecumenical movement, and similar manifestations, on the one hand, and our great concern with the widespread social tensions and revolutions which are springing up in all parts of the world and are keeping us poised on the brink of another world war.

As in all periods of exceptional social tension and revolution, leaders look for guidelines in the past and study the profiles of courageous men of action. Although the dramatic conflicts of the sixteenth century were enfolded in a microcosm when compared with the extent of our own, there are sufficient parallels to warrant a renewed preoccupation with the period, its problems, its leaders, and its solutions. This becomes obvious especially when we realize that many of our political, economic, and social as well as religious institutions had their beginnings in the late medieval and early modern

Harold J. Grimm, "Social Forces in the German Reformation," *Church History* 31 (1962): 3–13, the presidential address delivered before the American Society of Church History. Used by permission of the editors of *Church History.*

periods and can be examined with great profit because they then existed in relatively simple forms.

If one examines previous discussions of the interrelation of religious and social phenomena of the Reformation, one finds few guides to a helpful appraisal. Although much has been done, both qualitatively and quantitatively, to trace the religious and the social changes, there still is no satisfactory general study of their interrelation. Too often historians treat a succession of events as *ipso facto* causes and effects and parallel movements as intrinsically interrelated. Whereas conservative church historians tend to discuss social questions as incidental to theology, liberal historians usually point to the social-democratic characteristics of the revolts of the period and Marxists dwell on the economic motives, portraying the social movements in terms of a class struggle.

Karl Lamprecht, who provides us with a thorough study of the economic and social changes in Germany during the Reformation, based on a careful examination of the sources, speaks anachronistically of the journeymen not attached to guilds as "a striving proletariat" which "had the sympathy of the masses in the lower classes and became unusually conscious of the difference between the rich and the poor." Kurt Kaser likewise calls attention to the "proletariat masses" who, in the social revolts of the fifteenth century, blindly joined revolts in any kind of crisis, political, economic, or religious. He pictures the revolutionary movements of the Reformation period as prompted by anticlerical sentiment, demands for moderate reforms, and radical communist programs.

The greatest stimulus to an analysis of the interaction between the social and economic movements and the rise of Protestantism came from Max Weber. Strongly attracted to Werner Sombart's hypothesis that the "spirit of capitalism," already present in the period of the Reformation, was responsible for the rise of modern capitalism, Weber came to the conclusion that this dynamic spirit gained much of its impetus from the activistic religious ethic of Calvinism. It is he who called attention to the fact that Luther first used the word *Beruf,* or calling, in the sense of a divinely established work, thereby giving it a religious significance which later became an important aspect of Calvinist activism.

Ernst Troeltsch, a theologian, asserted that the Reformation was at the outset free of social distinctions yet was strongly influenced by its direct connections with the development of the urban middle class and the unorganized poor townsmen. It is this distinction, with its assumption that the upper classes favored the moderate Reformation initiated by Luther and that the lower classes followed the radical leaders, which became the basis of subsequent attempts to interpret the latter movements as proletarian revolts. Troeltsch's contention that Luther later in his life "deliberately decided in favor of the Territorial Church," thereby making the Reformer responsible to a large degree for the evolution of a territorial social doctrine within Lutheranism, was ably attacked by Karl Holl.

R. H. Tawney, an economic historian, modified considerably the Weber thesis by pointing to the relationships between capitalism and all forms of Protestantism and to general political, social, and economic as well as religious conditions as responsible for the development of the new capitalist spirit. Although he underestimated Luther's understanding of business practices, his findings stimulated considerable research in the economic and social life of the Reformation. The ablest arguments recently marshalled against the Weber thesis are those of Winthrop S. Hudson, H. M. Robertson, Henri Sée, Albert Hyma, and Amintore Fanfani.

R. Pascal goes much further than Troeltsch and Tawney in connecting Luther with a definite social class, that is, the small, settled, middle-class townsmen, and in deriving the Reformer's economic and social theories from this connection. He maintains that Luther, while considering himself essentially a theologian, developed his moral doctrines in harmony with the aims of the new bourgeois conservatives who, while seeking greater economic freedom, believed their security lay in the preservation of the existing social order and the continued suppression of the lower classes who were clamoring for a greater share in government and profits. He concludes that the reformer, by supporting this class and the sacredness of private property, "abandoned Christian principle, and accepted the basis of capitalistic society."

The distortion of history by Nazi historians has had little influence on the thinking of our own time. Yet it is instructive to learn from it how easily historical data can be interpreted to support political theories. Since these historians were preoccupied with finding in history the bases for the growth of the authoritarian state, they credited Luther with strengthening the territorial state and the territorial princes, with determining the development of economic, social, and religious, as well as political, events, as far far back as the thirteenth century when, as Fritz Rörig shows, no closed territorial state existed on German soil.

As might be expected, the Marxist historians of Soviet Russia and its satellites today interpret the late medieval and early modern history of Europe from the point of view of dialectic materialism. M. M. Smirin, for example, brands the outstanding European historians of the Reformation from Ranke to the present as "perverters of history" and, with the works of Marx, Engels, Lenin, and Stalin as his authorities, proposes to treat "the true, scientific history" of the period as resting basically on the revolutionary struggles of the oppressed peoples. Johannes Schildhauer, in an important, carefully documented work, calls attention to the era of the Protestant Reformation and Peasants' Revolt as a high point in the history of the German people and of great significance in general history since at that time occurred the first great movement of opposition of the townsmen against feudalism and, within the towns, a social revolution for democracy and egalitarianism. While not denying the significance of the religious developments, he bases these on social developments, arguing that historians should proceed from the standpoint of historical materialism for a better understanding of the period. On such a basis he makes many significant observations, even though he underestimates constitutional developments, the sincerity of religious convictions, and the elements which traditionally bound together the various classes in the towns.

This brief survey of the historiography concerned with the interrelation of the social and religious history of the Reformation illustrates the need for studies by historians with no ax to grind who are willing to examine both the social and the religious developments of the Reformation. There should be no doubt concerning the priority of theology in the minds of the reformers, for all attempts to attribute to them economic and other motives have failed. On the other hand, it is equally futile to attribute the spread of the Reformation solely to religious motives.

Seldom in the development of Western civilization was there so much universal dissatisfaction as at the beginning of the sixteenth century, particularly in Germany. To attempt to describe this dissatisfaction in terms of a class struggle, a conflict between the rich and the poor, is not only too facile but misleading.

That the explosion that did much to change Europe was set off by an Augustinian monk's theological formulation of the solution to his personal religious problems is not so strange as it might seem on the surface. In the first place, sixteenth-century religious life was closely interwoven with all other aspects of society, and religious standards were applied to all activities and institutions until well into the next century.

In the second place, the principles evolved by the reformers in their struggles to maintain their beliefs were applicable in other areas of thought and action, while their slogans could be taken over by social and political groups in promoting their respective reform programs. For example, the word "liberty," so effectively used by Luther in his widely read pamphlets, was employed by the German territorial princes and free imperial cities in their struggles with the emperor, by the nobles and towns in their conflicts with territorial rulers, by the peasants in their revolts against their feudal landlords, and by the lesser townsmen in their opposition to the ruling classes of the cities and towns. The word "gospel" likewise was used to convey social and political as well as religious meanings, while "the Word of God" provided members of all social groups with a dynamic hope for the future ordering of European life which dispelled much of the apocalyptic gloom of the late Middle Ages.

Finally, the word "class" should not be used in the modern sense of the word when speaking of the social groups of the Reformation era. Luther and his contemporaries usually spoke of these as "estates," conceiving of each estate as being an essential part of the entire social structure, a stratum of people with a common outlook on life and similar functions in society In no revolutionary program of that time is there a suggestion that one estate should liquidate the others and assume sole control.

Probably the most significant political changes necessitating great economic and social adjustments were those associated with the development of the territorial state, a process which was well under way in western Europe by 1500. Whereas in most countries this de-

velopment was furthered by kings, supported in the main by townsmen, in Germany it was led by princes, both ecclesiastical and lay,
and frequently in opposition to the cities. The territorial princes maintained their "liberty" by retaining control of the imperial diet while
at the same time establishing police powers with uniform justice, administration, and protection throughout their lands. The nobility, or
knights, who were being made subjects rather than vassals, retained
control over the granting of new subsidies in some territorial assemblies and held a share of the administrative posts, especially of those
having to do with taxes. As a group, the princes were inclined to
cling to all that they considered good in the old order, carrying out
conservative social and economic policies typical of the medieval
period. Yet by developing territorial states they were in effect furthering changes of revolutionary proportions.

Whereas a large number of princes became conscientious Lutherans, others adhered to Catholicism. Both continued to extend
their authority over administrative functions of the church, but some
of the Protestant princes influenced also theological developments. In
other words, the princes, rather than the king-emperor, faced the
realities of the age by forming a number of dynamic political states
in lieu of one strong royal authority. Although some studies have
been made of the motives of rulers who became Protestant and although archival materials of most of them are available, often in
printed form, much still remains to be done in this respect.

Throughout Western Europe the lesser nobles were adversely affected by the development of the territorial state and the rise of a
wealthy and influential class of townsmen. Their places in the courts
of kings and other territorial rulers were being taken by nonnobles
skilled in finance and administration and trained in law; in military
affairs they were being restricted to the role of captains of merce-
naries in the service of their rulers; and the income from their feudal
holdings was becoming insufficient to meet their needs in a changing
world. In Germany the plight of most knights was desperate by 1500.
While their political authority and social prestige were being sharply
reduced by the territorial princes, they were being ruined economi-
cally by the growth of capitalism and the concomitant decline of their
agrarian economy as well as by the accumulation of lands and
wealth by the church. Whereas some knights sank to the level of

serfs, others became robber barons, preying on merchants. Still others sought service as warriors, ambassadors, and counselors in the courts of secular and ecclesiastical princes.

To improve their position in face of the activities of princes, townsmen, and churchmen, the leaders of the knights produced reform pamphlets and sought to create effective unions of knights with a common program of action. Like the well known *Reformatio Sigismundi* of 1439, these reform programs called for no class struggle but primarily for the reestablishment of medieval order, justice, peace, and the common welfare under the emperor, while at the same time demanding the secularization of church lands and the abolition of monopolies and other capitalist abuses. Some programs, such as those of Eberlin von Günzberg and Hartmuth von Kronberg, were motivated basically by a firm faith in Lutheranism, the Gospel and Word of God providing optimism and hope despite the dismal outlook of the knights.

When it came to creating unions of knights, however, it became apparent that little agreement could be found with respect to a positive program of action. Although all the knights were convinced of the need of cooperation in preserving their estate, they were hopelessly divided by their territorial, economic, and religious differences. The so-called Knights' War of 1522–1523, for example, was no general uprising of the lower nobility, but a feud led by Franz von Sickingen and Ulrich von Hutten against the ecclesiastical prince, the Archbishop of Trier. Any hopes cherished by the leaders that their having embraced Lutheranism would lead to a widespread support of their cause were soon dispelled, for many Lutheran knights refused to support the feud. Furthermore, economic considerations had little or nothing to do with the attitudes of men like Eberlin and Hartmuth, who demonstrated that the knights need not constitute a reactionary status group but could adjust themselves to the needs and forces of their day. Like the reformers, however, they wanted a reform from above, not a revolution from below.

Lutheranism also aroused considerable hope among the peasants. Their leaders soon translated religious demands for freedom, the Word of God, and divine justice into social terms, despite Luther's warning against such action. Efforts to interpret the Peasants' Revolt of 1524–1525 as primarily a class struggle have failed, for there was no demonstrable class consciousness motivated basically by a hatred of economic exploitation.

The grievances and reform programs of the peasants varied from region to region. In the main, however, they called for the reestablishment of the peace, order, and justice of an earlier period rather than an overthrow of their landlords. Even the Christian communism of such men as Thomas Müntzer had little in common with a dictatorship of the proletariat. Moreover, the peasants attacked not only the feudal knights but princes, towns, and the church, particularly the monasteries.

Even more formidable is the task of discovering the interrelation of religious and social concerns among the townsmen of the Reformation era. Much has been written about the development of medieval German cities as states within states in a feudal sense, the rise of capitalism and the capitalist spirit, and the conflicts among patricians, guilds, and unorganized citizens. A few excellent biographies of influential townsmen have been published which give us insights into their broad religious, cultural, and economic interests. City chronicles also have been examined with the purpose of ascertaining the attitudes of medieval townsmen toward the major issues of their day. There still remains, however, the great task of searching the printed and manuscript works of leaders of the various classes within the cities to determine motives behind their embracing or opposing the Protestant Reformation and assessing the impact of Reformation doctrines on their society.

The patrician class, comprising the wealthy merchants and property owners who had gotten control of the city governments and whose monopoly was being challenged by the craft guilds in revolutionary movements after the middle of the fourteenth century, were not uniformly conservative opponents of the Reformation. Like the knights, the patricians, particularly those of the free imperial cities, were inclined to think of the common welfare of both their citizens and the empire as a whole. Convinced that they were by tradition and experience best qualified to serve the common welfare and aware of the widespread changes going on in their dynamic society, they made significant adjustments, often assuming functions once the prerogatives of the church, emperors, or territorial princes. To understand their attitudes toward the Reformation, therefore, one must

FIGURE 4. *A Knight Captured by Peasants.* This woodcut shows peasants capturing a nobleman during the great revolt of 1524–1525. The *Bundschuh,* or bound sandal, on the pennant was the symbol of their revolutionary movement. Taken from Hanns Lilje, *Martin Luther: Eine Bildmonographe,* Furche-Verlag, Hamburg, by permission.

evaluate not only their economic interests but also their political thought, intellectual pursuits, and religious concerns. Moreover, one must take into consideration their practical experience prior to the Reformation in dealing with religious matters such as furtherance of monastic reforms, selection of local clergy, supervision of morals, control of education, and care of the poor and sick.

Lazarus Spengler, *Ratsschreiber,* or chancellor, of the city council of Nuremberg, where the patricians had retained their control throughout the Middle Ages, best illustrates the complexity of interests involved in bringing the Reformation to this city. Educated in law, he joined Nuremberg's humanist circle which came under the strong influence of the mystic piety of the Augustinian prior Johann von Staupitz and finally of Luther's doctrines. By 1521 he had become a staunch Lutheran who in four years brought his city firmly into the Lutheran camp with the able assistance of Caspar Nützel, who had translated Luther's Ninety-five Theses for publication, and Jerome Ebner. Although Spengler, like the city council, remained loyal to the empire, he consistently supported Lutheranism to the end of his life.

The role of the patricians in the city councils varied from place to place at the beginning of the sixteenth century. In some cities, such as Nuremberg, Frankfurt a.M., Rostock, Stralsund, and Wismar, they were in complete control of the councils. In Augsburg, Ulm, Strassburg, Regensburg, Rothenburg, and Schwäbisch Hall they shared control with the guilds. In Speyer and Schlettstadt the guilds were in complete control. But in all cities they continued to exercise considerable authority, for they were more likely than the members of other classes to be financially independent and therefore able to accept positions requiring much time and frequent absence from their cities. In virtually all cities there were patricians who accepted Lutheranism at an early date. Few did so because of purely economic or social motives and some did so despite them.

The councils of the German cities of the Reformation were fully conscious of the fact that they were the organs of government for all citizens, although not in the sense of popular sovereignty. Whether or not they ruled autocratically, the councilmen were aware of their obligation to serve the welfare of their entire communities. By including in this a responsibility for the cultural and religious welfare of their fellow citizens, they anticipated by many years similar concerns on the part of the German territorial states. With the adoption of Lutheranism it was a relatively simple matter to enlarge their religious responsibilities to include the supply of ministers, the administration of church business, and the supervision of church discipline and even doctrine. But they did this in the name of all the citizens. In no case did they introduce the Reformation against the will of the majority and in many cases they justified their Reformation changes by stating that the suppression of Lutheranism would have led to revolt.

There is no doubt that Luther's doctrines did much to raise the economic hopes of those classes not represented in the city councils, above all of the guildsmen, despite the fact that such a support was furthest from Luther's mind. Guildsmen had revolted against patrician control before, especially after the middle of the fourteenth century. They accused the patricians of ruling in the interests of their own class, monopolizing city offices, mismanaging finances, in short, of not serving the common welfare. They also joined the patricians in their complaints against the clergy and the church. But in those cities in which they gained control or a share of the control of the city councils, usually with the aid of the unorganized citizens, they did not liquidate the patricians as a class but permitted them to remain as influential citizens.

To state that "the same classes which supported the Reformation had as their political goal the democratization of the city government" is a misleading generalization. No artisan was more vocal in his concern for the interests of the middle and lower classes than Hans Sachs, the Meistersinger-cobbler of Nuremberg. His conversion to Lutheranism was sincere and he remained constant to this faith throughout his long life, believing firmly with Luther that the Gospel would remake society. He never supported violence for the attainment of social goals, even when the patrician council warned him "to stick to his last" and not to attack the economic practices of some of the errant Nuremberg patricians. With the exception of a relatively few big merchants and financiers, Germans of the sixteenth century seemed unconcerned about production for profit and remained satisfied with making a modest living. Guildsmen also felt a responsibility for the common welfare of their communities and identified themselves with their cities and the empire, not as individuals but as members of their guilds.

City councils partially or completely under guild control tended to become as autocratic and exclusive as they had been under patrician control. Therefore the city revolts during and after the Peasants' Revolt were aimed at guild as well as patrician rule. Most revolutionary in outlook were the unorganized workers who had failed to find security and a "good living" within the guild system of production, particularly the journeymen, who had some elementary education and training in a skill but no prospects of becoming masters. The growing exclusiveness of the craft guilds and the development of the entrepreneurial system forced many of them into the ranks of day laborers. In their economic and social demands they usually had the support of the lowest classes, that is, the free laborers, recent immigrants to the city, and a floating population of beggars.

In 1500 about half of the population of Augsburg owned no property and 3 percent were beggars, while one fifth of the population of Hamburg lived in extreme poverty. It was among these lower classes that the distinction between rich and poor was most advanced and that preachers of radical religious and social reform gained many followers who were willing to use violence in achieving their goals. Although it is misleading to label this pathetic and incendiary group a proletariat in the nineteenth-century meaning of the term, its revolts under radical leaders often bore resemblance to modern revolutions. Among this group such Protestant slogans as Gospel, Word of God, brotherly love, divine justice, freedom, and equality were appropriated in support of revolutionary social programs. But this class had no uniform program or plan of action. Consequently its revolts were suppressed with relative ease.

An examination of the extant studies of the social forces of the Reformation indicates the many problems which must be solved before we can make definitive generalizations concerning their interrelationship with Reformation doctrines. We know for certain that all classes were being compelled to make adjustments which caused wide-spread dissatisfaction and that the Reformation provided many people in all classes with a dynamic hope that their difficulties could be solved. It is reasonable to assume that Reformation doctrines, ideas, and slogans were applied to individual class interests. Yet these cannot be described simply in terms of class conflict or dialectic materialism.

Before further progress can be made toward a clear understanding of the interrelation of the social and religious forces of the Reformation, much research must be done concerning the political, economic, and social status of all the classes; the cultural interests and social aims of their spokesmen; and the impact of the Reformation on them.

Henry Charles Lea

THE EVE OF THE REFORMATION

Henry Charles Lea, American journalist and historian, was born in 1825 in Philadelphia, where he also died in 1909. He wrote a sketch of sacerdotal celibacy and of auricular confession and indulgences, but he is best known for his multivolumed history of the Inquisition in the Middle Ages, the history of the Inquisition in Spain, and the history of the Inquisition in the Spanish dependencies.

As the sixteenth century opened, Europe was standing unconscious on the brink of a crater destined to change profoundly by its eruption the course of modern civilization. The church had acquired so complete a control over the souls of men, its venerable antiquity and its majestic organization so filled the imagination, the services it had rendered seemed to call for such reverential gratitude, and its acknowledged claim to interpret the will of God to man rendered obedience so plain a duty, that the continuance of its power appeared to be an unchanging law of the universe, destined to operate throughout the limitless future. To understand the combination of forces which rent the domination of the church into fragments, we must investigate in detail its relations with society on the eve of the disruption, and consider how it was regarded by the men of that day with their diverse grievances, more or less justifying revolt. We must here omit from consideration the benefits which the church had conferred, and confine our attention to the antagonisms which it provoked and to the evils for which it was held responsible. The interests and the motives at work were numerous and complex, some of them dating back for centuries, others comparatively recent, but all of them growing in intensity with the development of political institutions and popular intelligence. There has been a natural tendency to regard the Reformation as solely a religious movement; but this is an error. In the curious theocracy which dominated the Middle Ages, secular and spiritual interests became so inextricably intermingled that it is impossible wholly to disentangle them; but the

From H. C. Lea, "The Eve of the Reformation," *The Cambridge Modern History*, vol. I (Cambridge, 1931), pp. 653–692. Used by permission of the Syndics of the University Press, Cambridge.

motives, both remote and proximate, which led to the Lutheran revolt were largely secular rather than spiritual. So far, indeed, as concerns our present purpose we may dismiss the religious changes incident to the Reformation with the remark that they were not the object sought but the means for attaining that object. The existing ecclesiastical system was the practical evolution of dogma, and the overthrow of dogma was the only way to obtain permanent relief from the intolerable abuses of that system.

In primitive society the kingly and the priestly functions are commonly united; the church and the state are one. Development leads to specialization; the functions are divided; and the struggle for supremacy, like that between the Brahman and Kshatriya castes, becomes inevitable. In medieval Europe this struggle was peculiarly intricate, for, in the conversion of the Barbarians, a strange religion was imposed by the conquered on the conquerors; and the history of the relations between church and state thenceforth becomes a record of the efforts of the priestly class to acquire domination and of the military class to maintain its independence. The former gradually won. It had two enormous advantages, for it virtually monopolized education and culture, and, through its democratic organization, absorbed an undue share of the vigor and energy of successive generations by means of the career which it alone offered to those of lowly birth but lofty ambition. When Charles the Great fostered the church as a civilizing agency he was careful to preserve his mastership; but the anarchy attending the dissolution of his empire enabled the church to assert its pretensions, as formulated in the False Decretals, and, when the slow process of enlightenment again began in the eleventh century, it had a most advantageous base of operations. With the development of scholastic theology in the twelfth century, its claims on the obedience of the faithful were reduced to a system under which the priest became the arbiter of the eternal destiny of man, a power readily transmuted into control of his worldly fortunes by the use of excommunication and interdict. During this period, moreover, the hierarchical organization was strengthened and the claims of the pope as the Vicar of Christ and as the supreme and irresponsible head of the church became more firmly established through the extension of its jurisdiction, original and appellate. The first half of the thirteenth century saw the power of these agencies fully developed, when Raymond of Toulouse was humbled with fleshly arms, and John of England with spiritual weapons, and when the long rivalry of the papacy and empire was virtually ended with the extinction of the House of Hohenstaufen. The expression of the supremacy thus won is to be found in the Gloss of Innocent IV on the Decretals and was proclaimed to the world by Boniface VIII in the bull *Unam Sanctam.*

This sovereignty was temporal as well as spiritual. The power of the pope, as the earthly representative of God, was illimitable. The official theory, as expressed in the *De Principum Regimine,* which passes under the name of St. Thomas Aquinas, declared the temporal jurisdiction of kings to be simply derived from the authority intrusted by Christ to St. Peter and his successors; whence it followed that the exercise of the royal authority was subject to papal control. As Matthew of Vendôme had already sung—

> *Papa regit reges, dominos dominatur, acerbis*
> *Principibus stabili jure jubere jubet.*

The arguments of Marsiglio of Padua, intended to restore the imperial system of a church subordinate of the state, were of some assistance to Louis of Bavaria in his long struggle with the papacy; but at his death they virtually disappeared from view. The Councils of Constance and Basel were an effort on the part of the prelates and princes to limit the papal authority, and if they had succeeded they would have rendered the church a constitutional monarchy in place of a despotism; but the disastrous failure at Basel greatly strengthened papal absolutism. The superiority of councils over popes, though it continued to be asserted by France in the Pragmatic Sanction of 1438, and from time to time by Germany, gradually sank into an academic question, and the popes were finally able to treat it with contempt. In 1459, at the Congress of Mantua, Pius II, in his speech to the French envoys, took occasion to assert his irresponsible supremacy, which could not be limited by general councils and to which all princes were subject. In his extraordinary letter to Monammed II, then in the full flush of his conquests, Pius tempted the Turk to embrace Christianity with the promise to appoint him Emperor of Greece and of the East, so that what he had won by force he might enjoy with justice. If the pope could thus grant kingdoms, he could also take them away. George Podiebrad, King of Bohemia, committed the offence of insisting on the terms under which the Hussites had been reconciled to the church by the Fathers of Basel; whereupon Pius II in 1464, and Paul II in 1465, summoned him to Rome to stand trial for heresy; and the latter, without awaiting the expiration of the term assigned, declared him deprived of the royal power, released his subjects from their allegiance and made over his kingdom to Matthias Corvinus of Hungary, with the result of a long and devastating war. Julius II, in his strife with France, gave the finishing blow to the little kingdom of Navarre by excommunicating in 1511 those children of perdition, Jean d'Albret and his wife Catherine, and empowering the first comer to seize their dominions—an act of piety for which the rapacious Ferdinand of Aragon had made all necessary preparations. In the bull of excommunication Julius formally asserted his plenary power, granted by God, over all nations and kingdoms; and this claim, amounting to a quasi-divinity, was sententiously expressed in one of the inscriptions of the consecration of Alexander VI in 1492—

> *Caesare magna fuit, nunc Roma est maxima. Sextus*
> *Regnat Alexander: ille vir, iste Deus.*

While it is true that the extreme exercise of papal authority in making and unmaking kings was exceptional, still the unlimited jurisdiction claimed by the Holy See was irksome in many ways to the sovereigns of Europe and, as time wore on and the secular authority became consolidated, it was endured with more and more impatience. There could be no hard and fast line of delimitation between the spiritual and the temporal, for the two were mutually interdependent, and the convenient phrase, *temporalia ad spiritualia ordinata,* was devised to define those temporal matters, over which, as requisite to the due enjoyment of the spiritual, the church claimed exclusive control. Moreover it assumed the right to determine in doubtful matters the definition of this elastic term and the secular ruler constantly found himself inconveniently limited in the exercise of his authority. The tension thence arising was increased by the happy device of legates and nuncios, by which the Holy See established in every country a representative whose business it was to exercise supreme spiritual jurisdiction and to maintain the claims of the church, resulting in a divided sovereignty, at times exceedingly galling and even incompatible with a well-ordered state. Rulers so orthodox as Ferdinand and Isabel asked the great national Council of Seville, in 1478, how they could best prevent the residence of legates and nuncios who not only carried much gold out of the kingdom but interfered seriously with the royal preeminence. In this they only expressed the desires of the people; for the Estates of Castile, in 1480, asked the sovereigns to make some provision with respect to the nuncios who were of no benefit and only a source of evil.

Another fruitful source of complaint, on the part not only of the rulers but of the national churches, was the gradual extension of the claim of the Holy See to control all patronage. Innocent III has the credit of first systematically asserting this claim and exploiting it for the benefit of his cardinals and other officials. The practice increased, and Villani tells us that, in 1319, John XXII assumed to himself the control of all prebends in every collegiate church, from the sale of which he gathered immense sums. Finally the assertion was made that the Holy See owned all benefices and in the rules of the papal chanceries appear the prices to be charged for them, whether with or without cure of souls, showing that the traffic had become an established source of revenue. Even the rights of lay patrons and founders were disregarded and in the provisions granted by the popes there was a special clause derogating their claims. Partly this patronage was used for direct profit, partly it was employed for the benefit of the cardinals and their retainers, on whom pluralities were heaped with unstinted hand, and the further refinement was introduced of granting to them pensions imposed on benefices and monastic foundations. Abbeys, also, were bestowed *in commendam* on titular abbots who collected the revenues through stewards, with little heed to the maintenance of the inmates or the performance of the offices. In the eager desire to anticipate these profits of simony, vacancies were not awaited, and rights of succession, under the name of expectatives, were given or sold in advance. The deplorable results of this spiritual commerce were early apparent and formed the subject of bitter lamentation and complaint, but to no purpose. . . .

In this absorption of patronage the feature most provocative of friction with the sovereigns was the claim gradually advanced to nominate bishops; for these prelates were mostly temporal lords of no little influence, and in the political schemes of the papacy the character of its nominees might well create uneasiness in the state. Quarrels over the exercise of this power were of frequent occurrence. . . .

These cases have a double interest as illustrating the growing tension between the Holy See and secular potentates and the increasing disposition to meet its claims with scant measures of respect. It was constantly arrogating to itself enlarged prerogatives and the sovereigns were less and less inclined to submission. But, whether exercised by king or pope, the distribution of ecclesiastical patronage had become simple jobbery, to reward dependents or to gain pecuniary or political advantage, without regard to the character of the incumbent or the sacred duties of the office. These evils were aggravated by habitual and extravagant pluralism, of which the Holy See set an example eagerly imitated by the sovereigns. Bishoprics and benefices were showered upon the cardinals and their retainers, and upon the favorites of the popes in all parts of Europe, whose revenues were drawn to Rome, to the impoverishment of each locality; while the functions for which the revenues had been granted remained for the most part unperformed, to the irritation of the populations. . . .

There was another of the so-called liberties of the church which brought it into collision with temporal princes—the exemption from taxation of all ecclesiastical property, so vigorously proclaimed by Boniface VIII in the bull *Clericis laicos.* Although, under pressure from Philip the Fair, this declaration was annulled by the Council of Vienne, the principle remained unaffected. The piety of successive generations had brought so large a portion of the wealth of Europe—estimated at fully one third—into the hands of the church that the secular power was becoming more and more disinclined to exempt it from the burdens of the state. . . .

The incompatibility between the papal pretensions and the royal prerogative was intensified not only by the development of the monarchies but by the increasing secularization of the Holy See. It had long been weighted down by its territorial possessions which led it to subordinate its spiritual duties to its acquisitive ambition. When, about 1280, Nicholas III offered the cardinalate to the Blessed John of Parma, he refused it, saying that he could give good counsel if there was anyone to listen to him; but that in Rome salvation of souls was of small account in comparison with wars and intrigues. So it had been and so it continued to be. The fatal necessity of defending the patrimony of St. Peter against the assaults of unscrupulous neighbors and the even more fatal eagerness to extend its boundaries governed the papal policy to the virtual exclusion of loftier aims. Even the transfer to Avignon did not serve to release the Holy See from these chains which bound it to the earth, as was seen in the atrocious war waged by Clement V to gain Ferrara, in the long contest of John XXII with the Visconti, and in the bloody subjugation of revolted communities by Cardinal Albornoz as legate of Urban V. The earlier half of the fifteenth century was occupied with the Great Schism and the struggle between the papacy and the general councils; but, on the final and triumphant assertion of papal absolutism, the popes became to all intents and purposes mere secular princes, to whom religion was purely an instrument for supplementing territorial weakness in the attainment of worldly ends. Religion was, in fact, a source of no little strength, increasing the value of the papacy as an ally and its power as an enemy. Among the transalpine nations, at least, there was still enough reverence felt for the Vicar of Christ to render open rupture undesirable. Then there remained the sentence of excommunication and interdict, a force in reserve always to be borne in mind by hostile states. There was also the supreme authority to bind and to loose, whereby a pope could always release himself from inconvenient agreements and was absolved from observing any compacts, while, if the conscience of an ally chanced to be tender, it could be relieved in the same manner. Still more important was the inexhaustible source of revenue derived from the headship of the church and the power of the keys—the levying of annates and tithes and the sale of dispensations, absolutions, and indulgences. These were exploited in every way that ingenuity could suggest, draining Europe of its substance for the maintenance of papal armies and fleets and of a court unrivalled in its sumptuous magnificence, until the Holy See was everywhere regarded with detestation. It was this temporal sovereignty which rendered possible the existence of such a succession of pontiffs as disgraced the end of the fifteenth and commencement of the sixteenth century—such careers as those of Alexander VI and Cesare Borgia, such a catastrophe as the sack of Rome in 1527. Even before these evils had grown to such appalling magnitude, Dante had expressed the opinion of all thoughtful men in deploring the results which had followed the so-called Donation of Constantine. By the middle of the fifteenth century Lorenzo Valla, in his demonstration of the fraud, assumed that the corruption of the church and the wars which desolated Italy were its direct consequence, and few more eloquent and powerful indictments of the papacy are to be found than the bold utterances in which he warned the Holy See that princes and peoples could not much longer endure its tyranny and wickedness. Remonstrances and warnings were in vain; the papacy became more and more secularized, and, as the pressure grew more inexorable, men asked themselves why, if the headship of St. Peter were founded on Christ's injunction to feed his sheep, St. Peter's successor employed that headship rather to shear and slaughter.

Papal history, in fact, as soon as the Holy See had vindicated its supremacy over general councils, becomes purely a political history of diplomatic intrigues, of alliances made and broken, of military enterprises. In following it no one would conclude, from internal evidence, that the papacy represented interests higher than those of any other petty Italian prince, or that it claimed to be the incarnation of a faith divinely revealed to ensure peace on earth and goodwill to man—save when, occasionally in a papal letter, an unctuous expression is employed to shroud some peculiarly objectionable design. . . .

In every way the revenues thus enjoyed and squandered by the curia were scandalous and oppressive. To begin with, the cost of their collection was enormous. The accounts of the papal agent for first-fruits in Hungary, for the year 1320, show that of 1913 florins collected only 732 reached the papal treasury. With a more thorough organization in later periods the returns were better; but when the device was adopted of employing bankers to collect the proceeds of annates and indulgences, the share allotted to those who conducted the business and made advances was ruinously large. In the contract for the fateful St. Peter's indulgence with the Fuggers of Augsburg,

their portion of the receipts was to be 50 *percent*. Even worse was it
when these revenues were farmed out, for the banker who depended
for his profits on the extent of his sales or collections was not likely
to be overnice in his methods, nor to exercise much restraint over
his agents. Europe was overrun with pardon-sellers who had purchased letters empowering them to sell indulgences, whether of a
general character or for some church or hospital; and for centuries
their lies, their frauds, their exactions, and their filthy living were the
cause of the bitterest and most indignant complaints.

Even more demoralizing were the revenues derived from the sale
of countless dispensations for marriage within the prohibited de-
grees, for the holding of pluralities, for the numerous kinds of "ir-
regularities" and other breaches of the canon law; so that its
prescriptions might almost seem to have been framed for the purpose
of enabling the Holy See to profit by their violation. Not less destructive to morals were the absolutions, which amounted to a sale of
pardons for sin of every description, as though the Decalogue had
been enacted for this very purpose. There was also a thriving business done in the composition for unjust gains, whereby fraudulent
traders, usurers, robbers, and other malefactors, on paying to the
church a portion of their illegal acquisitions, were released from the
obligation of making restitution. In every way the power of the keys
and the treasure of the merits of Christ were exploited, without any
regard for moral consequences.

Deplorable as was this effacement of the standards of right and
wrong, all these were at least voluntary payments which perhaps
rather predisposed the thoughtless in favor of the church who so
benignantly exercised her powers to relieve the weakness of human
nature. It was otherwise, however, with the traffic in benefices and
expectatives which filled the parishes and chapters with unworthy
incumbents, not only neglectful of their sacred duties but seeking
to recoup themselves for their expenditure by exactions from their
subjects. A standing grievance was the exaction of the annates,
which, since their regulation by Boniface IX and the fruitless effort
of the Council of Basel to abolish them, continued to be the source
of bitter complaint. They consisted of a portion, usually computed at
one half, of the estimated revenue of a benefice, worth twenty-five
florins or more, collected on every change of incumbents. . . .

An even more potent, because more constant, source of antagonism was the venality of the curia and its pitiless exactions from the multitudes who were obliged to have recourse to it. This had always been the case since the Holy See had succeeded in concentrating in itself the supreme jurisdiction, original and appellate, so that all questions concerning the spirituality could be brought before it. At the Council of St. Baseul, in 992, Arnoul of Orleans unhesitatingly denounced Rome as a place where justice was put up to auction for the highest bidder; and similar complaints continued through the Middle Ages with ever-increasing vehemence, as its sphere of operations widened and its system became more intricate and more perfect. . . .

The whole machinery was thus manifestly devised for the purpose of levying as large a tax as possible on the multitudes whose necessities brought them to the curia, and its rapacity was proverbial. The hands through which every document passed were multiplied to an incredible degree and each one levied his share upon it. Besides, there were heavy charges which do not appear in the rules of the chancery and which doubtless enured to the benefit of the papal camera, so that the official taxtables bear but a slender proportion to the actual cost of briefs to suitors. . . .

The pressing necessities of the papacy had found another source of relief which did not bear so directly on the nations but was an expedient fatally degrading to the dignity and character of the Holy See. This was the sale of the highest office in the church next to the papacy itself—the red hat of the cardinalate. The reputation of the Sacred College was already rapidly deteriorating through the nepotism of the pontiffs, who thrust their kinsmen into it irrespective of fitness, or yielded to the pressure of monarchs and appointed their unworthy favorites in order to secure some temporary political advantage. Thus its decadence and secularization were rapid through the second half of the fifteenth century; but a lower depth was reached when, in 1500, Alexander VI created twelve Cardinals from whose appointment Cesare Borgia secured the sum of 120,000 ducats, and whose character may readily be surmised. . . .

Under such influence it is no wonder that Rome had become a center of corruption whence infection was radiated throughout Christendom. In the middle of the fourteenth century Petrarch exhausts his rhetoric in describing the abominations of the papal city of Avignon, where everything was vile; and the return of the curia to Rome transferred to that city the supremacy in wickedness. In 1499 the Venetian ambassador describes it as the sewer of the world, and Machiavelli asserts that through its example all devotion and all religion had perished in Italy. In 1490 it numbered 6000 public women—an enormous proportion for a population not exceeding 100,000. The story is well known how Cardinal Borgia who, as vice-chancellor, openly sold pardons for crime, when reproved for this, replied that God desires not the death of sinners but that they should pay and live. If the *Diary* of Infessura is suspect on account of his partisanship, that of Burchard is unimpeachable, and his placid recital of the events passing under his eyes presents to us a society too depraved to take shame at its own wickedness. The public marriage, he says, of the daughters of Innocent VIII and Alexander VI set the fashion for the clergy to have children, and they diligently followed it, for all, from the highest to the lowest, kept concubines, while the monasteries were brothels. . . .

In fact, one of the most urgent symptoms of the necessity of a new order of things was the complete divorce between religion and morality. There was abundant zeal in debating minute points of faith, but little in evoking from it an exemplary standard of life—as Pius II said of the Conventual Franciscans: they were generally excellent theologians but gave themselves little trouble about virtue. The sacerdotal system, developed by the dialectics of the Schoolmen, had constructed a routine of external observances through which salvation was to be gained not so much by abstinence from sin as by its pardon through the intervention of the priest, whose supernatural powers were in no way impaired by the scandals of his daily life. Except within the pale of the pagan Renaissance, never was there a livelier dread of future punishment, but this punishment was to be escaped, not by amendment but by confession, absolution, and indulgences. . . .

A priesthood trained in this formalism, which had practically replaced the ethical values of Christianity, secure that its supernatural attributes were unaffected by the most flagitious life, and selected by such methods as were practiced by the curia and imitated by the prelates, could not be expected to rise above the standards of the community. Rather, indeed, were the influences, to which the clergy were exposed, adapted to depress them below the average. They were clothed with virtually irresponsible power over their subjects, they were free from the restraints of secular law, and they were condemned to celibacy in times when no man was expected to be continent. For three hundred years it had been the constant complaint that the people were contaminated by their pastors and the complaint continued. . . .

That a reform of the church in its head and its members was necessary had long been generally conceded. For more than a century Europe had been clamoring for it. . . .

While thus the primary cause of the Reformation is to be sought in the all-pervading corruption of the church and its oppressive exercise of its supernatural prerogatives, there were other factors conducing to the explosion. Sufficient provocation had long existed, and since the failure at Basel no reasonable man could continue to anticipate relief from conciliar action. The shackles which for centuries had bound the human intellect had to be loosened before there could be a popular movement of volume sufficient to break with the traditions of the past and boldly tempt the dangers of a new and untried career for humanity. The old reverence for authority had to be weakened, the sense of intellectual independence had to be awakened and the spirit of inquiry and of more or less scientific investigation had to be created, before pious and devout men could reach the root of the abuses which caused so much indignation, and could deny the authenticity of the apostolical deposit on which had been erected the venerable and imposing structure of scholastic theology and papal autocracy.

It was the New Learning and the humanistic movement which supplied the impulse necessary for this, and they found conditions singularly favorable for their work. The church had triumphed so completely over her enemies that the engines of repression had been neglected and had grown rusty, while the popes were so engrossed in their secular schemes and ambition that they had little thought to waste on the possible tendencies of the fashionable learning which they patronized. Thus there came an atmosphere of free thought, strangely at variance with the rigid dogmatism of the theologians, and even in theology there was a certain latitude of discussion permissible, for the Tridentine decrees had not yet formulated into articles of faith the results of the debates of the Schoolmen since the twelfth century. It is a remarkable proof of the prevailing laxity that Nicholas V commissioned Gianozzo Manetti to make a new translation of the Bible from the original Hebrew and Greek, thus showing that the Vulgate was regarded as insufficient and that it enjoyed no such authority as that attributed to it at Trent. . . .

The dissemination of the Scriptures and the propagation of the antisacerdotal views of the humanists naturally led to questioning the conclusions of scholastic theology and to increased impatience of the papal autocracy, these being regarded as the source of the evils so generally and so grievously felt. The new teachings found a wide and receptive audience, fully prepared to carry them to their ultimate conclusions, in the numberless associations, partly literary and artistic, partly religious, which existed throughout the Teutonic lands. In the Netherlands there were everywhere to be found "Chambers of Rhetoric," exercising a powerful influence on public opinion, and these had long been hostile to the clergy whose vices were a favorite subject of their ballads and rondels, their moralities and farces. Less popular, but still dangerously influential, were the so-called Academies which sprang up all over Germany with the revival of learning, and which cherished tendencies adverse to the dogmas of the church and to her practical use of those dogmas. In 1520, Alexander includes among the worst enemies of the papacy the grumbling race of grammarians and poets which swarmed everywhere throughout the land. There were also numerous more or less secret societies and associations, entertaining various opinions, but all heretical to a greater or less degree. These were partly the representatives of mysticism which, since the days of Master Eckart and Tauler, had never ceased to flourish in Germany; partly they were the survivors of Waldensianism, so pitilessly persecuted yet never suppressed. Zwingli, Oecolampadius, Bucer, and other leaders of the reform had received their early impressions in these associations, and the sudden outburst of Anabaptism shows how numerous were the dissidents from Rome who were not prepared to accept the limitations of the Lutheran creed. The Anabaptists, moreover, were but a portion of these Evangelicals, as they styled themselves; for adult baptism was not a feature of their original tenets, and when it was adopted as a doctrine it led to a division in their ranks. The influence of art as well as of literature in stimulating opposition to Rome is seen in the number of artists belonging to the Evangelical bodies. . . .

The combination of all these factors rendered an explosion inevitable, and Germany was predestined to be its scene. The ground was better prepared for it there than elsewhere, by the deeper moral and religious earnestness of the people and by the tendencies of the academies and associations with which society was honeycombed. In obedience to these influences the humanistic movement had not been pagan and aesthetic as in Italy, but had addressed itself to the higher emotions and had sought to train the conscience of the individual to recognize his direct responsibility to God and to his fellows. But more potent than all this were the forces arising from the political system of Germany and its relations with the Holy See. The Teutonic spirit of independence had early found expression in the *Sachsenspiegel* and *Sächsisches Weichbild*—the laws and customs of northern Germany—which were resolutely maintained in spite of repeated papal condemnation. Thus not only did the church inspire there less awe than elsewhere in Europe, but throughout the Middle Ages there had been special causes of antagonism actively at work.

If Italy had suffered bitterly from the *Tedeschi,* Germany had no less reason to hate the papacy. The fatal curse of the so-called Holy Roman Empire hung over both lands. It gave the emperor a valid right to the suzerainty of the peninsula; it gave the papacy a traditional claim to confirm at its discretion the election of an emperor. Conflicting and incompatible pretensions rendered impossible a permanent truce between the representatives of Charlemagne and St. Peter. Since the age of Gregory VII the consistent policy of Rome had been to cripple the empire by fomenting internal dissension and rendering impossible the evolution of a strong and centralized government, such as elsewhere in Europe was gradually overcoming the centrifugal forces of feudalism. This policy had been successful and Germany had become a mere geographical expression—a congeries of sovereign princes, petty and great, owning allegiance to an emperor whose dignity was scarce more than a primacy of honor and whose actual power was to be measured by that of his ancestral territories. The result of this was that Germany lay exposed defenseless to the rapacity and oppression of the Roman curia. Its multitudinous sovereigns had vindicated their independence at the cost of depriving themselves of the strength to be derived from centralized union. Germany was the ordinary resource of a pope in financial straits, through the exaction of a tithe, the raising of the annates, or the issue in unstinted volume of the treasure of the merits of Christ in the form of an unremitting stream of indulgences which sucked up as with a sponge the savings of the people. Nor could any steady opposition be offered to the absorption of the ecclesiastical patronage by the curia, through which benefices were sold or bestowed on the cardinals or their creatures, and no limits could be set on appeals to the Holy See which enlarged its jurisdiction and impoverished pleaders by involving them in interminable and ruinous litigation in the venal Roman courts.

It was in vain that in 1438 the Roman King Albert II endeavored to emulate Charles VII of France by proclaiming a Pragmatic Sanction defining the limits of papal authority. He died the next year and was followed by the feeble Frederick III, during whose long reign of fifty-three years the imperial authority was reduced to a shadow. It was probably to procure a promise of papal coronation that, in 1448, he agreed to a concordat under which the reservation of benefices to the pope, as made by John XXII and Benedict XII, was assured; the election of bishops was subjected to papal confirmation with the privilege of substituting a better candidate by advice of the Sacred College; canonries and other benefices falling vacant during the six uneven months were conceded to the pope and a promise was made that the annates should be moderate and be payable in installments during two years. This was a triumph of Italian diplomacy, for the leaven of Basel was still working in Germany, and the Basilian anti-pope, Felix V, was endeavoring to secure recognition. But Aeneas Sylvius notified Nicholas V that this was only a truce, not a permanent peace, and that the utmost skill would be required to avert a rupture, for there were dangerous times ahead and currents under the surface would call for careful piloting.

Advantageous as the Concordat was to Rome, the curia could not be restrained to its observance and, in 1455, the three Spiritual Electors of Mainz, Trier, and Cologne united in complaint of its violation. With other bishops and princes of the empire they bound themselves to resist a tithe demanded by Calixtus III and to send his pardoners back across the Alps with empty purses; they agitated for the enforcement of the canons of Constance and Basel and urged Frederick III to proclaim a Pragmatic Sanction. Various assemblies were held during the next two years to promote these objects and, in 1457, Dr. Martin Meyer, chancellor of the Archbishop of Mainz, in a letter to Aeneas Sylvius, bitterly complained of the papal exactions, whereby Germany was drained of its gold and that nation which, by its valor, had won the Roman Empire and had been the mistress of the world was reduced to want and servitude, to grief and squalor. Calixtus met the German complaints with a serene consciousness of the weakness of his adversaries. To the prelates he wrote threatening them with punishment, spiritual and temporal. To Frederick he admitted that mistakes might have been made in the pressure of business but there had been no intentional violation of the Concordat. It was true that the Holy See was supreme and was not to be fettered by the terms of any agreement; but still, out of liberality and love of peace and affection for the person of the emperor, the compact should be observed. No one must dare to oppose the Roman Church; if Germany thought it had reason to complain it could appeal to him. The result corresponded to the expectations of Calixtus; the confederates suspected their leader, Archbishop Dietrich of Mainz, of desiring to sell them; and after some further agitation in 1458 the movement fell to pieces.

It was promptly followed by another of even more dangerous aspect. Dietrich of Mainz died May 6, 1459, and was succeeded by Diether von Isenburg. Pius II, then Aeneas Sylvius, had negotiated the Concordat of 1448 which stipulated that annates should be moderate and be payable by installments, yet he refused to confirm Diether except on condition that he would satisfy the demands of the camera for his annates. Diether's envoys agreed, and the cost of the confirmation was fixed at 20,550 *gulden,* to be advanced on the spot by Roman bankers. These accordingly paid the shares of the pope, the cardinals, and the lower officials, taking from them receipts which bore that they would refund the money in case Diether failed to meet the obligations given by his agents. He claimed that the amount was largely in excess of all precedent, repudiated the agreement, and disregarded the consequent excommunication. The result of this scandalous transaction was a series of disturbances which kept Germany in turmoil for three years. Leagues were formed to replace Frederick III by George Podiebrad, and to adopt as the laws of the land the Basilian canons, one of which abrogated the annates. Gregor Heimburg was sent to France to arrange for common action against the Holy See, and there seemed to be a prospect that Germany at last might assert its independence of the curia. But the papal agents with profuse promises detached one member of the alliance after another, and finally Diether was left alone. He offered submission, but Pius secretly sent Adolf of Nassau, one of the canons of Mainz, a brief appointing him Archbishop and removing Diether. This led to a bloody war between the rivals until, in October 1463, they reached a compromise, Adolf retaining the title and conceding to Diether a portion of the territory. Thus the papacy triumphed through its habitual policy of dividing and conquering. There could be no successful resistance to oppression by alliances in which every member felt that he might at any moment be abandoned by his allies. Yet this fruitless contest has special interest in the fact that Diether issued, May 30, 1462, a manifesto calling upon all German princes to take to heart the example of injustice and oppression of which they might be the next victims, and this manifesto, we are told, was printed by Gutenberg—an omen of the aid which the new art was to render in the struggle with Rome.

Even more bitter was the conflict, lasting from 1457 to 1464, between Sigismund, Duke of Tyrol, and Cardinal Nicholas of Cusa, as Bishop of Brixen, arising from his praiseworthy attempt to reform his clergy. In this struggle Sigismund had the support of both clergy and people and was able to disregard the interdicts freely launched upon the land, as well as to resist the Swiss whom Pius II induced to take up arms against him. He held out bravely, and the matter was finally settled by an agreement in which he asked for pardon and absolution, thus saving the honor of the Holy See.

If this was a drawn battle between the secular power and the church, it did not lessen the effect of the triumphs which the curia had won in the contests with the great Archbishops of Mainz. Unsuccessful resistance leads to fresh aggression and it is not to be supposed that Rome failed to make the most of her victories over the

German church. At the great assembly of the clergy at Coblenz, in 1479, there were countless complaints of the Holy See, chiefly directed against its violations of the Concordat, its unlawful taxation, the privileges granted to the Mendicant Orders, and the numerous exemptions. It was doubtless this demonstration that led, in 1480, to the negotiation of an agreement between Sixtus IV and the Emperor Frederick, in which the latter was pledged to keep Germany obedient to the pope, while the pope was to sustain the emperor with the free use of censures. This meant encouragement to fresh aggressions; and the indignation of the clergy found expression in the grievances presented, in 1510, to the emperor-elect Maximilian. They asserted with scant ceremony that the papacy could be restrained by no agreements or conventions, seeing that it granted, for the benefit of the vilest persons, dispensations, suspensions, revocations, and other devices for nullifying its promises and evading its wholesome regulations; the elections of prelates were set aside; the right of choosing provosts, which many chapters had purchased with heavy payments, was disregarded; the greater benefices and dignities were bestowed on the cardinals and prothonotaries of the curia; expectatives were granted without number, giving rise to ruinous litigation; annates were exacted promptly and mercilessly and sometimes more was extorted than was due; the cure of souls was committed by Rome to those fitted rather to take charge of mules than of men; in order to raise money, new indulgences were issued, with suspension of the old, the laity being thus made to murmur against the clergy; tithes were exacted under the pretext of war against the Turks, yet no expeditions were sent forth; and cases which should be tried at home were carried without distinction to Rome. Maximilian was seriously considering a plan for releasing Germany from the yoke of the curia, and for preventing the transfer to Rome of the large sums which Julius II was employing to his special detriment; he thought of the withdrawal of the annates and of the appointment of a permanent legate, who should be a German and exercise a general jurisdiction. But Jacob Wimpheling, who was consulted by the emperor-elect, while expressing himself vigorously as to the suffering of Germany from the curia, thought it wiser to endure in the hope of amendment than to risk a schism. Amendment, however, in obedience to any internal impulse, was out of the question. The Lateran Council met, deliberated, and dissolved without offering to the most sanguine the slightest rational expectation of relief. The only resource lay in revolution, and Germany was ready for the signal. In 1521 the nuncio Aleander writes that, five years before he had mentioned to Pope Leo his dread of a German uprising, he had heard from many Germans that they were only waiting for some fool to open his mouth against Rome.

If Germany was thus the predestined scene of the outbreak, it was also the land in which the chances of success were the greatest. The very political condition which baffled all attempts at self-protection likewise barred the way to the suppression of the movement. A single prince, like the elector Frederick of Saxony, could protect it in its infancy. As the revolt made progress other princes could join it, whether moved by religious considerations, or by way of maintaining the allegiance of their subjects, or in order to seize the temporalities and pious foundations, or, like Albrecht of Brandenburg, to found a principality and a dynasty. We need not here inquire too closely into the motives of which the League of Schmalkalden was the outcome, and may content ourselves with pointing to the fact that even Charles V was, in spite of the victory of Mühlberg, powerless to restore the imperial supremacy or to impose his will on the Protestant states.

The progress of the Reformation, and still more so that of the counterreformation, lie outside the limits of the present chapter; but it may be concluded by a few words suggesting why the abuses which, in the sixteenth century, could only be cured by rending the church in twain, have to so large an extent disappeared since the Reformation, leading many enthusiasts to feel regret that the venerable ecclesiastical structure was not purified from within—that reform was not adopted in place of schism.

The abuses under which Christendom groaned were too inveterate, too firmly entrenched, and too profitable to be removed by any but the sternest and sharpest remedies. The task was too great even for papal omnipotence. The attempt of Adrian VI had broken down. In 1555, the future cardinal Seripando, in announcing to the Bishop of Fiesole the death of Marcellus II, who, in his short pontificate of twenty-two days, had manifested a resolute determination to correct abuses, says that perhaps God, in thus bringing reform so near and

FIGURE 5. *Portrait of Emperor Charles V,* by Anthony Van Dyck, engraved in Rome by H. Guttenberg. Reproduced from the Dr. Leon Kolb collection, Division of Special Collections, Stanford University Libraries. Used by permission.

then destroying all hope of it, has wished to show that it is not to be the work of human hands and is not to come in the way expected by us, but in some way that we have not been able to conjecture. In truth the slow operation was required of causes for the most part external. So long as the Roman Church held the monopoly of salvation it inevitably followed the practice of all monopolies in exacting all that the market would yield—in obtaining the maximum of power and wealth. When northern Europe had definitely seceded, and a large proportion of the rest of the continent was trembling in the balance,—when what was lost could not be regained and a strenuous effort was required to save the remainder,—the church at length recognized that she stood face to face with a permanent competitor, whose rivalry could only be met by her casting off the burdens that impeded her in the struggle. To this the Council of Trent contributed something, and the stern purpose of Pius V, followed at intervals by other pontiffs, still more. The permanent supremacy of Spain in Italy checked the aspirations of the Holy See towards enlarging its temporal dominions. The chief source of cause of advance, however, is the action of the secular princes who sustained the cause of the church during a century of religious wars. The Reformation had emancipated their power as well as the spirit of Protestantism. If the church required their support she must yield to their exigencies; she could no longer claim to decide peremptorily and without appeal as to the boundary line between the spiritual and the temporal authority in the dominions of each of them; and she could no longer shield her criminals from their justice. Together with the progress of the Reformation, a phase of absolute monarchy had developed itself through which the European nations passed, and the enforcement of the *regalia* put an end to a large part of the grievances which had caused the church of the fifteenth century to be so fiercely hated. Whether or not the populations were benefited by the change of masters, the church was no longer responsible; and for the loss of her temporal authority and the final secularization of her temporalities she has found recompense tenfold in the renewed vigor of her spiritual vitality.

Joseph Lortz
WHY DID THE REFORMATION HAPPEN?

Joseph Lortz, ecumenical Catholic church historian, was born in Luxemburg in 1887. Formerly at the University of Münster, he is now director of the division for religious history at the Institute for European History in Mainz, Germany. He is best known for his history of the church, currently in its twenty-third edition, and for his two-volume history of the Reformation in Germany.

The historical way of thinking, if it wishes to some extent to press to the roots, does not simply take cognizance of what and how things were. Rather, it pursues the process of becoming and describes that which has come to be. History is rewarding only if the human past is understood reflectively.

If one wishes to maintain this position, one does well to take the approach to the events to be described from as far back as possible. For the term "historical cause" means much more than immediate causation. The problematics of the "historical cause" is much more complicated than can be developed in this present context. But in order to rule out a possible misunderstanding at least the following must be added: nothing has only one simple meaning except pure quantity taken in its most external function of enumeration. Nothing real is one-sided. The historical cause, too, is in its essence multivalent. We shall see, for example, that late medieval piety belongs to the causal sequence of inner Catholic reform as well as of the Reformation. It is, however, frequently (or always?) not possible to determine where the limit of an historical effect lies, which classes of mankind, which times, and so forth, were *not* affected. That is to say, it is impossible to grasp the total effective range of a historical factor and to circumscribe it precisely. If, therefore, one speaks of historical cause, one means with this that only *one* line of actions is thrown into relief. In setting up our causal sequences we do not intend an exhaustive presentation of the periods of history treated. This could be done only through *many kinds* of causal sequences.

The immediate cause of the Reformation was Martin Luther. But

Translated by Lewis W. Spitz from Joseph Lortz, *Wie kam es zur Reformation?*, 3rd ed. (Einsiedeln, 1955). Used by permission of the Johannes Verlag, Einsiedeln.

prior to this narrower ring of immediate causes comes the broad area of preparatory factors, the preconditions which first give rise to the possibility of an epochal event. That is true also of revolutions and even of the highly gifted creative personalities. We can study it also in the case of Martin Luther. The individual theological elements which he acquired from his study do not at first glance prove much regarding the vivid occurrence of the reformatory changes which turned the Catholic monk into a reformer. The breakthrough arises apparently directly out of irrational depths. Ultimate impulses of the human vis-à-vis the Deity are in play, neither explainable nor essentially bound to the contemporary historical particulars of theological thought. The event remains a secret, mysterious generation, mysterious birth. And yet the origin of this very event is demonstrably bound to these very theological elements of the time; so much and so deeply that it could not have come at all without them. Luther outside of the monastery, outside of theology, Luther filled with the theology of St. Thomas or of the Roman missal instead of with theology of an Ockhamist stamp—his reformatory turn could never have taken place. That inner friction which led to inflammation and then to rending crisis would have remained completely inexplicable. Not even Luther's inner oppression by anxiety over sin and judgment could have experienced that precipitous sharpening which alone provides the lever for his new perceptions. And if it had, it would never have awakened from the dullness of personal anguish to a structured form and to an historical effective power.

If one takes the concept of "historical cause" in this sense (as preparatory and immediately occasioning), then there appears that colorful episodical fullness of history, that apparently arbitrary emergence and disappearance in historical development elevated to a certain historical necessity, an *historical,* not an absolute necessity, which exists in human history only in the indiscussible purely materialistic conception of history. Historical existence is never in itself a justification in the absolute sense. Not even the most secular figures and formations contain through their mere historical existence an absolute right in themselves. To put it another way, there exists not merely an historical fullness of meaning, which is bound to truth and right, but there is also the kind which is tied to error and guilt. Even the most numerous accumulation of historical causes merely furnishes the proof that the *coming* of a particular event had become necessary and unavoidable, but the inner absolute justification of this event is not thereby pronounced. If we, therefore, see the causes of the Reformation mounting up so that at last a powerful revolt against the old church can no longer be avoided, then with that not a word has as yet been said about the right or wrong of the new teachings announced by the Reformation.

The question of why the *Reformation* came about can now be posed more precisely: How did there arise in the Western family of peoples, which was conscious of being bound to the Roman church as the norm established by God, a lag of powers (above all of the psychical-spiritual powers), a way of thinking that made it possible at all for a large part of this community of peoples to set itself against the church? What had happened that Western peoples, which knew Christendom only as church under the pope came to the notion that there could be a Christendom outside of this church and without the pope?

A preliminary general answer goes: the Reformation arose out of the dissolution of the basic medieval principles. That appears to be banal. Correctly developed however, this sentence shows the whole enormous abundance of elements which one can appeal to as causes of the Reformation. The complete presentation of the "medieval" embraces, to be sure, only a short span of time. That is, as soon as the medieval in the classical sense, the actual high Middle Ages, has lifted itself out of the laborious fermentation process of the fifth to the tenth centuries and out of the process of evolution of the eleventh century, a comprehensive process of shifting begins and spreads which, with respect to its church-history side, reveals itself as a *movement of withdrawal from the church.*

To describe and analyze this movement of withdrawal is to present the causes of the Reformation in a comprehensive manner. It takes its course in very different forms, which in part are as different as faithful followers and opponents on principle can be. The most important thing about it is this: it has to do with a displacement of powers which takes place in the *heart of the church.* Long before the Reformation, things "reformatory" existed in Western Christendom and in the Roman church.

In order to avoid all misunderstandings, we want in this case to place "reformatory" in quotation marks. What is meant has little to do with the word formerly so often misused, "pre-reformers," at that time, e.g., when one referred to Francis and Savonarola as types of evangelical piety. But long before the Reformation events began within the Western ecclesiastical area, measures were encountered and ideas advanced which made the coming of a widespread revolt against the papal church easier, rendered it possible, provoked, and then even immediately gave rise to it. They brought a large part of Christendom little by little to the point where an existence free of the pope seemed to them no longer impossible, no longer unchristian, so that the new teachings, consequently, when they were pronounced in the sixteenth century, no longer seemed to them simply strange and unheard of, but they were able to listen to them with assent, often as something expected. And when finally the reformers expounded their theses or demands, much in them harmonized with what was already somehow familiar to the external and inner senses of the West.

Without the centuries-long preparation through the *pre-reformation* the Reformation could not have come. And without giving it a very extensive place in the analysis, it is impossible to make the origin of the Reformation intelligible.

Out of the multiplicity of events we shall select three great complexes and with them confirm in order the theses laid down.

1. First of all, the *medieval unity.* The Reformation is the breaking-up of the Western Christian-ecclesiastical unity. For a long time before, however, this unity was already greatly weakened, its destruction decisively prepared for.

Medieval unity was, to be sure, often exaggerated. The Middle Ages in the full sense of the word lasted perhaps a century and a half to two centuries. Not only is the development up to the eleventh century a very laborious and rather sporadic ascent, but in the thirteenth already such a mass of strong countercurrents set in, so many tears reveal themselves, that from then on the full unity of the Middle Ages is already gone. But the Western Christian-ecclesiastical unity was nevertheless present in everything which we call Middle Ages and indeed as authoritative character and power and, in spite of what has been said, as strong as ever before or since. For above all it was essentially present in the unity of one faith under the one church government. And this unity of the church government was in turn represented in the unity between state and church, between *sacerdotium* and *imperium.* And if this latter was exceptionally full of tensions, it was nevertheless by no means a creature of caprice or of chance, but an expression of the *essence.* . . .

What the destruction of unity in the thirteenth century and in Avignon meant at the deepest level, however, first became evident with the decisive fruit of Avignon: the *schism in the West.* One knows that the Western schism was that period in which there were two popes, each with its curia, the one residing in Rome, the other in Avignon. This duality of popes, which indeed increased to an "accursed threesome" of popedom, was ended above all through the effort of the German Emperor Sigismund at the reform Council of Constance (1414). That figures. But the actual importance is thereby not yet estimated at all.

For the development of the church the Western schism means an unheard of, and almost universal uncertainty, lasting for decades, about deciding where the legitimate pope and therefore where the legitimate church was to be found. The fact is that for long decades a situation existed in which two popes put each other and their followers under the ban, so that actually the whole of Christendom found itself under a ban; that both popes referred to each other as antichrist and probably also their mass as idolatry. And this situation of a monstrous, inconceivable scandal, despite its inner impossibility, despite all the sharpest protests from all sides, appeared to be simply insurmountable. The restoration of unity failed ever and again. And often over such inferior, egoistic points of resistance!

The split was immeasurably far removed from being merely a theological, academic affair. It extended to the total public and private life, the economic in no way excluded, but decisively involved in many ways (above all through the conflicts over prebends). The split ran through the church provinces, the orders, the universities, even through individual monasteries and parishes. It was a matter of a decades-long deep experience which affected all sectors of life and involved them. . . .

It was an experience of the whole West, an experience that could no longer disappear from the Western consciousness and actually for a century did no longer disappear. The importance for the effect of the Reformation doctrines is clear without further comment. When Luther made the assertion that the Roman pope is not the legitimate successor of Peter and that the church is not coextensive with popedom, these were, to be sure—as they were intended and supported —new words. But decisive elements in them had long since been anticipated. And for many they sounded very familiar to the ear. Long before the Reformation, deeply disintegrating reformatory actions in the church had undermined the Western Christian-ecclesiastical unity.

2. The Reformation is in the second place an expression of a most comprehensive *dissatisfaction* with conditions in the church. At least from 1200 A.D. on the church experienced the cry never again silenced for a "reform in head and members," the cry "back to the apostolic church!" We hear this cry from all classes. It is not as though only a few circles of disaffected Christians had expressed their dissatisfaction. Rather what is ever and again the moving and decisive thing is that the demand for reform, the expressions of criticism from the church itself become loud, from true and most faithful servants of the papacy, even from such as were attached to curialism and hyper-curialism. And we hear these demands from them often in a radicality which surprises us. . . .

The complaints made against the curia at the beginning of the fourteenth century continued to increase. By the end of the fifteenth century the world is filled with impatient or furious, sadly revolutionary, defiant *outcries against the rule* of Rome and the clergy, against their suppression and exploitation, against their arbitrary action. And against their all too sensualist existence.

One must naturally ask the question whether these complaints were actually justified or whether an unrestrained aggressiveness did not rather exaggerate very, very many things in an inadmissible way. Nevertheless, no matter how much one may reduce the justification of the charges in many points, unfortunately too much that is offensive and less than Christian remains. And as far as the historical effect goes, moreover, one must confirm that, whether justified or not, the revolt is there. The dissatisfaction expressed itself everywhere, in literature, in the pulpit, in pamphlets and songs, in the diets. Where these demands or also aspersions should or must find a limit, that was completely unclear to many. It appeared rather that one could not be too radical at all and would still always be assured of much approval on all sides. Again, it is evident to what extent also here minds were prepared for a fundamental uprising against Rome, against the estate of the priests. When Luther came, he appeared to thousands and tens of thousands only as the final redemption of the old demands for reform which were long due and long generally recognized as justified.

3. Finally, the most important thing. The Reformation is above all the disavowal of Catholic dogmas. Also in this respect there was in the church reformatory movement before the Reformation. At first that appears to be a paradox. One supposes that *within* the Catholic church it could not have come to such a dissolution. The teachings advocated were certainly *eo ipso* no longer Catholic. We shall soon see that matters lay much deeper.

I believe that one must make the proof of a decisive thesis not easy, but as difficult as possible, so that it then really stands firm. We shall try to follow this method. We shall, therefore, disregard the actual heretical or heresy-like movements of the Middle Ages (thus e.g., the advance of the Arabic pantheistic wisdom, of the Waldensians and Cathari, of Wycliffism and Hussitism). We shall select for our examination only the area indubitably *within* the church and for this we shall set up the thesis: in the ecclesiastical realm itself there was from the fourteenth century on an increasing *theological uncertainty*.

This thesis, too, naturally requires a host of qualifications, which can only be presented in a history of late medieval theology (which is still lacking), but not here. I merely point out that the thesis just formulated is valid in different measures for the lands of Western Christendom. For Italy and Spain which still had a lively theological tradition—be it from Thomas or from Augustine—it is not nearly so applicable as for central Europe and England. Up until now this has been seen all too little. And yet it describes *the* cause which first made the Reformation possible. The foundation of the Reformation from which it rose up and a large part of the Reformation movement itself was formed not merely of religious, but of decisive theological factors. . . .

First of all mention must be made of an increasing freedom and arbitrariness of constructing and disputing within theology at that time, an arbitrariness which not infrequently seemed to lead to a certain aimlessness and which was often connected with a regrettable slipping off into peripheral questions. . . .

But what has been said reveals itself comprehensively in the development of theology to the Ockhamism of the fourteenth and fifteenth centuries, that is, the theology of the English Franciscan William Ockham and his school (both still insufficiently studied). I, therefore, expressly include in this development, which—together with important intellectual achievement—was a disintegration of theology, also the Ockhamism of the fifteenth century correctly inclined toward the church, which indeed was very far from being a unified quantity. For it included in its content as in its way of thinking propositions which, if consistently followed out, had to lead away from church doctrine. . . .

Measured against this basis [the Roman missal], Ockhamism is no longer fully Catholic. The missal knows nothing of an arbitrary God. It knows nothing of a one-sided threatening, cruel judge, nothing of an unbearable God dealing on the basis of *punitive* righteousness, but also nothing of a man capable of satisfying God on the basis of his own powers. Rather, it reveals to us a man who is a child of God *and* a sinner who seeks the Father through the Son and his grace, not in his own merits, but in loving awe before God, and is accepted by God.

Ockhamism teaches an arbitrary God instead of the Father-God; a God who without an objective criterion destines the one for heaven, the other for hell, who only by chance has named the one good and the other bad, who likewise could have commanded what today is forbidden as evil or could have forbidden what today is praised as good.

Ockhamism (for example, Pierre d'Ailly, Gabriel Biel, Gregory of Rimini) acknowledges a strong, yes, immeasurable upgrading of the powers of man within the process of salvation, and this precisely against that arbitrary God. The theological consequence had to be the minimizing of grace; and thereby one would end up with a downright false interpretation of Christianity.

Ockhamism, which rejected the authority of Aristotle, is finally characterized by the tearing apart of nature and the supernatural, almost to the point of the proposition of the double truth. That is, it acknowledges the conception that something can be true theologically (because it is in revelation) and at the same time can be refuted philosophically or can be demonstrated to be impossible.

To be sure, this direction was condemned in the fourteenth century in Avignon. But the little that we know about it does not leave the impression that at the time the danger was recognized even with approximate clarity. The decisive proceeding against Ockham undoubtedly concerned much more the church politician who sided with Emperor Ludwig the Bavarian than the theologian. In any case, the awareness of a danger did not get through to a wide theological circle. On the contrary, the nominalistic way of thought basic to Ockhamism became in the fifteenth century a great power within scholastic theology and, where it prevailed, its fate. This way of thinking from the superficial nominalistic was not adequate for supernatural realities. Its individualizing and atomizing thinking, which tore apart the elements of tension and made them too sharply one-sided, is in addition not capable of conceiving of the sacramental organism "Church" and its sacramental life and rendering them theologically understandable. "Church" is only the sum of individual believers; these constitute the Church; they are not born out of the Church, which is more than the sum of its members. Faith might even, as Clémanges said, disappear so completely that it would exist finally only in a little old lady. The theological consequences of this in the direction of a radical ecclesiastical democracy and of the destruction of the correctly understood intermediary role of the priest are completely incalculable—*if* they are followed through consistently.

These consequences became evident in Luther in many ways, as well in the development of the young Luther (namely as a starting point which was explosive and which made the spiritual tensions unbearable) as in the way of viewing things which Luther retained permanently (as in his battle with reason in his theory of imputation); and they became evident again in his attack upon old church theologians in the question of the Sacrament of the Altar and the sacrifice of the mass. His conflict with Eck reveals the tragedy of the situation: both are thinking in nominalistic terms. Luther proceeds from this way of thinking with due consistency to the denial of Catholic dogmas. Eck, proceeding from the same nominalistic thought, is unable to illuminate theologically even in a measure satisfactorily the Catholic theses to which he firmly holds. His gigantic accumulation of proofs for Catholic teaching on the sacrifice of the mass remains unfruitful. One may ask reflectively whether precisely this theologically inadequate manner of Eck's did not necessarily strengthen in Luther the conviction that he possessed the religious riches of revelation in a greater fullness than his theological opponent from the Roman papal church.

The lack of theological clarity in the late Middle Ages reveals itself especially strongly in the obscuring of the idea of the *papal primacy.* Think back to what was said about the Western schism and recall in addition the discussions or rather battles about the conciliar idea which penetrated with unusual energy deeply into the spiritual and theological universal consciousness of the period. . . .

Let us now summarize: at the end of the Middle Ages a dangerous lack of theological clarity existed. It was of such a kind that it was relatively easy for a theologically independent person to become a heretic. . . .

Now it would be fitting to fill in with particulars the scope surveyed so far. We would have to pursue the movement sketched in general in the area of the political, of the church political, of the social, and of the economic. We would have to familiarize ourselves especially with the crystallization of the powers in the territorial church. But we wish to limit ourselves and bring into consideration only the *spiritual-religious* life and that in the fifteenth century. We therefore approach more closely the forces which immediately caused the Reformation. . . .

The fifteenth century is distinguished spiritually in Germany as a *time of contradictions* and thereby as a time of dissolution as well as of seeking for renewal. To be sure, nearly all history is full of overlappings; much always comes to an end, while at the same time other things build up, originating far away. But there are, nevertheless, times which are more self-contained and appear to rest more in their peculiarity. And there are other times in which the inherited possession has become essentially uncertain, for which it is less satisfactory, which are much more fundamentally on the search for new shores. To these the fifteenth century belongs. . . .

The strongest proof for the contradictions asserted as well as for the excited nature of the time and for its seeking for a fundamental new foundation is *humanism*.

What is humanism? It is almost impossible to describe it adequately in a few sentences. Let us at least attempt a hint!

Humanism is first of all a complete change, a fundamental change, and an enthusiasm. It is expectation and desire. It fears with its age the coming end of the world. Above all, however, it awaits, wishes, and greets and wants to be the making of a new man. Disgusted with the past, it feels itself to be proudly superior to it and turns with a self-conscious feeling to the new.

Humanism says that man stands in the center, that is, in contrast to the medieval world which thought from God on out. It is well known that this awakening of the individual began already in the high Middle Ages. . . .

But those were only isolated beginnings. Now, in humanism, they already characterize the time so much that one can denote them as an essential part of the total picture. Even now the Middle Ages are not at an end. Naturally there was at first also much that was medieval in humanism. And therefore it is also self-evident that one does not find pure individualistic subjectivism in it. For the full and pure presentation of the new never exists in the incubation period. But the direction decides for the future. The direction of humanism points not to God but to the world, to man. And this was not in the sense of the medieval balance, as in Thomas Aquinas, but already in the sense of modern one-sidedness which disturbs and finally destroys that equilibrium. The fact that in the baroque, significant counterforces set in, holds up the dominant consequences for a time. The seed still ripens. The Enlightenment will come. That the victory of the new affirmation of the world comes here was decisively prepared for in humanism. It would not alone, to be sure, have led to this result. But the intellectual loosening which we call humanism participates also in the formation of the other powers which thereby became effective.

That is true not least of all of the Reformation. In an especially direct way humanism is the cause of the Reformation. Can one really say that the Reformation destroyed humanism too early, in its youth? It appears rather that had the tumult and the revolution of ecclesiastical revolt not revealed the danger (I am not now speaking of the positive religious content of the Reformation), there are clear indications present that after 1524 an Erasmus would not have held back. He would have criticized destructively and mocked further.

In humanism, therefore, man moves into the center of things. We stand before the decisive historical *tendency* to the subjective anthropocentric. Man is still not simply the measure of things, but he begins to become that. In the center of the discussions is the concept of *virtù*. An unflaggingly variated theme reads: "On the dignity of man." But *this "dignitas hominis"* is intended entirely differently than that which we praise in the mass in the preparation of the chalice. Humanism means that man to whom the Father in heaven gave the powers to create a new man out of himself. . . .

Humanism once more, then, as a pagan movement? Certainly not. It is not the secret knowledge of a few people that built up humanism with Christian people. At its roots, in spite of everything, are the Christian conceptions of new birth, of a new becoming, of the bath of regeneration and of the new creation through the descending Holy Spirit. There was even an honest north German early humanism which restricted itself almost entirely to pedagogical renewals and which one can confidently still ascribe to the Middle Ages. And I know as well as others do that also in later and in the very last years a large number of humanist personalities took their formal principle from Christianity.

No, humanism was not pagan, also not there where individual humanists and even whole groups speak and live in a pagan manner. But it is deeply marked by a pronounced spiritual, moral, and—if the expression is allowed—religious secularization. One can not answer the proposed question, if one is satisfied to point out that at that time there was *still* something Christian or much Christian in humanism. For one can never thoroughly characterize a spiritual power, a movement, an idea, merely by estimating the finding arrived at here and now statistically. The direction decides the tendency toward which the force to be described is gravitating, the tendency which holds it in motion and prevails. One must ask: what would have come of it, if the novel implicit in it had developed completely from within itself? If we pose the question in this way to humanism, then for us Catholics there is an answer as unequivocal as distressing. It reads: Renaissance popes and their culture. Is there anybody who sees in this a Christianizing of the world and not much more a dangerous secularization of the sacred?

Christian ideal solutions such as St. Thomas More or the humanism of the *devotio moderna* pose a special problem, but do not prove the least against these conclusions.

By its very nature, humanism was also an attack, that is, against the immediate past.

To be sure, humanism is not *only* a break with the Middle Ages. Like the Renaissance—one thinks of north Italy—humanism, too, is deeply rooted in the Middle Ages. One need merely mention Dante, Petrarch, and early German humanism, to become conscious of this. Nevertheless, above all else it is revolt and a conscious turning away from the immediate preceding times and criticism of them.

Humanism lives in large part on its manifold criticism of the ecclesiastical, especially of monasticism and of scholasticism. In both it finds missing the living spirituality, the culture of learning and inner mobility, which it believes it possesses and it actually did achieve in many a thing. Scholasticism itself was responsible for this criticism in many respects. In it a proceeding took place similar to that which we established earlier in the case of curialism: the confusion of the temporally bound form with the absolute content. The scholastics had after all sometimes operated as though their theology were synonymous with the Christian faith. Therefore, the attack of humanism unfortunately hit not only the form, but also the content.

One can counter this with: this whole criticism is not to be taken so tragically. Humanism is known to have been an aristocratic movement. Only a very thin upper stratum was affected by it. First of all, this judgment is only partially valid. Strong movements are not at all effective only there where they are consciously taken up and given expression; they work through a thousand channels. Also humanism was effective in this way religiously and to a degree theologically through the *devotio moderna* then newly arising and affected by humanism. But beyond that a development took place which appeared to make that thin stratum the spokesman for the whole general public and in Germany precisely the most radical circle, Erfurt humanism, succeeded in this. But here the criticism of the ecclesiastical became *radical* and slid over into the area of doctrine. *This* humanism is already extensively detached from the sacramental Roman papal church. It lives in no small part upon a deep hatred against the priestly church. Its criticisms of monasticism turned against the monastic existence as such. Its representatives live practically as heathen.

One must now establish serious tendencies toward a *misinterpretation of Christianity.* For, in the first place, these circles and their works, as said above, stand at a radical distance from the praying and sacrificing of the church. Secondly, the Stoic presuppositions take effect. Also the apologists of the second century had by putting aside the person and work of the Redeemer seen the essence of Christianity in its monotheism. But they had arrived at this "monotheistic selection" on tactical grounds. The Erfurt humanists are different and they can in a measure be pronounced forerunners of the Enlightenment. Christianity is monotheism, to be sure. But the definition is immediately fundamentally false, if one reverses it and if one formulates as has so often happened in recent times: monotheism is Christianity. Then the one decisive and indispensable element is lacking in Christianity: Jesus Christ. Then all of the higher religions become more or less of equal value. The result is an undervaluing of dogma, and relativism threatens.

And further: through its contact with antiquity humanism came to see man above all in his own power and to emphasize his will and its ability. As was true already of that monotheistic interpretation, also this new point of departure did not see Redemption at all, or at least not sufficiently as central. Grace moved to the periphery. From both sides the reinterpretation of Christianity as an ethic threatens. From this point on, humanism became one of the decisive forces disintegrating Christianity into the modern. In all this we come upon an isolation of the demand: "better inner righteousness" of the synoptic gospels, and, indeed, in such a way that this demand is conceived philosophically and stoically and besides that is stripped of its religious, unconditional seriousness.

This radical company of humanists, so small in number, succeeds in being effective in a wide area. In the battle around Reuchlin regarding the protection of Jewish theological learning, immediately before and at the outbreak of the Reformation, there originated the infamous "Letters of Obscure Men." Moving, clever, ironic, often awkward, malicious, but ever and again light of touch and appealing to the reader, far removed from all pedantry, clumsiness and even more from all monotony, these letters, which twisted the truth in such an alarming manner and carried on evil defamation on a large scale, succeeded in bringing to the public the opinion: we are the modern, we alone count; the others are antiquated.

Humanist theology in general is not deep. It cannot, seen as a whole, remotely compare with Scholasticism. Precisely also the Erfurt humanists are not at all able to enter into a serious competition here. But their case shows that as timeless as truth is, as independent as it is in itself from form as far as its effect is concerned, it is still decisively bound to form. Insofar as it is supposed to be nourishment, truth is decisively dependent upon it, whether it is expressed in a lively manner or not. Monotony or clumsiness damages the very profoundness itself. . . .

If that is all true, then we must say of Erasmus that he represented a serious threat for the church.

In Rome at the time the humanist pope Leo X was living, who had a high regard for Erasmus. The danger which threatened from his side was not seen. Thus it was possible that the papal emissary Aleander had to report from the Diet at Worms, 1521, to Rome: "For God's sake, do not send us any more such privileges for Erasmus! That man injures us more than Luther can ever hurt us." It was none other than Luther, then, who expelled the danger threatening from the humanist side. With the enormous force of his one-sidedness he led away from the cultural religiosity of Erasmus back to the faith religion of Paul.

The decisive question reads: with how much religious power or impotence did the church enter into the Reformation storm?

It is difficult to give a really suitable answer. Ever and again one must make additions and qualifications, brighten up dark facts with whatever pleasing thing is available, remain conscious of how enormously difficult it is precisely in the area of piety to win an exact picture of the powers. One must also not forget how different the situation was in the individual cities and provinces. The religious life had by no means fallen so absolutely into decline as one formerly often asserted.

In spite of this one can ask oneself what then decisively charac-

FIGURE 6. *The Dream of Frederick the Wise.* This woodcut of Elector Frederick's dream at Schweinitz in 1517, which Luther also mentioned in *Table Talks,* shows Luther's quill, writing the Ninety-five Theses, growing so long that it knocks the crown from Pope Leo X's head. In the foreground John Hus, the goose, is burning. From Hanns Lilje, *Luther and the Reformation* (Philadelphia: Fortress Press, 1967). Used by permission of the Furche-Verlag H. Rennebach KG (Hamburg).

terized the situation. Was it the religiously sound or was it the *abuses?*

In recent times it has been asserted that the theme of the abuses has been treated all too frequently and too thoroughly. I can in no way agree to this. This has to do with the existence or nonexistence of that which is actually Christian in the church. It all depends merely upon this—that one proceeds from the correct concept of abuse.

When the subject is ecclesiastical abuses, many think readily or even exclusively of the so-called "wicked" popes, of the scandals of Alexander VI and his kind.

Assuredly it is most significant—precisely for the situation among the Catholic clergy—whether that sort of thing has taken place in the house of God or not. Nevertheless, that is not the finally decisive thing. Not the religious-*moral* decomposition, but the correct or false *structural* tendency is decisive.

It is naturally also not a matter of questioning as to some kind of subjective guilt, whether of the popes or bishops or of the lower clergy. We ask rather as to the objective balance of power and impotence. We inquire into the objective cause and after that as to what extent it became historically powerful. And we ask whether a given decadence remains merely an accident and episode or whether it has perhaps somehow grown out of the structure of the institution. And we determine that it unfortunately is not merely a matter of accidental phenomena, but that very important structural elements are at play, perhaps the influence of political power on the ecclesiastical-religious, the predominant interest which the economic (as in the case of prebendaries) had won in the church. We do not overlook that also political interests of the secular powers, egoism and epicureanism of extrachurchly circles are here to be taken into account. But we will not conclude from this that things were less bad, but rather worse. Otherwise one could also represent the interpretation that there were no actually sick people, but only the wicked microbes, which destroy the healthy organisms. The question, however, is precisely whether the church had enough inner strength to kill those microbes which so extensively poisoned its organism.

To what extent did at that time the idea of the church, the idea of the priestly, the idea of monasticism exist in pure form? How much cure of souls existed at that time? How much of the priestly? And further—were the positive forces creatively strong or were they tired? Was life in its center and forceful or was it external, peripheral?

Let one bear in mind here that mere correctness would not suffice, when the problem of the religious power of the church before the Reformation is at stake. Mere correctness, the absence of errors, is no Christian category. Christianity is power and truth, inwardness and fullness. . . .

And now the concrete situation in the individual estates and levels of the church.

In the first place the *secularization* prevailing at the Roman curia must be mentioned. In order to recognize its extent, one must look less at Alexander VI than at Julius II, and better yet, at Leo X. Though he personally can be accused of no gross excesses, we recognize him as the typical representative of a curialism, which with its whole secularization was considered to be legitimate without any restriction. . . .

It would be possible now to go through the individual strata of the ruling and teaching church: the cardinals, the bishops, and the lower clergy, which stood in such an unwholesome separation from the higher clergy and in so many ways had become a spiritual proletariat. In all of these levels the healthy Christian spirit does not prevail, but the inadequacies grow too luxuriantly by far. . . .

The whole difficulty of describing the situation precisely first becomes evident when we turn to *popular piety.* In this superfluity of pious devotions, in this mixture of externalization and inwardness, of solid churchliness and spiritualistic piety, of true faith and crude superstition—what is genuine, what is not genuine? And the second question: What *function* at any given time do the one and the other possess in bringing about the Reformation?

Before us stands a gigantic flowering of churchly phenomena of piety, stand countless imposing new buildings and endowments, which would not have been possible without a mighty reservoir of powers and most significant sacrifice in money and labor. And yet all that does not give the conclusive proof for true Christian power. Also much egoism and boasting, much competition manifest themselves here. Worse is that the sacramental life is so in decline. That in all lands the lack of religious knowledge in the people is frightening, and this in spite of the educational work of the church, in spite of its picture-preaching on the walls of churches or of the picture Bibles. What appears as popular piety characterizes itself to a large extent as moralism or even as crass externalization, which in practice often expresses itself in work-righteousness and superstition. The economic-egotistical conception of their office by the clergy, which the Council of Trent (*sessio* 25) was to pillory for its harmful effect on souls, here found its counterpart.

Once more: all that exists in the midst of a genuine rise of "churchliness" and of the true doctrine. The fifteenth century remains, therefore, a classic time of contradictions. Next to the blossoming "churchliness" there exists as though without a transition a strong dissatisfaction of the people with the clergy. The church had "long since been a deadly hated capitalistic power, which with its interest service held the common man in its claws" (W. P. Fuchs). The threats of the revolting peasants against the interest-taking monks speak clearly enough. . . .

Let us rather see matters once from the other side. Much, incomparably more than the world of the clergy, popular religious piety shows that which is religiously healthy. There are two realms which are available to all for testing and demonstration: devotional literature and Christian art. . . .

What, then, to put the question once again, gives the tone to the popular piety of the time? If formerly one represented work-righteousness, indeed crass externalization, as its distinguishing feature, that was simply a fable. This was not last of all created by Luther himself, whereby he succumbed to his most singular world of ideas and experience, to his drive to stress one aspect and to outbid, and also to the influence of Ockhamist theology. In spite of everything we cannot avoid the conclusion for very many people and for wide areas of existence: one lived as though one could earn salvation in an external sense.

Why is it, though, that also specialists struggle so stubbornly against this description and the conclusions drawn from it? To be sure, an anxious, faint-hearted, overemphatic apologetic stand plays a part. But there are also factual reasons: the finding is in itself remarkably divided. This multivalence of the fact explains its varying evaluation. It explains already the point-blank enormous opposition of the church renewers of the sixteenth century and of the Catholic polemical theologians in the description of the historical situation and in its evaluation. A passion for exaggeration, massive Grobianism played a role; but it is against all probability that the pillorying in well-known things had been *only* lies. And yet also the establishment of the deep duality of meaning is not adequate. Things of that time are not merely ambivalent, they are in the end ready to collapse. What stands has the strange character of a façade.

Wilhelm Neusz is completely right: if we, without having any notion of the Reformation, were suddenly to be placed bodily into the religious churchly conditions of the year 1500, what would we see? A Catholic world with a rich, very rich churchly life, numerous clergy and numerous monasteries. The church and no one else is the unchallenged leader of life in all sectors of public and private life. And this world collapses in an inconceivably sudden catastrophe. Until yesterday the mothers of Nuremberg had brought their daughters to the Clarissa convent so that they would as nuns lead a life of perfection. And "today" the same mothers appear with horse and wagon, crying out and scolding, in order to lead their daughters with force out of a convent full of idolatry. Thousands of monks overnight forget their vows; marry; and with Luther rail at "monkishness" in a way which could not be worse. What happened? Life had long since changed fundamentally, only one did not yet know it. Life was in its outward appearance still Catholic, but it was a deceptive picture.

Revolutions are not made by propaganda. Even the ever so powerful, ever so earnest sounding call of a single great man is not able to bring it about. The totality, a large part of the general public must be basically prepared for it. Revolutions are not freely created, they are set loose.

And precisely the frighteningly extensive and surprisingly quick revolt is best proof that the time had become ripe.

Gerhard Ritter

WHY THE REFORMATION OCCURRED IN GERMANY

Gerhard Ritter, Protestant church historian, was born in 1888. Educated at the universities of Munich, Leipzig, Berlin, and Heidelberg, he served as professor of modern history at Freiburg University. Phenomenally productive, he was best known for his political biography of Stein, his evaluation of Luther and of the world-wide significance of the Reformation, his study of More, Machiavelli, and the corrupting influence of power, and his volume on the new formation of Europe in the sixteenth century. He died in 1967.

At the end of the Middle Ages, the moral prestige of the old papal church was severely shaken in all the countries of Europe. Open criticism of its moral shortcomings and its organizational defects had been going on for centuries. To its diverse splinter movements of heretical sects (which were never wholly suppressed) had been recently added the great reform movements of the Wyclifites and the Hussites. But even they had brought about no lasting and widespread upheaval. Ultimately the old hierarchy had always prevailed. Why then did the Germans, a people slow to be aroused, fond of order, and faithful to the church, take it upon themselves to carry out the most prodigious revolution in the church? And why did only their revolt against the papal church have such vast and enduring consequences?

By way of answer, it is of course not enough to cite the adverse outcome of the council proceedings, particularly in Germany, the "gravamina of the German nation," and the reformatory efforts of the German territorial governing bodies. For these complaints and reform efforts made no headway in the direction in which the Lutheran Reformation was later to move—towards a renewal of church life in its innermost regions, one which would start from a new understanding of the Christian revelation rather than from patchwork improvement of the outward deficiencies of the ecclesiastical system.

Translated from the original "Kirche und geistiges Leben in Deutschland um 1517" (Chap. 8 of the author's *Die Neugestaltung Europas im 16. Jahrhundert,* Berlin, 1950), by G. H. Nadel. Used by permission of the editors of *Church History.* It was published in that journal in the June 1958 issue, volume 27, pp. 99–106.

It is true that this decisively new impetus to reform was entirely the personal deed of an individual of genius, without example or precedent: the deed of Martin Luther. But how did it happen that in Germany it was not immediately branded as heresy and stamped out, but met with a loud response, which did not even abate when it became universally evident that the attack shook the dogmatic foundations of the old priestly church? Could this response perhaps become intelligible in the light of the special nature of German Christian piety?

A person coming at this time across the Alps from Italy would sense immediately the vastly greater intensity of ecclesiastical and religious life among the Germans. The secularization of existence, the fading of the Christian ascetic ideals of the Middle Ages, encountered at the Renaissance courts of the South are not yet felt. All life is still consummated in the shadow of the mighty cathedrals, which dominate the panorama of the German city. With unbroken force the Christian teaching of the world to come still determines all forms of life; its influence, indeed, seems to wax continuously. Pious foundations become alarmingly numerous. Hundreds of clerical benefices, many dozens of altars, accumulate in the great churches; in Cologne, a good third of built-up ground was said to have been church property, and in some other places every tenth inhabitant was said to have belonged to the clergy. The sumptuous furnishings even of small village churches and the daily influx of churchgoers never cease to astound foreign travelers. The ecclesiastical organization of the masses pushes rapidly ahead. All kinds of lay brotherhoods, for the care of the poor and the sick, for the erection of homes, for common devotions, increase in number and magnitude with extraordinary speed. Every mendicant order attracts such associations; but still others spring up like weeds, and their spiritual control and supervision cause the church authorities no little concern. These groups teach their members unselfish service of their neighbors, but at the same time an outward sanctimoniousness which is shrewdly calculated to secure for itself certain salvation in the next world by multiplying prayers and oblations. Church devotions have become popular, the most sacred has become commonplace; very often, religious excitation is combined with a rank mania for sensation and miracle. The system of pilgrimages and relics, with its thousand frauds, the spread of the belief in witches, the alarming frequency of religious epidemics, of eschatological states of excitement in the masses—all these are repellent enough. But who could on their account overlook the numerous testimonies of profound and genuine piety, the deep poetic touches of the cult of Mary with its reflections in poetry and the plastic arts and the moral effects of spreading the church's teachings among the people?

Now what is peculiar is how closely this very vigorous popular piety is combined with severe, even embittered, criticism of the church and of her clergy; this attitude contrasts very noticeably with the blind devotion of the Spanish masses to the church. This criticism, voiced with equal severity among all classes of the German people, is itself a testimony, not perhaps of diminishing, but rather of live and increasing interest in religion and the church. There is, indeed, nothing which excites public opinion more than the church and its preaching. Among the masses, and in particular among the peasants, the preaching of the radical mendicant friars of the ideal of the propertyless church, in contrast to the prelates grown rich and unscrupulous, is most effective; in the agitation carried on by nameless hole-and-corner preachers, this ideal is not infrequently combined with communistic ideas in the style of the Hussites and with apocalyptic expectations of the imminent end of the world. Among the urban middle classes there is primarily the sound common-sense criticism of excessive church privileges and of the contradiction between the claims of the clergy to spiritual authority and its scandalous manner of life; finally, there is also the misuse of mass devotion by the sellers of relics and indulgences, whose fraudulent practices do not deceive the burgher's sober business sense. The lazy dronelike existence of monastics and of so many recipients of church benefices arouses the ire of the diligent artisan; the democratic consciousness of the new age offers resistance to the aristocratic, dignified, and contemplative mode of life of the higher clergy. The burgher is also apt to be critical of the overly artful scholastic sermon whose content is often overloaded with theological subtleties, of the involved casuistry of canon law and its procedures of penance; he desires an unsophisticated form of Christian teaching accessible to all, a straightforward handling, intelligible to the layman, of the church's authority to punish. The noble too has his bitter complaints against papal administration of benefices and financial practices. And finally, among men of letters—that is to say, above all among the members of the universities, academic graduates, the more studious clerics, and certain of the urban patriciate—the humanists' criticism of church tradition gradually gains ground.

For in Germany too the reverence of the Italian humanists for classical greatness of soul, for the beauty of classical forms of life, art, and poetry, found enthusiastic followers. At princely courts here and there, in the patrician houses of the great south-German imperial cities, and at most of the universities, the imitation of Italian patronage of arts and letters, of Italian "academies" and literary circles was begun; letters and poems were exchanged in artful and laboriously turned Latin; old authors, ancient coins, and all sorts of antiquities were unearthed and collected. The best fruit of these scholarly and semischolarly efforts was a literature which for the first time sought after the historical origin of the German character. It traced and published German historical sources of the Middle Ages, collected old-German folk-customs, proverbs, and the like, and created an ideal of a genuine Germanic character which in its essentials went back to the *Germania* of Tacitus. Together with this went all kinds of empty rhetoric, false pathos, courtly flattery (especially in the service of the house of Hapsburg), fanciful creation of legends, and even deliberate falsification of history. Yet German national historiography received its first strong impetus from the semidilettante efforts of Celtis, Cuspinian, Trithemius, Wimpfeling, Bebel, Nauclerus, Peutinger, Pirckheimer, and many others. Chroniclers like Aventin and scholarly antiquaries like Beatus Rhenanus rose far above the craft of the medieval chronicler. Such juridical learning as Ulrich Zasius' and Bonifacius Amerbach's challenged for the first time the heretofore undoubted preeminence of the Italian jurists. Cosmographers like Sebastian Münster and Martin Waldseemüller, orientalists like Reuchlin and Pellican founded new branches of learning. The rigid formula of scholastic tradition was attacked from all possible angles, and ample scope was obtained for new branches of knowledge, for a new, freer view of the world. All this added considerably to the strengthening of the national self-consciousness of educated Germans. They would no longer allow themselves to be called "barbarians" by the southern people. It became a favorite theme of patriotic literature to praise the ancient virtues of the German character by calling on Tacitus and to contrast German bravery and fidelity with Latin cunning and frivolity. Thus humanistic literature soon gained a keenly nationalistic trait. It turned against the "hereditary enemy," France, in the service of imperial foreign politics, and against the Roman curia, in the service of the German imperial estates and their "gravamina." But it met invariably with greatest approval when it treated the favorite theme of the time: the faults of the church.

The humanists' own contribution to this theme was chiefly the derision of the paltry education of the average cleric. There was mockery of the "barbarous" Latin, the peasantlike bearing, and the "stinking cowls" of the mendicant friars, and the like, closely combined, naturally, with the usual jokes on concubinage, public immorality, and the high living of the priests. The most pointed satire of this kind was the collection of the fictitious *Dunkelmännerbriefe,* produced by Hutten's circle of friends. In it the new literary estate, whose self-respect was severely offended by the church's censorship of the great scholar Reuchlin and of his propaganda for Hebrew literature, gave vent to its need for vengeance in quite unmeasured and obscene terms. Among the criticism of the church must also be reckoned the humanists' fight against scholastic learning and theology with its empty subtleties and artificialities. But this fight remained fruitless as long as it would merely destroy without erecting a truly all-embracing new ideal of learning and culture which went beyond the introduction of new style forms and new academic subjects (such as Greek and Hebrew grammar). Only two of the humanists on German soil, however, were capable of this: Rudolf Agricola, who died in his youth in 1485, and Desiderius Erasmus. Both belonged to the cultural circle of the Netherlands.

What the German humanists at once understood and took from the lifework of the Great Dutchman was first its satirical, condescending criticism of the outward aspect of the late medieval church: the scandalous mode of life and ignorance of her priests, especially of the monks, the dull superstition of the populace, the excess of her ritual, her misuse of spiritual power for secular purposes, and the degeneration of her theological learning. In his *Praise of Folly* he could put more cleverly and aptly than anyone else the doubts and objections which the sound common sense of the German burgher had long raised. The new wide outlook on the world and on life which stood behind this admittedly went over the heads of most German readers as far as its final aims were concerned. It was the ideal of an intimate union of humane and liberal culture, of humanity in the sense of the old Hellenic and old Roman patrician society, with the Christian ethic of love as defined in Jesus' Sermon on the Mount. The "philosophy of Christ," as Erasmus imagined it, set out to reconcile the consciousness of the natural dignity and moral strength of man, newly sprung up in Italy, with the teaching of Christ's act of redemption and our duty to follow it; it set out to unite the belief in the unique value of the Christian revelation with the recognition of religious truth in the great spiritual creations of all peoples and all times. This was possible only with the aid of many ambiguous, often contradictory, theological formulations which barred the great mass of German readers from a deeper understanding of the Erasmian ideals of life. They exercised their strongest influence outside territorial Germany: we shall meet them in the path of the Swiss and Dutch Reformation and also repeatedly in the Latin countries and in England. Erasmus was in any event far removed from the emphatic nationalism of the German humanists and from their crude contentiousness; he lived in a cosmopolitan world of learning beyond all nationalistic boundaries and shunned nothing more than any threatened intrusion of the noise of great political struggles into the edifying calm of his scholarly existence. If in Germany he was despite this hailed with extravagant enthusiasm as leader, indeed as prophet and champion of a new age, this was largely a misunderstanding. Erasmus' tender, subdued philosophy of life and his dignified and delicate scholar's personality were not made for the severe and decisive spiritual and political battles towards which Germany now advanced. Yet his theology showed certain genuinely German traits, which separate him clearly from Italian humanism and which help to explain the astonishingly powerful effect he had on Germany despite all his cool cosmopolitan restraint.

Even the most passionate and most embittered German criticism of the church could still be called the anger of disillusioned love. The very heat of the Germans' zeal proves how much the message of the church meant to them, how heavily the decadence of spiritual life weighed on their soul. The indifference of most Italian humanists to this question was incomprehensible to them, as indeed it was to Erasmus, who would have nothing to do with any kind of neopaganism. The moral abuses in the life of the late medieval clergy (which are witnessed by testimonies far too voluminous to allow of doubt) were certainly no greater in Germany than in other countries; such monstrous profligacies as those of the papal court of Alexander VI were still inconceivable among the German prelates. But nowhere was the zeal of spiritual and secular authorities to improve these faults greater than in Germany, and nowhere did they inspire more vehement invective. But the more vehement it was, the less progress could any outward reformation make toward its goal. For the root of the evil was deeper: the church, as a Roman legal institution for the administration of means of grace and for the execution of magical, sacred acts, could no longer satisfy the religious needs of the German soul.

In order to understand the special nature of the German piety of that time in contrast to other forms of worship, particularly the Latin, one might best begin with a comparison of religious works of art. What is obscured in theological literature, dominated as it must be by the universal ideas and thought-forms of Scholasticism, immediately becomes visible in art: the striving of the German temper for a direct personal appropriation of salvation. Italian religious art preferred scenes of the glorification of the church, her means of grace, her holy fathers and martyrs, and her triumphs; it liked to represent the Mother of God as a princely personage, surrounded where possible by her heavenly retinue. Altar pictures of this kind are found in Germany too, but far more popular are representations of a more intimate kind which move the pious heart: scenes, perhaps, from the life of Mary, with pictures in a middle-class setting, but especially Christ's passion, depicted with the most intimate participation in the suffering of the Man of Sorrows. The *Vesperbild* or *Pietà*,

---

FIGURE 7. *The Passion of Christ and the Antichrist* (following pages). These four pairs of woodcuts, with captions by Luther, are selections from the twenty-six presented in the original tract published in mid-May 1521. They contrast the humility and goodness of Christ with the pride and worldliness of the pope. Reproduced from *Dr. Martin Luther's Sämmtliche Schriften,* ed. J. G. Walch, vol. 14 (*St. Louis: Concordia Publishing House, 1898),* cols. 206–209, 222–225, 226–229, 246–249.

A. The Lord washed his disciples' feet,

B. The pope makes others kiss his feet.

C. Christ devoted himself to his sheep,

D. Antichrist lives in lust and pride.

E. In poverty and peace Christ was born,

F. For war and arrogance the pope is chosen.

G. Christ ascended from this world,

H. The pope falls to the netherworld.

the representation of the Mother of Sorrows with the dead Son on her knee, is the only German contribution to the rich treasury of motives of late medieval religious art. The Last Judgment, too, with its horror, and the story of the wise and foolish virgins, with its strong appeal to conscience, never failed to move German artists very deeply.

Even this cursory observation indicates intellectual and spiritual connections which it would be easy to confirm by further examples and to trace through the entire Middle Ages. Time and again a buried antagonism comes to light, a contest between the spirit of Latin churchdom, with its outward legalism, and German piety, with its strong temperamental needs and intense seriousness of conscience. Throughout the Middle Ages, the Roman church developed more markedly into a legal institution, whose rigid juridical-theological apparatus bound the religious procedure of salvation increasingly to the execution of outward sacred acts and the fulfillment of external sacred norms. But this very development serves to conceal even further the genuine, pristine essence of religion as the direct personal experience of God. The conscience of the deepest and purest German spirits had already revolted against this in the Middle Ages. Outward exhibition of religious experience in glowing ecstasies and visions, in new and striking forms of monastic asceticism, had always been rarer in Germany than the tendency to the most intimate submersion in the divine secrets. None of the founders of the great medieval orders was a German. There was, however, a German mysticism of great historical significance, which can be traced throughout the entire late Middle Ages.

The lay piety of upper Germany and the Netherlands (in which Erasmus too was nurtured), now turning towards more mystic edification, now towards more practical and efficacious piety, shows a common trend in its most varied forms: to relegate the church's sacramental apparatus of grace to lesser importance than the personal assurance of salvation which is sought and experienced by the individual believer in direct intercourse with his God. This, of course, need by no means lead to an attitude of opposition to the church. But the more emphatically the church stressed the indispensability of priestly mediation and juridically extended the concept of the power of the keys, the closer lay the danger that the pious soul

would feel this intervention as a disturbing impediment, as an interference of alien power in the innermost secrets of the heart. The
boundary between mysticism and heresy was never clearly drawn
and was easily transgressed; indeed Germany in the fifteenth century was almost overflowing with mystical heretical sects. And even
among the great mass of church people, where heretical inclinations
were lacking, the priestly performance of the sacraments could be
regarded more or less indifferently and pushed aside. The more
easily this was done, the lower the moral prestige of the priesthood
sank, and the misuse of the power of the keys for secular purposes
became manifest. Finally, there was no lack of opposition-minded reformers who were able to justify on theological grounds such a
rejection or at least devaluation of priestly mediation in salvation.
In the writings of the so-called early reformers, especially of the
Dutchman Wessel Gansfort, one can already discover a revolutionary
bent which resembles the Lutheran conception of the process of
salvation. Also outside the mystic tradition, Wyclifite ideas, which
proposed to set a new community of saints in place of the hierarchi-
cally conceived priestly church, continually excited and engaged
German theologians. The conviction that all reform in theology must
begin with a return to the oldest and most original truths of Christianity, intelligible to the layman, was disseminated in the widest circles;
it too was among the basic teachings of Erasmus and through the
instrumentality of his writings it took hold of a very broad stratum of
scholars, theological as well as lay. On the eve of the Reformation
there were throughout Germany pious men and women to whom,
from the point of view of their personal faith, the church with its
splendid hierarchy appeared as a place of downright sale and corruption. They lived in a religion of quiet inwardness, in uncertain
groping and seeking, of which hardly anything was expressed
publicly. But because here was undoubtedly the greatest religious
vitality, they too constituted a dangerous threat to the dominance of
the old church. It was only a matter of combining the new religious
vitality of the "devout in the land" with the already mentioned loud
criticism and political opposition, which filled the whole age, against
the outward aspects of the church. Once this combination had been
accomplished the revolutionary momentum could no longer be
arrested.

In retrospect we see both currents of church opposition at work simultaneously though at first independently. The one struggles against manifest abuses and insists on reforms, but in practice does not go beyond a patchwork improvement of institutions. Though it does not reach down into spiritual depths, it is nevertheless most impassioned, impelling, and popular. The other current is less concerned with the outward appearance of the church, but instead touches on the substance of religion and the spiritual roots of church life. Those in power long underestimate its significance because at first it lacks any prospect of practical effect. But at the same time, it has the advantage that practical power can do nothing against it. In the figure of Martin Luther the two currents combine for the first time. He is a man of the people, an agitator in grandest style, and the most popular speaker and writer that Germany has ever produced; possessed of unprecedented hitting power and coarseness of language, of boundless anger and fighting zeal, he sways the masses most forcefully. He shares the moral indignation of his contemporaries over the outward corruption of the church; he uses all the slogans of anticlerical and antipapal opposition of the preceding hundred years and still outdoes them—but at the same time he is the most brilliant and profound theological thinker, the most powerful and strong-willed prophet-figure of his people, and a religious genius whose experience of faith is of unprecedented inwardness and intimacy.

This combination is plainly unique. And thus Luther became incomparably the most formidable opponent of the old church.

Karl Barth
REFORMATION AS DECISION

"When the curtain is rung down on the twentieth century," writes John D. Godsey, "and the annals of its church history are complete, there will surely be one name that will tower above all others in the field of theology—that of Karl Barth." Born in Basle in 1886, he was educated at the universities of Bern, Berlin, Marburg, and Tübingen. From 1911 to 1921, he served the Reformed Church in Safenwil, near Zurich, as parish pastor. The terrible events of the World War I shook his confidence in liberal views of the goodness of man and led him to an earnest study of the New Testament and the writings of the great reformers, Luther and Calvin. In 1919 he published a commentary on the Epistle of St. Paul to the Romans, enlarged in the second edition of 1922. He criticized the lack of realism in liberal theology, stressed man's sinfulness and finitude, and the need to acknowledge the holiness and majesty of God. Barth taught at the universities of Göttingen and Bonn until 1935, when the Nazi government forced him to leave Germany. He then taught at the University of Basle until 1962 and died in 1968. He wrote "Reformation as Decision" in the fateful year 1933.

At no time during the four hundred years of its existence has our Evangelical church found it possible to refrain entirely from remembering the Reformation of the sixteenth century, from recalling its historical image and impressing it upon itself anew, from emphasizing and cultivating its own relation with it, and from desiring an understanding of itself as the church of that very Reformation. Often it was not at all self-evident that this should occur. Often enough It took place in opposition to the prevailing spirit of the times and was therefore more or less artificial and forced. But it did occur. One after another and side by side Orthodox, Pietists, adherents of the Enlightenment, Idealists, representatives of Romanticism, Positivists, and many others imprinted the marks of their character upon our church. None of them could refrain from giving their attention again and again to the events and conditions of those former days and, if possible, to feel themselves to be and to pose as the true heirs of its spirit. Hardly any important personality or movement within Protes-

From Karl Barth, "Reformation als Entscheidung," 2nd ed., published in *Theologische Existenz heute,* edited by Karl Barth and Eduard Thurneysen, 1933. Copyright by Theologischer Verlag Zürich. Used by permission. Translated by Lewis W. Spitz, Sr.

tantism would have desired to build the church entirely without
Luther or in the Reformed sphere without Calvin. No wonder then
that no one desires to do so today! The question arises, by what
right did this occur or does this occur now? Who may appeal to the
Reformation? Who may fully regard himself at one with it? The
answer to this question obviously depends on the answer to the
other question: By what potency, by what magnetic attraction does
the Reformation have this seemingly inevitable overall importance in
our Evangelical church?

There is a law of unforgetfulness, or persistent founding personalities and founding events, in the history of religion. But appealing to
this general phenomenon would be more a characterization than an
explanation of the mysterious fact noted above. That in fact is the
very thing that was founded in the Reformation church, was founded
anew in the church itself. From the Reformation period, in fact, was
derived its special, its willing or unwilling, understanding or lack of
understanding, normative position vis-à-vis the later epochs of the
church. What is it that gives the Reformation the status and dignity
of an ecclesiastical founding? We must in fact ask just that way. And
precisely because the question must be formulated that way, the
answer to the question is so difficult, for thereby many answers that
appear at first sight are excluded from the outset.

Some have tried to be convinced and in part still try to be, that it
is the cultural, the political, and today one emphasizes particularly
the national element of the Reformation, that make it especially
memorable. One cannot deny that it actually had such a component.
But from these points of view one cannot speak of the Reformation
with such conviction, as one would like to, for the very reason that it
is after all a matter of great controversy, and will remain so, as to
whether one should in the final analysis welcome or deplore its cultural, political, and national consequences. One may find it difficult,
to mention only one example, to say that the actual consequence of
the life work of Martin Luther has been beneficial to the internal and
external unity of the German people. The same difficulty would also
arise for a Frenchman who would attempt to exalt Calvin on the basis
of French national history. But even the person who might be in a
position to enjoy the effects of the Reformation in these areas by way
of some such interpretation would still not be able on those grounds

to explain the existence of the Evangelical church and its persistent relation to those specific men and events.

The same applies to the attempt to base the significance of the Reformation on an appreciation of the great, the heroic, and creative personalities of its leading founders, an effort made famous by Thomas Carlyle. The Reformers, after all, were not poets, philosophers, or kings. One would have to idealize and correct their actual character in a remarkable way in order to obtain the necessary breath and good conscience to honor them from this point of view. And although—and this again shall not be controverted—they were in their way "great men," men of unusual stature of will and achievement, this still does not justify or make clear why they founded a church and are able to this very day to be a law-giving and judicial court in the church.

But one does not get much farther by describing the time of the Reformation as a time in which fountains welled up and the forces of inwardness burst out, as a classical time of profound and direct reflection on the ultimate reasons of human existence, as one of the supreme periods of living religion. In the actual Reformation, as far as one can see, things developed much more externally also in the intimate life of the Reformation itself. For instance, they wrangled, disputed, dogmatized, and politicized also among themselves much more than might be regarded as proper by the lovers of a religion and metaphysic of the heart when viewed close up. One should not say Luther when one means Eckhart, Suso, or Tauler! And even insofar as it might in part be possible and justified to understand the Reformers as virtuosos of religion (as is now gladly conceded also by Catholics, specifically regarding Luther)—as virtuosos of religion due to their fervent heart or due to their inner essentiality, due to their mysticism in the best and most comprehensive sense of this concept —if the Reformers perhaps had possessed some quality like the saints (precisely in the sense of Catholicism), they could not have become the fathers of our church by virtue of these attributes.

One certainly came much closer to the truth of the matter when in previous centuries one simply perceived the merit and greatness of the Reformers in the fact that they again proclaimed certain Christian truths, forgotten or half-forgotten in the church, and thereby restored the church: the glory and authority of the Bible, the lordly majesty of God the Creator, the significance of Jesus Christ as the reconciler of sinful man, the power of faith in this Christ, the freedom of the Christian in the world, the necessary humility and the necessary courage of the true church. In fact, if one asks the Reformers themselves about the importance which they attribute to their willing and doing, one gets the simple answer that they were concerned about the pure teaching of these truths, and, in and with this pure doctrine, about the correct obedience, the right life, the right form of the church, or negatively, about its true liberation from the papacy as a form of church worship, church law, and church morals which was not in accord with this pure doctrine. We can take this for granted in answer to our question: the Evangelical church in the Reformation sense is there and only there where the concern is for the pure teaching of the Christian truths, where the whole life of the church is determined and measured by this one task. But one must pay close attention. The Reformers were concerned about the *pure* teaching of those truths. These were indeed not wholly unknown to the Christian medieval age. The present-day Catholic church also grants them some significance. They were presumably taught in the Evangelical church in later times as well. The Reformers however taught them purely. This certainly was not the case in Catholicism and is not so now, whereas in all later times this was and is the key question for the Evangelical church, whether these truths were taught purely, or perhaps were once again taught impurely, and that at once means that they were taught not at all. For one cannot deal with these truths as one pleases. One cannot indiscriminately give them either this or that sense, emphasis, and relation. They must be taught in a fully determined sense and form, otherwise they are no longer those truths. This is what founded the church in the time of the Reformation, namely that thousands and thousands were then convinced, that they suddenly heard those truths proclaimed in the one correct and therefore necessary sense and form. Now they suddenly heard them proclaimed as actually commanding and saving truths, which had not been the case for many centuries. With this conviction that "here we hear the old Christian truths in a pure and therefore superior and salutary proclamation"—with this conviction the Evangelical church was there, at first within the papal church and later, when the papal church refused to see and tolerate the rising sun, outside of it, on her own foundation. This is what has made the Reformation so important to the Evangelical church, which regards it as the determining factor for all times: the clear or the dim remembrance of that indelible extraordinary element that could be heard in the proclamation of the church at that time, and was heard, that extraordinary element which at that time stamped the seal of *the* truth on *those* truths. The mystery of this extraordinary element was and is the mystery of the Reformation. This would then at all times constitute the right for one to appeal to the Reformation, to be aware of one's unity with it—there where the awareness of this extraordinary element is and where there is not only the awareness of it, but where this extraordinary element of the Reformation proclamation lives on, is honored and is made fruitful, where it is not a light standing under a bushel, but a light on the stand, shining for all that are in the house. But what is it about this extraordinary element? What was it about this one right and therefore necessary form and meaning of the church proclamation that one then thought one saw suddenly flaring up like a bolt of lightning? What does *pure* teaching of the Christian truth mean?

In order to give a correct answer to this question it will be helpful to recall still another explanation of the Reformation. Next to the explanation of the Reformers themselves it is the oldest explanation. It is, if you please, also the most naive. But it is instructive. When Luther had died, it was customary in the Evangelical church simply to say: A prophet like Elijah or John the Baptist was among us, a man of God, a lightbearer, a theologian who had his theology a priori, that is, from revelation. Luther himself had occasionally come quite close to similar expressions regarding his own mission and preparation. Calvin's *Institutes,* too, after his death were boldly characterized as a book the likes of which had not appeared since the writings of the Apostles. Stylistically all this smacks of the Renaissance. But it is nevertheless worthwhile to think about it. This could in fact have been that extraordinary element, the supreme purity of the Reformation doctrine, namely that it had something very specific in common with the doctrine of the Prophets and Apostles, common not only in content, but also in the form and meaning in which it was presented. If at that time things happened rightly, if this extraordinary element really founded the church, then it could indeed not have been otherwise, then this extraordinary element, this purity, must have existed in the prophetic-apostolic manner of that teaching. Had it been of a different kind, we would have to say that it was something else than church, Christian church, that was founded here. Extraordinary elements of Christian doctrine other than just the prophetic-apostolic do not customarily found church but heresy. If at that time a legitimate founding or rather refounding, reformation, that is, reconstruction of the one true Christian church, occurred, if the church at that time returned from heresy to its true self, then it must have been the voice of the Prophets and Apostles that was being heard. And the fact that one heard *this* voice, was actually and originally what made the Reformation memorable and normative for the entire later Evangelical church, still makes it so and must make it so ever again. We must therefore now ask another question: What then precisely was this prophetic-apostolic kind of Reformation proclamation?

Now the simple answer can be given: The Christian thinking and speaking of the Reformers, as it was expressed in their doctrine, was like that of the Prophets and Apostles, a thinking and speaking that issued from a decision reached at that moment. This thinking and speaking did not want to be anything else in content than an announcement and defense of the decision reached at that moment. A decision has been reached at the point where once and for all a person comes to the end of reflection on and the consideration of various possibilities, to the end of inquiry about their total deeper unity or even the supposed knowledge of such a unity. A decision has been reached where one has come to a judgment, to a choice, to a definite preference or rejection, to placing things higher or lower. To reach a decision means to surrender one's freedom in freedom. Whoever has reached a decision has bound himself. That kindly protecting darkness or also the eminent height, where one could still do one thing or the other lies behind him. Having stepped out or climbed down into the sober light of day, he must now say yes or no, want this or that, stand here or there. The Reformers were such men bound by decision. They had chosen. They now abandoned the position where they still had many possibilities. Therefore their teaching had only one dimension, one concern, one purpose. It was in part a call to all to reach a decision together with them, in part a vindication of the content of this decision over against those who did not want to reach a decision with them, in part an understanding with those who had already reached a decision with them. Reformation doctrine did not retreat from their decision by a single word, and so it must not be understood in a single word apart from their decision. Reformation teaching does not issue from some higher level. It does not compare, does not weigh, does not discuss. But it presents, it explains, it disputes. This is what gives it iron and power. This is what it has in common with the proclamation of the Prophets and Apostles. This is what was lacking in the Catholic church before the Reformation and is still missing since the Reformation. This is what has made the Reformation unforgettable to the Evangelical church, even though and inasmuch as it has at all times been doubtful and at some times more than doubtful, and still is, whether one still knew and knows: Reformation is decision, and the church of the Reformation is there and only there where there is a decision.

But there are various kinds of decisions. The Reformers, like the Prophets and Apostles, arose from one absolutely definite decision that must not be confused with any other. All human decisions, even the most serious and important ones—with but a single exception—are of such a nature that man can, as long as he has the time, overhaul, correct, or simply replace them with new decisions. We have indeed often experienced how many a man stood firmly only yesterday and seemed to stand with the greatest determination and then—behold!—today he, too, is able to do otherwise. But it is also comforting to realize that even for the strongest resolves of today there is a tomorrow that can change much or everything. That is due to the fact that man in all of his decisions—with the exception of a single one—grasps one of his own possibilities and goes to bat himself for this one chosen possibility and so fetters himself on the basis of his decision. The loss of his freedom that he suffers by his decision is at all times—with a single exception—at the same time also a triumph of his freedom. As long as he has the time he is able to bind himself in this lost freedom differently today from yesterday and tomorrow differently from today. An unchangeable decision, that is one in which man finds himself irreversibly bound, in which he would now really sacrifice his freedom, would at the same time be one on the basis of which he no longer would have time—at least absolutely no more time for a revision of this decision. This decision—if we may exclude here the border-line case of suicide—can be no other than the decision for the Christian faith. In this decision man has bound himself irrevocably without any prospect of doing otherwise in the future, without any remaining possibility of overhauling this decision in the future. If he is otherwise, if he is bound less firmly, then his decision was not *this* decision. This decision in contrast with all others is the ultimate decision. For in this decision man has sacrificed his freedom, that is, precisely the possibility of being able to do otherwise in the future. Both for the reason that he who has decided for the Christian faith has no time, no more time available to him to depart from the faith. For the decision for the Christian faith is the decision for *God* as the Lord of man. And so his, man's time is no longer in his own hands but in God's hands. Therefore the way to other decisions in the future is barred to him, for he has now actually and ultimately surrendered his freedom not to believe, "You cannot serve God and mammon" [Matt. 6:24]. Note that it does not say, "You *should* not!" but "You *cannot!*" Jesus Christ said that to his disciples. The situation is a world apart from that other where Elijah asks the people: "How long will you go limping with two different opinions?" and where the answer had to be: "And the people did not answer him a word" [1 Kings 18:21]. Here the answer is already given: "You cannot." You can indeed do something entirely different than my disciples. You can do something entirely different than believe, but you cannot believe and still always want to be free in the faith, free not to believe at another time. You are captured in this decision. Every future decision, viewed from it, can only be its repetition and confirmation. You *are* God's! Coming from the decision to the Christian faith, man says with the Prophets: "O Lord, thou hast deceived [persuaded] me, and I was deceived [persuaded]; thou art stronger than I, and thou hast prevailed" [Jer. 20:7]. Therefore man says with the Apostles: "One thing I do, forgetting what lies behind and straining forward to what lies ahead" [Phil. 3:13]. The movement that is described with these words is an unambiguous and irreversible movement. The person who is caught in this movement can give as little attention to the direction he is going as a child longing for its mother, because he is in fact totally reversed and becomes such a child. He now exists in that direction and therefore he can have a future only in that direction. Only the decision for death or indeed the decision for God the Lord in the Christian faith can have this unconditioned character. But the decision from which the Reformation doctrine came has this character and this is the extraordinary element, the pure in the Reformation teaching of the Christian truths. I shall try to make this clear with several examples.

The Reformation doctrine deals with the Holy Scriptures as the sole testimony to the actual and determinative revelation of God concerning the simple realization that God is to be found by us there where it has pleased him to seek us. Hence not there where we think we can seek him, not within reach of our own possibilities, be it called reason or experience, nature or history, internal or external universe. Not where we think we should in our wisdom speak of him, but where he in his wisdom spoke to us. He did speak to us once and for all. And of this perfect tense: *Deus dixit* [God has spoken] the Sacred Scriptures testify and they alone. Therefore the proclamation of the Christian church neither can nor may in any sense be a philosophy, that is an elaboration of any kind of self-discovered world-view and view of life. Therefore it is bound as an interpretation of the Scriptures. All other doctrine has neither right nor promise in the church. This Reformation doctrine of the Sacred Scriptures is immediately intelligible to the man who understands that they speak on the basis of the ultimate decision. They declare that after God sought us in the wonder of his condescension in Jesus Christ, whose witnesses the Prophets and Apostles are, all our efforts to find him from within ourselves have not only become baseless but demonstrated to be in themselves impossible. After God has spoken to man, man simply has no more time to want to instruct himself regarding God. On the basis of the decision that had been reached the doctrine of the Sacred Scriptures actually could not be otherwise than as it was presented by the Reformers in great severity, but also with even greater joy. On the basis of the decision reached there could not and cannot exist the least need for any natural theology.

The Reformation doctrine of original sin furthermore deals with the simple realization that inasmuch as God the Creator, Reconciler, Savior, inasmuch as God's command and God's comfort has revealed itself to us through his word, our judgment has been spoken. From this there is no excuse and no escape. For as we hear this word we must let it tell us that the use which we make of our freedom within the compass of our birth from Adam on is, within the compass of our own personal possibilities, including the use we may regard as the very best, an evil use that at all times means enmity against God and hatred against our neighbor. We have—and that is in fact our boundless guilt—actually no freedom for God. We are at the very root of our being and essence such as have willfully cast away that freedom and so lost it. This Reformation doctrine also speaks on the basis of the decision rendered with finality. It declares that after God's humiliation in Jesus Christ proved itself as the only way between God and man, man's godless, unholy, unrighteous way must no longer be denied but confessed. Whoever at best must depend on pity is just pitiful. The Reformation doctrine declares that the man who has been reached and struck by God's real word must acknowledge that because he cannot have any time, any breath, any air to have any illusions regarding himself, regarding the use he knows to make of his freedom and therefore regarding the actual fact of his freedom. How else could the doctrine of man be different on the basis of this decision than that his imagination is evil from his youth, his will an unfree will. Whoever understands it on this basis will not for a moment fail to hear in it, besides the audible dismay of man, who must confess himself lost, also the endless jubilation of the child of God saved from his lostness. The Reformation doctrine furthermore deals with the *justification* of sinful man through faith, the simple realization that for the very reason that we, using our own freedom, will never within the scope of our own possibility do what is right before God—for that very reason we may seek our righteousness only there where God has given and offered it to us: in the condescension in which he took our place in Jesus Christ in order to make good what we make bad. That indeed means believing: decision for *God* as our Lord. If he is our Lord, then he is also our righteousness, then we can base our confidence of becoming righteous before him only on him alone. Here again everything depends on our understanding that we are here speaking on the basis of the ultimate irreversible decision. The Reformation doctrine declares that inasmuch as God has demonstrated his honor and glory in the fact that in Jesus Christ he gave us nothing less than himself, our veneration, our gratitude, and our obedience must consist in fleeing from all of our own righteousness to his righteousness. The man who lets God be God, as he is God for us in the manger at Bethlehem and on the cross of Golgotha—that man simply has no time and no room for still wanting to justify himself with his own works, that is, with his attitude and bearing, his seriousness, his behavior, his ability. How could the doctrine of salvation be otherwise on the basis of the "rendered decision" than that man, inasmuch as his sins have been forgiven him, is bound to the obedience of faith, the deeds of which are good in God's gracious judgment and not in man's own evaluation. On the basis of the decision rendered, it is no longer possible to look for any other grace than the grace of God.

Thus the Reformation doctrine of election or predestination deals with the realization, most simple but nevertheless fundamental, that the decision for this Christian faith in the divine condescension which has occurred, in the revealed mercy of God, is indeed a decision of man, but not in fact one of the decisions that he makes In and by his own freedom. It is just this that distinguishes it from all other decisions, namely that the decision is for God the Lord, that therefore the freedom of man is sacrificed in it. This makes of it a firm bond to the absolutely necessary and irrefutable decision. But who then himself decides for God the Lord? Just he who really does it, just he believes, just he will never give credit to his freedom for it. But this is the doctrine of the Christian faith regarding itself, namely that it rests on the altogether unmerited and incomprehensible election of him in whom it believes, that man is not free to believe or not to believe, but that God is indeed free to be merciful or to harden according to his pleasure. Once more, every word also of this Reformation doctrine is based on the decision reached. Whoever merely thinks about faith will never, whoever thinks from within faith must ever come to the conclusion expressed in this doctrine. The Reformers thought from within the faith, which justifies because in it all honor is given to God. Therefore they—Luther and Calvin fully of one mind in this matter— taught the unconditional, the double predestination. That means the total freedom of God. This doctrine declares that as Jesus Christ himself, so also faith in him is none of man's own possibilities, but the great saving possibility of God for him. It is the wonder of the Holy Spirit that no one can take for himself. Believing man really has no time for desiring to take his faith from anywhere. He has his hands full with the task of receiving and ever again receiving. That is the decision of faith that man receives the gift from within the mystery of

God to regard God for his Lord. On the basis of this decision the doctrine of faith can hardly be expressed differently than it was formulated by the Reformers.

What has just been said was not by any means intended to represent what the Reformers taught in full or even only about these individual points of the Christian faith. The intention was merely to show
by means of the four chosen points in which special direction their
teaching was moving. This direction was the extraordinary element,
the purity, the prophetic-apostolic manner of their doctrine and the
mystery of the entire Reformation. This direction was to the old and is
to the new Catholicism intolerable. This direction has made the Reformation unforgettable in the Evangelical church.

But we have already heard that this direction was at times quite
often intolerable also to the prevailing movement even within the
Evangelical church. Because the direction of the prevailing movement in the Evangelical church was often enough secretly or openly,
mildly or severely, exactly the opposite! Peculiar times then began.
The Reformation remained in its dignity and meaning, but the manner
in which one dealt with it aroused the strong suspicion that basically
the chief concern was to escape the protest which seemed to arise
from that distant event like a thunderstorm against that which the
current age thought and desired. The Reformation was indeed loved
and praised, but this love and praise, carefully avoiding the focal
point, was accorded to those points on the basis of which the reformation of the church just could not have happened. The Reformers,
particularly when an anniversary came around again, were zealously
quoted and extolled, their tombs were built energetically and
adorned, and, like Samuel's spirit summoned by the witch at Endor,
Luther actually appeared here and Calvin actually appeared there in
the midst of the festive conjuries. But then there was no mistaking
how happy everyone was, when the disappearance of these noble
spirits made it possible to return again to the order of the day. The
actual life of the church, as it appeared particularly in its public
proclamation and to the extent that it was determined by the prevailing movement, always actually took a totally different direction. In all
of these peculiar times it was bound to be more or less questionable
whether the church was in truth still what it presumed to be then and
now—Evangelical church.

One must speak of another direction in the church opposed to the Reformation where that extraordinary element, that purity, that prophetic-apostolic kind of Reformation teaching has been lost to the thinking and speaking of the church, but that means where the thinking and speaking of the church, in spite of every pretension and the good will to be believing, no longer comes from that decision rendered for the Christian faith. The estrangement of the Evangelical church from the Reformation will in such times not consist in the fact that the Christian truths which the Reformation again raised on the candle stick are perhaps not at all being proclaimed or are even denied. Indeed not! Precisely in such times one will rather hear the affirmation, and indeed the honest affirmation, at every streetcorner that the confession must remain untouched, that now as always the Gospel should prevail and be heard in the church. Precisely at such times—it has happened more than once—a conservative, not to say a reactionary trend, regarding the traditional articles of faith will pass through the church. At such times an altogether too-open liberalism shall beware lest it become the victim of attempted murder, which seems to be in style precisely in such a period. One thing that can happen is that after convulsive efforts in this sense, sooner or later peculiar perforations and changes in the traditional articles of faith will develop quite unintentionally. But basically and primarily this is never the real concern when the Evangelical church once again becomes unfaithful to the Reformation. Rather, basically and primarily it is then always the case that in all good faith one fundamentally thinks and speaks differently than the Reformation. That is, one no longer thinks and speaks on the basis of the decision rendered, but on the basis of reflection and comparison, on the basis of the greater unity of two possibilities, of which the Christian faith is only one—perhaps a strongly and honestly emphasized one, but still only one. One has not surrendered the faith, but one has once again gained one's freedom in the face of it. One's freedom! So then liberalism anyway? Indeed, basically, regarding the point on which everything depends, nevertheless liberalism, no matter how strongly one might detest it. But this is the liberalism in the church, that one chooses the faith for reasons, with seriousness and conviction, but one chooses it as one of one's own possibilities. One confesses it, but one also does not want to overlook the many other possibilities besides the faith that one could also choose in the same freedom. One basically still has, or once again has, time for them. One certainly wants to serve God and God only, but one now wants to do it again from that higher place of safety, viewed from which the service of mammon, too, is a serious possibility. Also and precisely because one still wants to serve God, one's own freedom, in which one basically stands in the middle, triumphs. This middle is maintained. One has time to compare, to weigh, in brief, time for one's self. In basically having time for one's self and one's own possibilities one now also wants to understand and confess, explain, and proclaim the Christian faith. But that means that one now understands and confesses, one explains and proclaims it in relation to that understanding of one's self and one's own possibilities for which one just has time, in other words, which is just then opportune. One must understand it with regard to morals, so they said at one time. Then with regard to reason, then with regard to humanity, then with regard to culture, and today notably with regard to nationality and the state. As a child of this or that time, as a partaker of its history, its spirit, its particular meanings and convictions one has affirmed and grasped this or that evaluation of man as the only right one at the time, and faith—well, faith must now under all circumstances stand in relation to man evaluated in that way. Otherwise it would be, and that cannot be—so one must now presumably sigh—in a vacuum. That it must be in that relationship, that is, that under all circumstances it must be a moral or rational or humanitarian or today also a nationalistic faith—this has quietly become remarkably certain and important. Must one not say this has become just as certain and important as the other point, namely that it must be faith? Yes, must one perhaps not say, even much more certain and important than this other? Frankly, what is more certain and important in such times, the relation of faith to morals, to reason, to humanity, to culture, to nationalism and to the state, in brief, to man in any one of the evaluations that he gives himself, or faith itself? This is certain in any case, that all interest, all zeal, all passion in such times concern such relations of faith, not faith itself, not its confession. Faith and confession are then as a rule proposed as being self-evident! It need not even then be necessary that faith in this confrontation should get the short end of it. It is only necessary that the two necessities confront each other in equilibrium like the lever arms of an empty balance, but man in his freedom may regard himself as the little indicator on the balance. But precisely at that point faith itself has become something different. It is now discussible like the other possibilities for which man can decide, discussible because now indeed the relation to these other possibilities in which one wishes to place it, and therewith these other possibilities themselves, become his own conditions. It is now no longer free. It can now only be what it can be by virtue of man's freedom and what it can be in that relation. Even if it is still a most orthodox faith—already in the eighteenth century there was a glorious orthodoxy in such a situation—it is nevertheless viewed from the point of its opposite, measured by it, in duty bound to answer the questions that are put to it, to satisfy the concerns that are brought to it from there. If it does not do this, if it does not appear as moral, rational, and conformable to a national manner and function, then already notice is privately served on it that it may be fired. It may perhaps be a carefully and zealously cultivated faith, but nevertheless it is still a domesticated, an imprisoned faith, a faith that is put into foreign service. And the more so if man in his freedom takes the liberty to encompass the human possibilities that are opposite faith with a religious luster, to trace it back to some pristine revelation, to identify it with the order of creation or, still further, with God's law or ultimately directly with the Holy Spirit, who, as is well known, lives in all of us. If man is really in a position to conceive his own definition as God's Word, as he sees fit to understand it, how then could God's Word, which he supposes must be understood in faith, in the long run penetrate to him as God's Word? How could it in the long run be anything else than a word which he speaks to himself, and which he therefore shapes to accord with that which he has to say to himself, or wishes to say. This faith that permits itself to be given check by reason, culture, nation, and state, and that can now appear only in this rational situation, has become a different faith. Understood and known, explained and proclaimed from that other starting point, it will with the best intention present itself and prove itself to be that faith in which man can serve God and mammon, and then actually must serve. The direction opposed to the Reformation, wherever one has once entered upon it, has sooner or later always become apparent in the fact that in faith and in life one actually became totally estranged from the Reformation. "If the mantle falls, the duke must follow!" When one has once lost that direction, then one will ultimately in vain want to be orthodox. How should one then, just to name those four mentioned points once more, in matters of the authority of the Sacred Scriptures, in matters of original sin, in matters of justification, in matters of predestination, still be able to teach as the Reformers did? Will one at all still be able to understand their doctrine which came altogether from elsewhere? Will it not of necessity appear absurd, first secretly and then openly? Will one not have to bend and weaken it all along the line until it just about again sounds as it sounded in Catholicism, from which the Reformation came forth, and until today still sounds? Is separation from the papacy then still right and necessary? We can only say: Yes, so things have always developed wherever one had lost the Reformation direction that wanted to do justice to God's freedom in favor of the other direction that wants to favor God's freedom and man's freedom together, and which results in man's freedom alone. Actually something different, altogether different is the result: a different faith, a different Christ, a different proclamation, a different church. One may then argue whether one wants rather to rear this different church as a humanist or a national or state church, whether its proclamation is oriented better to the individual or to the public. Needless quarrel! The church that is not born of the decision for the Christian faith, of the word of God, will one way or another not be the church of the Reformation, but it will one way or another be the church of natural theology, triumphing secretly or openly, of optimism, of work-righteousness, of human presumption, which is never greater than when it is also religious—a parallel to the papacy in spite of all anti-Roman raving, which one will still here or there hear in its halls.

One must not joke with the Reformation. It is certainly in order to ask seriously whether the Reformers with the refounding of the church did not attempt something that they should not have attempted, inasmuch as European humanity was not equal to this attempt. Whether they did not leave us an inheritance which, as it is, we do not know what to make of, because it means an unbearable expectation for us, because it demands a faith from us which we cannot produce, because it does not do justice to what just happens to be our concern at the moment. One can ask this in all seriousness. Whoever thinks that he must see matters thus, let him stick to it as an honest man and instead of building the church with the Reformers on the foundation of Jesus Christ, let him build the church on the better foundation of revelation and reason, faith and knowledge, Gospel and nationalism. But one should then likewise honestly give up all claim to the unity of a church constructed that way with the Reformation. One should then no longer be ashamed of unity with Roman Catholic thinking and striving. And Luther festivals—yes, Luther festivals should then perhaps rather be discontinued.

But if we cannot discontinue them, if we still want to be and remain the Evangelical church, the church of the Reformation, if we do not want to refuse its inheritance, if we do not want the Reformation itself to be different—really do not want the beginning of our church, still alive today, to be otherwise than it once was—how can we do otherwise than let the direction that *she* once had ask us how it is with the direction *we* now have. The Reformation as decision will then ask the Evangelical church of today about its decision. If we submit to this question, it will certainly become evident if there is still among us something like a "rendered decision" and therefore also a legitimate Reformation confession, pure Reformation doctrine, or still only an accommodation and therefore no right to appeal to the Reformation. If it were then to become evident that such a "rendered decision" is not to be found in the prevailing movement of the Evangelical church today, that this movement is nothing more than the last most fully completed form of the great New-Protestant unfaithfulness toward the Reformation—well, then at least all those who have not become victims of this movement would know exactly what to do. What should they do? Strengthened by what the Reformation has to say today, they must resist. In the name of the true church against the false Evangelical church prevailing in this movement! This resistance will consist in the fact that in opposition to the prevailing movement it will again recklessly and joyfully, as happened four hundred years ago, support the "rendered decision." I say recklessly, for whoever does not want anything altogether different and does not act altogether differently than this movement does, is of no use here. There cannot again be a compromise between decision and no decision, between Luther and the pope. There was also no compromise between Luther and the Enthusiasts. Compromise could here only mean going over to the enemy. Resistance should here be a happy one, for behind the "rendered decision" one travels happily along his way, and though one were the only one against a hundred, happily, because one need not fear his opponents. The case of the movement prevailing today is not a strong one. Whoever has lost the Reformation direction has lost his backbone, no matter how powerful he may pretend to be. He will not accomplish what he would like to accomplish. When the old Swiss at Sempach advanced against the armored phalanx of Leopold of Austria, one of them is said to have shouted: "Strike their spears, for they are hollow!" They are hollow! One should say that, even if one had to say it without any outward confidence. And it will, in fact, be even better, if one says it without any outward confidence. The danger of the destruction of the Evangelical church does not lie in any form, also not in that of today, one that can be met successfully with human resistance, with human recklessness, happiness, and confidence. The resistance offered today can appeal to the Reformation as decision only insofar as it can understand itself to be in accord with the words of Calvin (from his writing to Charles V of 1543. *Corp. Ref.* VI 510f.) with which I should now like to conclude: "The Reformation of the church is God's work and is as independent of human hope and intention as the resurrection of the dead or another miracle of this kind. Therefore, regarding the possibility of doing something for it, one must not wait for the good will of the people or changing circumstances, but must break forth through the midst of despair. God would have his Gospel preached. Let us obey this command and go where he calls us! What the success will be is none of our business."

Martin Luther

LUTHER'S ROAD TO THE REFORMATION

Martin Luther (1483–1546), the first evangelical reformer and the founder of Protestantism, was professor of theology at the University of Wittenberg. The author of over one hundred volumes of treatises, translations, commentaries, and correspondence, he spoke very openly about his inner struggles and the early events of the Reformation.

Martin Luther wishes the sincere reader salvation!

For a long time I strenuously resisted those who wanted my books, or more correctly my confused lucubrations, published. I did not want the labors of the ancients to be buried by my new works and the reader kept from reading them. Then, too, by God's grace a great many systematic books now exist, among which the *Loci communes* of Philip excel, with which a theologian and a bishop can be beautifully and abundantly prepared to be mighty in preaching the doctrine of piety, especially since the Holy Bible itself can now be had in nearly every language. But my books, as it happened, yes, as the lack of order in which the events transpired made it necessary, are accordingly crude and disordered chaos, which is now not easy to arrange even for me.

Persuaded by these reasons, I wished that all my books were buried in perpetual oblivion, so that there might be room for better ones. But the boldness and bothersome perseverance of others daily filled my ears with complaints that it would come to pass, that if I did not permit their publication in my lifetime, men wholly ignorant of the causes and the time of the events would nevertheless most certainly publish them, and so out of one confusion many would arise. Their boldness, I say, prevailed and so I permitted them to be published. At the same time the wish and command of our most illustrious Prince, Elector, etc., John Frederick was added. He commanded, yes, compelled the printers not only to print, but to speed up the publication.

But above all else, I beg the sincere reader, and I beg for the sake

"Preface to the Complete Edition of Luther's Latin Writings, Wittenberg, 1545," translated by Lewis W. Spitz, Sr., in *Luther's Works*, vol. 34 (Philadelphia, 1960), pp. 327–338. Used by permission of the Fortress Press.

of our Lord Jesus Christ himself, to read those things judiciously, yes, with great commiseration. May he be mindful of the fact that I was once a monk and a most enthusiastic papist when I began that cause. I was so drunk, yes, submerged in the pope's dogmas, that I would have been ready to murder all, if I could have, or to cooperate willingly with the murderers of all who would take but a syllable from obedience to the pope. So great a Saul was I, as are many to this day. I was not such a lump of frigid ice in defending the papacy as Eck and his like were, who appeared to me actually to defend the pope more for their own belly's sake than to pursue the matter seriously. To me, indeed, they seem to laugh at the pope to this day, like Epicureans! I pursued the matter with all seriousness, as one who, in dread of the last day, nevertheless from the depth of my heart wanted to be saved.

So you will find how much and what important matters I humbly conceded to the pope in my earlier writings, which I later and now hold and execrate as the worst blasphemies and abomination. You will, therefore, sincere reader, ascribe this error, or, as they slander, contradiction to the time and my inexperience. At first I was all alone and certainly very inept and unskilled in conducting such great affairs. For I got into these turmoils by accident and not by will or intention. I call upon God himself as witness.

Hence, when in the year 1517 indulgences were sold (I wanted to say promoted) in these regions for most shameful gains—I was then a preacher, a young doctor of theology, so to speak—and I began to dissuade the people and to urge them not to listen to the clamors of the indulgence hawkers; they had better things to do. I certainly thought that in this case I should have a protector in the pope, on whose trustworthiness I then leaned strongly, for in his decrees he most clearly damned the immoderation of the quaestors, as he called the indulgence preachers.

Soon afterward I wrote two letters, one to Albrecht, the archbishop of Mainz, who got half the money from the indulgences, the pope the other half—something I did not know at the time—the other to the ordinary (as they call them) Jerome, the bishop of Brandenburg. I begged them to stop the shameless blasphemy of the quaestors. But the poor little brother was despised. Despised, I published the *Theses* and at the same time a German *Sermon on Indulgences,* shortly thereafter also the *Explanations,* in which, to the pope's honor, I developed the idea that indulgences should indeed not be condemned, but that good works of love should be preferred to them.

This was demolishing heaven and consuming the earth with fire. I am accused by the pope, am cited to Rome, and the whole papacy rises up against me alone. All this happened in the year 1518, when Maximilian held the diet at Augsburg. In it, Cardinal Cajetan served as the pope's Lateran legate. The most illustrious Duke Frederick of Saxony, Elector Prince, approached him on my behalf and brought it about that I was not compelled to go to Rome, but that he himself should summon me to examine and compose the matter. Soon the diet adjourned.

The Germans in the meantime, all tired of suffering the pillagings, traffickings, and endless impostures of Roman rascals, awaited with bated breath the outcome of so great a matter, which no one before, neither bishop nor theologian, had dared to touch. In any case that popular breeze favored me, because those practices and "Romanations," with which they had filled and tired the whole earth, were already hateful to all.

So I came to Augsburg, afoot and poor, supplied with food and letters of commendation from Prince Frederick to the senate and to certain good men. I was there three days before I went to the cardinal, though he cited me day by day through a certain orator, for those excellent men forbade and dissuaded me most strenuously, not to go to the cardinal without a safe conduct from the emperor. The orator was rather troublesome to me, urging that if I should only revoke, everything would be all right! But as great as the wrong, so long is the detour to its correction.

Finally, on the third day he came demanding to know why I did not come to the cardinal, who expected me most benignly. I replied that I had to respect the advice of those very fine men to whom I had been commended by Prince Frederick, but it was their advice by no means to go to the cardinal without the emperor's protection or safe conduct. Having obtained this (but they took action on the part of the imperial senate to obtain it), I would come at once. At this point he blew up. "What?" he asked. "Do you suppose Prince Frederick will take up arms for your sake?" I said, "This I do not at all desire." "And where will you stay?" I replied, "Under heaven." Then he, "If you had the pope and the cardinals in your power, what would you do?" "I would," said I, "show them all respect and honor." Thereupon he, wagging his finger with an Italian gesture, said, "Hem!" And he left, nor did he return.

On that day the imperial senate informed the cardinal that the emperor's protection or a safe conduct had been granted me and admonished him that he should not design anything too severe against me. He is said to have replied, "It is well; I shall nevertheless do whatever my duty demands." These things were the start of that tumult. The rest can be learned from the accounts included later.

Master Philipp Melanchthon had already been called here that same year by Prince Frederick to teach Greek literature, doubtless so that I should have an associate in the work of theology. His works attest sufficiently what the Lord has performed through this instrument, not only in literature but also in theology, though Satan is mad and all his adherents.

Maximilian died, in the following year, '19, in February, and according to the law of the empire Duke Frederick was made deputy. Thereupon the storm ceased to rage a bit, and gradually contempt of excommunication or papal thunderbolts arose. For when Eck and Caraccioli brought a bull from Rome condemning Luther and revealed it, the former here, the latter there to Duke Frederick, who was at Cologne at the time together with other princes in order to meet Charles who had been recently elected, Frederick was most indignant. He reproved that papal rascal with great courage and constancy, because in his absence he and Eck had disturbed his and his brother John's dominion. He jarred them so magnificently that they left him in shame and disgrace. The prince, endowed with incredible insight, caught on to the devices of the Roman curia and knew how to deal with them in a becoming manner, for he had a keen nose and smelled more and farther than the Romanists could hope or fear.

Hence they refrained from putting him to a test. For he did not dignify with the least respect the Rose, which they call "golden," sent him that same year by Leo X, indeed ridiculed it. So the Romanists were forced to despair of their attempts to deceive so great a prince. The Gospel advanced happily under the shadow of that prince and was widely propagated. His authority influenced very many, for since he was a very wise and most keen-sighted prince, he could incur the suspicion only among the hateful that he wanted to nourish and protect heresy and heretics. This did the papacy great harm.

That same year the Leipzig debate was held, to which Eck had challenged us two, Karlstadt and me. But I could not, in spite of all my letters, get a safe conduct from Duke George. Accordingly, I came to Leipzig not as a prospective debater, but as a spectator under the safe conduct granted to Karlstadt. Who stood in my way I do not know, for till then Duke George was not against me. This I know for certain.

Here Eck came to me in my lodging and said he had heard that I refused to debate. I replied, "How can I debate, since I cannot get a safe conduct from Duke George?" "If I cannot debate with you," he said, "neither do I want to with Karlstadt, for I have come here on your account. What if I obtain a safe conduct for you? Would you then debate with me?" "Obtain," said I, "and it shall be." He left and soon a safe conduct was given me too and the opportunity to debate.

Eck did this because he discerned the certain glory that was set before him on account of my proposition in which I denied that the pope is the head of the church by divine right. Here a wide field was open to him and a supreme occasion to flatter in praiseworthy manner the pope and to merit his favor, also to ruin me with hate and envy. He did this vigorously throughout the entire debate. But he neither proved his own position nor refuted mine, so that even Duke George said to Eck and me at the morning meal, "Whether he be pope by human or divine right, yet he is pope." He would in no case have said this had he not been influenced by the arguments, but would have approved of Eck only.

Here, in my case, you may also see how hard it is to struggle out of and emerge from errors which have been confirmed by the example of the whole world and have by long habit become a part of nature, as it were. How true is the proverb, "It is hard to give up the accustomed," and, "Custom is second nature." How truly Augustine says, "If one does not resist custom, it becomes a necessity." I had then already read and taught the sacred Scriptures most diligently privately and publicly for seven years, so that I knew them nearly all by memory. I had also acquired the beginning of the knowledge of Christ and faith in him, i.e., not by works but by faith in Christ are we made righteous and saved. Finally, regarding that of which I speak, I had already defended the proposition publicly that the pope is not the head of the church by divine right. Nevertheless, I did not draw the conclusion, namely, that the pope must be of the devil. For what is not of God must of necessity be of the devil.

So absorbed was I, as I have said, by the example and the title of the holy church as well as by my own habit, that I conceded human right to the pope, which nevertheless, unless it is founded on divine authority, is a diabolical lie. For we obey parents and magistrates not because they themselves command it, but because it is God's will, I Peter 3 [2:13]. For that reason I can bear with a less hateful spirit those who cling too pertinaciously to the papacy, particularly those who have not read the sacred Scriptures, or also the profane, since I, who read the sacred Scriptures most diligently so many years, still clung to it so tenaciously.

In the year 1519, Leo X, as I have said, sent the Rose with Karl von Miltitz, who urged me profusely to be reconciled with the pope. He had seventy apostolic briefs that if Prince Frederick would turn me over to him, as the pope requested by means of the Rose, he should tack up one in each city and so transfer me safely to Rome. But he betrayed the counsel of his heart toward me when he said, "O Martin, I believed you were some aged theologian who, sitting behind the stove, disputed thus with himself; now I see you are still young and strong. If I had twenty-five thousand armed men, I do not believe I could take you to Rome, for I have sounded out the people's mind all along the way to learn what they thought of you. Behold, where I found one standing for the pope, three stood for you against the pope." But that was ridiculous! He had also asked simple little women and girls in the hostelries, what they thought of the Roman chair [i.e., See]. Ignorant of this term and thinking of a domestic chair, they replied, "How can we know what kind of chairs you have in Rome, wood or stone?"

Therefore he begged me to seek the things which made for peace. He would put forth every effort to have the pope do the same. I also promised everything abundantly. Whatever I could do with a good conscience with respect to the truth, I would do most promptly. I, too, desired and was eager for peace. Having been drawn into these disturbances by force and driven by necessity, I had done all I did: the guilt was not mine.

But he had summoned Johann Tetzel of the preaching order, the primary author of this tragedy, and had with verbose threats from the pope so broken the man, till then so terrible to all, a fearless crier, that from that time on he wasted away and was finally consumed by illness of mind. When I found this out before his death, I comforted him with a letter, written benignly, asking him to be of good cheer and not to fear my memory. But perhaps he succumbed a victim of his conscience and of the pope's indignation.

Karl von Miltitz was regarded as vain and his advice as vain. But, in my opinion, if the man at Mainz had from the start, when I admonished him, and, finally, if the pope, before he condemned me unheard and raged with his bulls, had taken this advice, which Karl took although too late, and had at once quenched Tetzel's fury, the matter would not have come to so great a tumult. The entire guilt belongs to the one at Mainz, whose smartness and cleverness fooled him, with which he wanted to suppress my doctrine and have his money, acquired by the indulgences, saved. Now counsels are sought in vain; in vain efforts are made. The Lord has awakened and stands to judge the people. Though they could kill us, they still would not have what they want, yes, they would have less than they have while we live in safety. This some of them who are not entirely of a dull nose smell quite enough.

Meanwhile, I had already during that year returned to interpret the Psalter anew. I had confidence in the fact that I was more skillful, after I had lectured in the university on St. Paul's epistles to the Romans, to the Galatians, and the one to the Hebrews. I had indeed been captivated with an extraordinary ardor for understanding Paul in the Epistle to the Romans. But up till then it was not the cold blood about the heart, but a single word in Chapter 1 [:17], "In it the righteousness of God is revealed," that had stood in my way. For I hated that word "righteousness of God," which, according to the use and custom of all the teachers, I had been taught to understand philosophically regarding the formal or active righteousness, as they called it, with which God is righteous and punishes the unrighteous sinner.

Though I lived as a monk without reproach, I felt that I was a sinner before God with an extremely disturbed conscience. I could not believe that he was placated by my satisfaction. I did not love, yes,

I hated the righteous God who punishes sinners, and secretly, if not blasphemously, certainly murmuring greatly, I was angry with God, and said, "As if, indeed, it is not enough, that miserable sinners, eternally lost through original sin, are crushed by every kind of calamity by the law of the decalogue, without having God add pain to pain by the Gospel and also by the Gospel threatening us with his righteousness and wrath!" Thus I raged with a fierce and troubled conscience. Nevertheless, I beat importunately upon Paul at that place, most ardently desiring to know what St. Paul wanted.

At last, by the mercy of God, meditating day and night, I gave heed to the context of the words, namely, "In it the righteousness of God is revealed, as it is written, 'He who through faith is righteous shall live.' " There I began to understand that the righteousness of God is that by which the righteous lives by a gift of God, namely by faith. And this is the meaning: the righteousness of God is revealed by the Gospel, namely, the passive righteousness with which merciful God justifies us by faith, as it is written, "He who through faith is righteous shall live." Here I felt that I was altogether born again and had entered paradise itself through open gates. There a totally other face of the entire Scripture showed itself to me. Thereupon I ran through the Scriptures from memory. I also found in other terms an analogy, as, the work of God, that is, what God does in us, the power of God, with which he makes us strong, the wisdom of God, with which he makes us wise, the strength of God, the salvation of God, the glory of God.

And I extolled my sweetest word with a love as great as the hatred with which I had before hated the word "righteousness of God." Thus that place in Paul was for me truly the gate to paradise. Later I read Augustine's *The Spirit and the Letter,* where contrary to hope I found that he, too, interpreted God's righteousness in a similar way, as the righteousness with which God clothes us when he justifies us. Although this was heretofore said imperfectly and he did not explain all things concerning imputation clearly, it nevertheless was pleasing that God's righteousness with which we are justified was taught. Armed more fully with these thoughts, I began a second time to interpret the Psalter. And the work would have grown into a large commentary, if I had not again been compelled to leave the work begun, because Emperor Charles V in the following year convened the Diet at Worms.

I relate these things, good reader, so that, if you are a reader of my puny works, you may keep in mind that, as I said above, I was all alone and one of those who, as Augustine says of himself, have become proficient by writing and teaching. I was not one of those who from nothing suddenly become the topmost, though they are nothing, neither have labored, nor been tempted, nor become experienced, but have with one look at the Scriptures exhausted their entire spirit.

To this point, to the year 1520 and 21, the indulgence matter proceeded. Upon that followed the sacramentarian and the Anabaptist affairs. Regarding these a preface shall be written to other tomes, if I live.

Farewell in the Lord, reader, and pray for the growth of the Word against Satan. Strong and evil, now also very furious and savage, he knows his time is short and the kingdom of his pope is in danger. But may God confirm in us what he has accomplished and perfect his work which he began in us, to his glory, Amen. March 5, in the year 1545.

Erik H. Erikson
YOUNG MAN LUTHER

Erik H. Erikson, born in 1902, a training psychoanalyst, is Professor of Human Development, emeritus, at Harvard University. His earlier book on childhood and society applied psychoanalysis to the field of cultural anthropology. Among his most widely discussed recent works is Ghandi's Truth: On the Origins of Militant Nonviolence.

We cannot leave history entirely to nonclinical observers and to professional historians who often all too nobly immerse themselves into the very disguises, rationalizations, and idealizations of the historical process from which it should be their business to separate themselves. Only when the relation of historical forces to the basic functions and stages of the mind has been jointly charted and understood can we begin a psychoanalytic critique of society as such without falling back into mystical or moralistic philosophizing.

Freud warned against the possible misuse of his work as an ideology, a *Weltanschauung;* but as we shall see in Luther's life and work, a man who inspires new ideas has little power to restrict them to the area of his original intentions. And Freud himself did not refrain from interpreting other total approaches to man's condition, such as religion, as consequences of man's inability to shake off the bonds of his prolonged childhood, and thus comparable to collective neuroses. The psychological and historical study of the religious crisis of a young great man renews the opportunity to review this assertion in the light of ego-psychology and of theories of psychosocial development.

As to the dichotomy of psychoanalysis and religion, I will not approach it like a man with a chip on each shoulder. Psychology endeavors to establish what is demonstrably true in human behavior, including such behavior as expresses what to human beings seems true and feels true. I will interpret in psychological terms whatever phenomena clinical experience and psychoanalytic thought have made me recognize are dependent on man's demonstrable psychic structure. This is my job, as a clinician and as a teacher—a job which (as I have pointed out) includes the awareness that psychoanalysis for historical reasons often occupies a position on the borderline of what is demonstrably true and of what demonstrably *feels* true. The fact that each new vital focus of psychoanalytic research inadvertently leads to a new implied value system obliges us to ask ourselves whether or not we mean what we seem to be saying. It obligates us, as well as our critics, to differentiate psychoanalysism from psychoanalysis, and to realize that ours is not only a profession recognized among professions, but also a system of thought subject to fashionable manipulation by molders of public opinion. Our very success suggests that our partisanship be judicial.

Religion, on the other hand, elaborates on what feels profoundly true even though it is not demonstrable: it translates into significant words, images, and codes the exceeding darkness which surrounds man's existence, and the light which pervades it beyond all desert or comprehension. This being a historical book, however, religion will occupy our attention primarily as a source of ideologies for those who seek identities. In depicting the identity struggle of a *young* great man I am not as concerned with the validity of the dogmas which laid claim to him, or of the philosophies which influenced his systematic thought, as I am with the spiritual and intellecutal milieu which the isms of his time—and these isms *had* to be religious— offered to his passionate search.

My focus, then, is on the "ideological." In modern history, this word has assumed a specifically political connotation, referring to totalitarian systems of thought which distort historical truth by methods ranging from fanatic self-deception to shrewd falsification and cold propaganda. Karl Mannheim has analyzed this word and the processes for which it stands from the sociological point of view. In this book, *ideology* will mean an unconscious tendency underlying religious and scientific as well as political thought: the tendency at a given time to make facts amenable to ideas, and ideas to facts, in order to create a world image convincing enough to support the collective and the individual sense of identity. Far from being arbitrary or consciously manageable (although it is as exploitable as all of man's unconscious strivings), the total perspective created by ideological simplification reveals its strength by the dominance it exerts on the seeming logic of historical events, and by its influence on the identity formation of individuals (and thus on their "ego-strength"). In this sense, this is a book on identity and ideology.

In some periods of his history, and in some phases of his life cycle, man needs (until we invent something better) a new ideological orientation as surely and as sorely as he must have air and food. I will not be ashamed then, even as I analyze what is analyzable, to display sympathy and empathy with a young man who (by no means lovable all of the time) faced the problems of human *existence* in the most forward terms of his era. I will use the word *existential* in this simplest connotation, mindful that no school of thought has any monopoly on it. . . .

The characteristics of Luther's theological advance can be compared to certain steps in psychological maturation which every man must take: the internalization of the father-son relationship; the concomitant crystallization of conscience; the safe establishment of an identity as a worker and a man; and the concomitant reaffirmation of basic trust.

God, instead of lurking on the periphery of space and time, became for Luther "what works in us." The way *to* Him is not the effortful striving toward a goal by "doing what you can"; rather, His way is what moves from inside: *via dei est, qua nos ambulare facit.* God, now less of a person, becomes more personal for the individual; and instead of constituting a threat to be faced at the end of all things, He becomes that which always begins—in us. His son is therefore always reborn: *"Ita et nos semper oportet nasci, novari, generari":* It therefore behooves us to be reborn, renovated, regenerated. To "do enough" means always to begin: *"Proficere est nihil aliud nisi semper incipere."* The intersection of all the paradoxes of the vertical and the horizontal is thus to be found in man's own divided nature. The two *regna,* the realist sphere of divine grace and the naturalist sphere of animality, exist in man's inner conflicts and in his existential paradoxes: *"Die zwo Personen oder zweierlei ampt,"* the two personalities and the two callings which a Christian must maintain at the same time on this earth.

It does not matter what these two personalities "are." Theologians, philosophers, and psychologists slice man in different ways, and there is no use trying to make the sections coincide. The main point to be made here is Luther's new emphasis on man in *inner* conflict and his salvation through introspective perfection. Luther's formulation of a God known to individual man only through the symbolism of the Son's Passion redefined the individual's existence in a direction later pursued in both Kierkegaard's existentialism and Freud's psychoanalysis—methods which lead the individual systematically to his own borders, including the border of his religious ecstasies.

Let us rephrase somewhat more psychologically what we have just put in theological terms. What we have referred to as the negative conscience corresponds in many ways to Freud's conceptualization of the pressure put by the superego on the ego. If this pressure is dominant in an individual or in a group, the whole quality of experience is overshadowed by a particular sense of existence, an intensification of certain aspects of subjective space and time. Any fleeting moment of really bad conscience can teach us this, as can also, and more impressively, a spell of melancholy. We are then strangely constricted and paralyzed, victims of an inner voice whispering sharply that we are far from that perfection which alone will do when the closely impending, but vague and unpredictable, doom arrives; in spite of that immediacy, we are as yet sinners, not quite good enough, and probably too far gone. Any temporary relief from this melancholy state (into which Luther, at the height of his worldly success, sank more deeply than ever before) is only to be had at the price of making a painful deal with the voice, a deal which offers the hope that maybe soon we will find the platform for a new start; or maybe at the hour of trial we will find that according to some unknown scale we will prove barely but sufficiently acceptable, and so may pass—pass into heaven, as some proud minds have asked, by just *getting by?* In the meantime, our obsessive scrupulosity will chew its teeth out and exercise its guts on the maybe-soons, the already-almosts, the just-a-bit-mores, the not-yet-quites, the probably-next-times. Not all minds, of course, naturally exercise themselves in this way; but everybody does it to some degree, and almost everybody can be prevailed upon to participate by an ideological system which blocks all exits except one, that one adorned with exactly matching symbols of hope and despair, and guarded by the system's showmen, craftsmen, and torturers.

To some individuals, however, such a state becomes, for personal reasons, habitual: from these people the religionists in any field are recruited. Whole peoples may elaborate this potential state into a world image. William James remarked that the Latin races seem to be able more easily to split up the pressure of evil into "ills and sins in the plural, removable in detail," while the Germanic races tend to erect one "Sin in the singular, and with a capital S . . . eradicably ingrained in our natural subjectivity, and never to be removed by any piecemeal operation." If this is true, climate may have much to do with it: the more decided retreat of the sun to the danger point of disappearance in the Nordic winter, the protracted darkness and the fatal cold which last over periods long enough to convey a sense of irretrievability or at any rate to enforce a totalistic adjustment to such a possibility. Just because Luther's periodic states of melancholy repeatedly forced him to accept despair and disease as final, and death as imminent, he may have expressed in his pessimistic and philosophically most untenable concepts (such as the total predestination of individual fate, independent of personal effort) exactly that cold rock bottom of mood, that utter background of blackness, which to northern people is the condition of spring:

> Der Sommer ist hart fuer der Tuer
> Der Winter ist vergangen
> Die zarten Blumen gehn herfuer;
> Der das hat angefangen
> Der wird es auch vollenden.

This only says that winter is gone and summer is at the door, and that the flowers are coming up; and that Whoever has begun such a process will surely complete it.

A predominant state of mind in which the ego keeps the superego in victorious check can reconcile certain opposites which the negative conscience rigidly keeps separate; ego-dominance tends to be holistic, to blend opposites without blunting them. In his state of personal recovery, Luther (like any individual recovering from an oppressive mental state) had recourse to massive totalisms from which he derived the foundation stones for a new wholeness. The whole person includes certain total states in his balances: we are, Luther proclaimed, totally sinners (*totus homo peccator*) and totally just (*totus homo justus*), always both damned and blessed, both alive and dead. We cannot thus strive, by hook or by crook, to get from one absolute stage into another; we can only use our God-given organs of awareness in the here and now to encompass the paradoxes of the human condition. Psychologically speaking, this means that at any given moment, and in any given act or thought, we are codetermined to a degree which can never become quite conscious by our drives *and* by our conscience. Our ego is most powerful when it is not burdened with an excessive denial of our drives, but let us enjoy what we can, refute what we must, and sublimate according to our creativity—always making due allowance for the absolutism of our conscience, which can never be appeased by small sacrifices and atonements, but must always remain part of the whole performance. Luther thus said in his terms what Freud formulated psychologically, namely, that only on the surface are we ever entirely driven *or* completely just; in our depths we are vain when we are most just, and bad conscience can always be shown to be at work exactly when we are most driven by lust or avarice. But this same inner psychological condition saves God (theologically speaking) from that impossible characteristic for which Martin had not been able to forgive him, namely, that of being The Father only in certain especially meritorious moments, rather than for all eternity, as he should be. To the ego, eternity is always now.

Luther's strong emphasis on the here and now of the spiritual advent, and on the necessity of always standing at the beginning (*semper incipere*), is not only a platform of faith, it is akin to a time-space quality dominating the inner state which psychoanalysts call "ego-strength." To the ego the past is not an inexorable process, experienced only as preparation for an impending doom; rather, the past is part of a present mastery which employs a convenient mixture of forgetting, falsifying, and idealizing to fit the past to the present, but usually to an extent which is neither unknowingly delusional nor knowingly dishonest. The ego can resign itself to past losses and forfeitings and learn not to demand the impossible of the future. It enjoys the illusion of a present, and defends this most precarious of all assumptions against doubts and apprehensions by remembering most easily chains of experiences which were alike in their unblemished presentness. To the healthy ego, the flux of time sponsors the process of identity. It thus is not afraid of death (as Freud has pointed out vigorously); it has no concept of death. But it *is* afraid of losing mastery over the negative conscience, over the drives, and over reality. To lose any of these battles is, for the ego, living death; to win them again and again means to the ego something akin to an assumption that it is causing its own life. In theological terms, *creaturae procedunt ex deo libere et voluntarie et non naturaliter:* what lives, proceeds from God freely and voluntarily, not naturally, that is, not by way of what can be explained biologically.

Luther's restatements about the total sinfulness and the total salvation which are in man at any given time can easily be shown to be alogical. With sufficient ill will they can be construed as contrived to save Martin's particular skin, which held together upswings of spiritual elations and cursing gloominess, not speak of lusts for power and revenge, women, food, and beer. But the coexistence of all these contradictions has its psychologic—as has also the fury of their incompatibility. Martin's theological reformulations imply a psychological fact, namely, that the ego gains strength *in practice,* and *in affectu* to the degree to which it can accept at the same time the total power of the drives and the total power of conscience—*provided* that it can nourish what Luther called *opera manum dei,* that particular combination of work and love which alone verifies our identity and confirms it. Under these conditions, apparent submission becomes mastery, apparent passivity the release of new energy for active pursuits. We can make negative conscience work for the aims of the ego only by facing it without evasion; and we are able to manage and creatively utilize our drives only to the extent to which we can acknowledge their power by enjoyment, by awareness, and through the activity of work.

If the ego is not able to accomplish these reconciliations, we may fall prey to that third inner space-time characterized by the dominance of what Freud called the *id.* The danger of this state comes from what Freud considered biological instincts which the ego experiences as beneath and outside itself while at the same time it is intoxicated by them. Dominance by the id means that time and space are arranged in one way—toward wish fulfillment. We know only that our tension rises when time and circumstances delay release and satisfaction, and that our drivenness is accelerated when opportunities arise. The self-propelled will tends to ignore all that has been learned in the past and is perceived in the present, except to the extent to which past and present add fuel to the goal-directedness of the wish. This id-intoxication, as Luther formulated so knowingly, can become total poisoning especially when it is haughtily denied.

Some monastic methods systematically descend to the frontiers where all ego dangers must be faced in the raw—where an overweening conscience is appeased through prayer, drives tamed by asceticism, and the pressure of reality is itself defeated by the self's systematic abandonment of its identity. But true monasticism is a late development and is possible only to a mature ego. Luther knew why he later said that nobody under thirty years of age should definitely commit himself to it. . . .

To relegate Luther to a shadowy greatness at the turbulent conclusion of the Age of Faith does not help us see what his life really stands for. To put it in his own words:

"I did not learn my theology all at once, but I had to search deeper for it, where my temptations took me." *"Vivendo, immo moriendo et damnando fit theologus, non intelligendo, legendo, aut speculando"*: A theologian is born by living, nay dying and being damned, not by thinking, reading, or speculating.

Not to understand this message under the pretense of not wanting to make the great man too human—although he represented himself as human with relish and gusto—only means to protect ourselves from taking our chances with the *tentationes* of our day, as he did with his. Historical analysis should help us to study further our own immediate tasks, instead of hiding them in a leader's greatness. . . .

When Luther challenged the rock bottom of his own prayer, he could not know that he would find the fundament for a new theology. Nor did Freud know that he would find the principles of a new psychology when he took radical chances with himself in a new kind of introspective analysis. I have applied to Luther, the first Protestant at the end of the age of absolute faith, insights developed by Freud, the first psychoanalyst at the end of the era of absolute reason; and I have mentioned seemingly incidental parallels between the two men. A few weightier connections must be stated in conclusion.

Both men endeavored to increase the margin of man's inner freedom by introspective means applied to the very center of his conflicts; and this to the end of increased individuality, sanity, and service to men. Luther, at the beginning of ruthless mercantilism in church and commerce, counterpoised praying man to the philosophy and practice of meritorious works. Subsequently, his justification by faith was absorbed into the patterns of mercantilism, and eventually turned into a justification of commercialism by faith. Freud, at the beginning of unrestricted industrialization, offered another method of introspection, psychoanalysis. With it he obviously warned against the mechanical socialization of men into effective but neurotic robots. It is equally obvious that his work is about to be used in furtherance of that which he warned against: the glorification of "adjustment." Thus both Doctor Luther and Doctor Freud, called great by their respective ages, have been and are apt to be resisted not only by their enemies, but also by friends who subscribe to their ideas but lack what Kierkegaard called a certain strenuousness of mental and moral effort.

Luther, as we saw, instituted a technique of prayer which eminently served to clarify the delineation of what we, to the best of our knowledge, really mean. Freud added a technique (totally inapplicable to people who do not really mean anything at all) which can make us understand what it means when we insist we mean what we, according to our dreams and symptoms, cannot mean deep down. As to prayer, Luther advocated an appeal to God that He grant you, even as you pray, the good intention with which you started the prayer: *ut etiam intentionem quam presumpsisti ipse tibi dat.* Centuries later Freud postulated an analogous rigor for genuine introspection, namely, the demand that one take an especially honest look at one's honesty.

Luther tried to free individual conscience from totalitarian dogma; he meant to give man credal wholeness, and, alas, inadvertently helped to increase and to refine authoritarianism. Freud tried to free the individual's insight from authoritarian conscience; his wholeness is that of the individual ego, but the question is whether collective man will create a world worth being whole for.

Luther accepted man's distance from God as existential and absolute, and refused any traffic with the profanity of a God of deals; Freud suggests that we steadfastly study our unconscious deals with morality and reality before we haughtily claim free will, or righteously good intentions in dealings with our fellowmen.

Luther limited our knowledge of God to our individual experience of temptation and our identification in prayer with the passion of God's son. In this, all men are free and equal. Freud made it clear that the structure of inner *Konflikt,* made conscious by psychoanalysis and recognized as universal for any and all, is all we can know of ourselves—yet it is a knowledge inescapable and indispensable. The devoutly sceptical Freud proclaimed that man's uppermost duty (no matter what his introspective reason would make him see, or his fate suffer) was *das Leben auszuhalten:* to stand life, to hold out.

In this book I have described how Luther, once a sorely frightened child, recovered through the study of Christ's Passion the central meaning of the Nativity; and I have indicated in what way Freud's method of introspection brought human conflict under a potentially more secure control by revealing the boundness of man in the loves and rages of his childhood. Thus both Luther and Freud came to acknowledge that "the child is in the midst." Both men perfected introspective techniques permitting isolated man to recognize his individual patienthood. They also reasserted the other pole of existence, man's involvement in generations: for only in facing the helplessness and the hope newly born in every child does mature man (and this *does* include woman) recognize the irrevocable responsibility of being alive and about.

Let us consider, then, what we may call the metabolism of generations.

Each human life begins at a given evolutionary stage and level of tradition, bringing to its environment a capital of patterns and energies; these are used to grow on, and to grow into the social process with, and also as contributions to this process. Each new being is received into a style of life prepared by tradition and held together by tradition, and at the same time disintegrating because of the very nature of tradition. We say that tradition "molds" the individual, "channels" his drives. But the social process does not mold a new being merely to housebreak him; it molds generations in order to be remolded, to be reinvigorated, by them. Therefore, society can never afford merely to suppress drives or to guide their sublimation. It must also support the primary function of every individual ego, which is to transform instinctual energy into patterns of action, into character, into style—in short, into an identity with a core of integrity which is to be derived from and also contributed to the tradition. There is an optimum ego synthesis to which the individual aspires; and there is an optimum societal metabolism for which societies and cultures strive. In describing the interdependence of individual aspiration and of societal striving, we describe something indispensable to human life.

In an earlier book, I indicated a program of studies which might account for the dovetailing of the stages of individual life and of basic human institutions. The present book circumscribes for only one of these stages—the identity crisis—its intrinsic relation to the process of ideological rejuvenation in a period of history when organized religion dominated ideologies.

In discussing the identity crisis, we have, at least implicitly, presented some of the attributes of any psychosocial crisis. At a given age, a human being, by dint of his physical, intellectual and emotional growth, becomes ready and eager to face a new life task, that is, a set of choices and tests which are in some traditional way prescribed and prepared for him by his society's structure. A new life task presents a *crisis* whose outcome can be a successful graduation, or alternatively, an impairment of the life cycle which will aggravate future crises. Each crisis prepares the next, as one step leads to another; and each crisis also lays one more cornerstone for the adult personality. I will enumerate all these crises (more thoroughly treated elsewhere) to remind us, in summary, of certain issues in Luther's life; and also to suggest a developmental root for the basic human values of faith, will, conscience, and reason—all necessary in rudimentary form for the identity which crowns childhood.

The first crisis is the one of early infancy. How this crisis is met decides whether a man's innermost mood will be determined more by basic trust or by basic mistrust. The outcome of this crisis—apart from accidents of heredity, gestation, and birth—depends largely on the quality of maternal care, that is, on the consistency and mutuality which guide the mother's ministrations and give a certain predictability and hopefulness to the baby's original cosmos of urgent and bewildering body feelings. The ratio and relation of basic trust to basic mistrust established during early infancy determines much of the individual's capacity for simple faith, and consequently also determines his future contribution to his society's store of faith—which, in turn, will feed into a future mother's ability to trust the world in which she teaches trust to newcomers. In this first stage we can assume that a historical process is already at work; history writing should therefore chart the influence of historical events on growing generations to be able to judge the quality of their future contribution to history. As for little Martin, I have drawn conclusions about that earliest time when his mother could still claim the baby, and when he was still all hers, inferring that she must have provided him with a font of basic trust on which he was able to draw in his fight for a primary faith present before all will, conscience, and reason, a faith which is "the soul's virginity."

The first crisis corresponds roughly to what Freud has described as orality; the second corresponds to anality. An awareness of these correspondences is essential for a true understanding of the dynamics involved.

The second crisis, that of infancy, develops the infantile sources of what later becomes a human being's will, in its variations of willpower and wilfulness. The resolution of this crisis will determine whether an individual is apt to be dominated by a sense of autonomy, or by a sense of shame and doubt. The social limitations imposed on intensified willfulness inevitably create doubt about the justice governing the relations of grown and growing people. The way this doubt is met by the grownups determines much of a man's future ability to combine an unimpaired will with ready self-discipline, rebellion with responsibility.

The interpretation is plausible that Martin was driven early out of the trust stage, out from "under his mother's skirts," by a jealously ambitious father who tried to make him precociously independent from women, and sober and reliable in his work. Hans succeeded, but not without storing in the boy violent doubts of the father's justification and sincerity; a lifelong shame over the persisting gap between his own precocious conscience and his actual inner state; and a deep nostalgia for a situation of infantile trust. His theological solution—spiritual return to a faith which is there before all doubt, combined with a political submission to those who by necessity must wield the sword of secular law—seems to fit perfectly his personal need for compromise. While this analysis does not explain either the ideological power or the theological consistency of his solution, it does illustrate that ontogenetic experience is an indispensable link and transformer between one stage of history and the next. This link is a psychological one, and the energy transformed and the process of transformation are both charted by the psychoanalytic method.

Freud formulated these matters in dynamic terms. Few men before him gave more genuine expression to those experiences which are on the borderline between the psychological and the theological than Luther, who gleaned from these experiences a religious gain formulated in theological terms. Luther described states of badness which in many forms pervade human existence from childhood. For instance, his description of shame, an emotion first experienced when the infant stands naked in space and feels belittled: "He is put to sin and shame before God . . . this shame is now a thousand times greater, that a man must blush in the presence of God. For this means that there is no corner or hole in the whole of creation into which a man might creep, not even in hell, but he must let himself be exposed to the gaze of the whole creation, and stand in the open with all his shame, as a bad conscience feels when it is really struck. . . ." Or his description of doubt, an emotion first experienced when the child feels singled out by demands whose rationale he does not comprehend: "When he is tormented in *Anfechtung* it seems to him that he is alone: God is angry only with him, and irreconcilably angry against him: then he alone is a sinner and all the others are in the right, and they work against him at God's orders. There is nothing left for him but this unspeakable sighing through which, without knowing it, he is supported by the Spirit and cries 'Why does God pick on me alone?' "

Luther was a man who would not settle for an easy appeasement of these feelings on any level, from childhood through youth to his manhood, or in any segment of life. His often impulsive and intuitive formulations transparently display the infantile struggle at the bottom of the lifelong emotional issue.

His basic contribution was a living reformulation of faith. This marks him as a theologian of the first order; it also indicates his struggle with the ontogenetically earliest and most basic problems of life. He saw as his life's work a new delineation of faith and will, of religion and the law: for it is clear that organized religiosity, in circumstances where faith in a world order is monopolized by religion, is the institution which tries to give dogmatic permanence to a reaffirmation of that basic trust—and a renewed victory over that basic mistrust—with which each human being emerges from early infancy. In this way organized religion cements the faith which will support future generations. Established law tries to formulate obligations and privileges, restraints and freedoms, in such a way that man can submit to law and order with a minimum of doubt and with little loss of face, and as an autonomous agent of order can teach the rudiments of discipline to his young. The relation of faith and law, of course, is an eternal human problem, whether it appears in questions of church and state, mysticism and daily morality, or existential aloneness and political commitment.

The third crisis, that of initiative versus guilt, is part of what Freud described as the central complex of the family, namely, the Oedipus complex. It involves a lasting unconscious association of sensual freedom with the body of the mother and the administrations received from her hand; a lasting association of cruel prohibition with the interference of the dangerous father; and the consequences of these associations for love and hate in reality and in phantasy. (I will not discuss here the cultural relativity of Freud's observations nor the dated origin of his term; but I assume that those who do wish to quibble about all this will feel the obligation to advance systematic propositions about family, childhood, and society which come closer to the core, rather than go back to the periphery, of the riddle which Freud was the first to penetrate.) We have reviewed the strong indications of an especially heavy interference by Hans Luder with Martin's attachment to his mother, who, it is suggested, secretly provided for him what Goethe openly acknowledged as his mother's gift—*"Die Frohnatur, die Lust zu fabulieren"*: gaiety and the pleasure of confabulation. We have indicated how this gift, which later emerged in Luther's poetry, became guilt-laden and was broken to harness by an education designed to make a precocious student of the boy. We have also traced its relationship to Luther's lifelong burden of excessive guilt. Here is one of Luther's descriptions of that guilt: "And this is the worst of all these ills, that the conscience cannot run away from itself, but it is always present to itself and knows all the terrors of the creature which such things bring even in this present life, because the ungodly man is like a raging sea. The third and greatest of all these horrors and the worst of all ills is to have a judge." He also said, "For this is the nature of a guilty conscience, to fly and to be terrified, even when all is safe and prosperous, to convert all into peril and death."

The stage of initiative, associated with Freud's phallic stage of psycho-sexuality, ties man's budding will to phantasy, play, games, and early work, and thus to the mutual delineation of unlimited imagination and aspiration and limiting, threatening conscience. As far as society is concerned, this is vitally related to the occupational and technological ideals perceived by the child; for the child can manage the fact that there is no return to the mother as a mother and no competition with the father as a father only to the degree to which a future career outside of the narrower family can at least be envisaged in ideal future occupations: these he learns to imitate in play, and to anticipate in school. We can surmise that for little Martin the father's own occupation was early precluded from anticipatory phantasy, and that a life of scholarly duty was obediently and sadly envisaged instead. This precocious severity of obedience later made it impossible for young Martin to anticipate any career but that of unlimited study for its own sake, as we have seen in following his path of obedience—in disobedience.

In the fourth stage, the child becomes able and eager to learn systematically, and to collaborate with others. The resolution of this stage decides much of the ratio between a sense of industry or work completion, and a sense of tool-inferiority, and prepares a man for the essential ingredients of the ethos as well as the rationale of his technology. He wants to know the *reason* for things, and is provided, at least, with rationalizations. He learns to use whatever simplest techniques and tools will prepare him most generally for the tasks of his culture. In Martin's case, the tool was literacy, Latin literacy, and we saw how he was molded by it—and how later he remolded, with the help of printing, his nation's literary habits. With a vengeance he could claim to have taught German even to his enemies.

But he achieved this only after a protracted identity crisis which is the main subject of this book. Whoever is hard put to feel identical with one set of people and ideas must that much more violently repudiate another set; and whenever an identity, once established, meets further crises, the danger of irrational repudiation of otherness and temporarily even of one's own identity increases.

I have already briefly mentioned the three crises which follow the crisis of identity; they concern problems of intimacy, generativity, and integrity. The crisis of intimacy in a monk is naturally distorted in its heterosexual core. What identity diffusion is to identity—its alternative and danger—isolation is to intimacy. In a monk this too is subject to particular rules, since a monk seeks intentional and organized isolation, and submits all intimacy to prayer and confession.

Luther's intimacy crisis seems to have been fully experienced and resolved only on the Wartburg; that is, after his lectures had established him as a lecturer, and his speech at Worms as an orator of universal stamp. On the Wartburg he wrote *De Votis Monasticis,* obviously determined to take care of his sexual needs as soon as a dignified solution could be found. But the intimacy crisis is by no means only a sexual, or for that matter, a heterosexual, one: Luther, once free, wrote to men friends about his emotional life, including his sexuality, with a frankness clearly denoting a need to share intimacies with them. The most famous example, perhaps, is a letter written at a time when the tragicomedy of these priests' belated marriages to runaway nuns was in full swing. Luther had made a match between Spalatin and an ex-nun, a relative of Staupitz. In the letter, he wished Spalatin luck for the wedding night, and promised to think of him during a parallel performance to be arranged in his own marital bed.

Also on the Wartburg, Luther developed, with his translation of the Bible, a supreme ability to reach into the homes of his nation; as a preacher and a table talker he demonstrated his ability and his need to be intimate for the rest of his life. One could write a book about Luther on this theme alone; and perhaps in such a book all but the most wrathful utterances would be found to be communications exquisitely tuned to the recipient.

Owing to his prolonged identity crisis, and also to delayed sexual intimacy, intimacy and generativity were fused in Luther's life. We have given an account of the time when his generativity reached its crisis, namely, when within a short period he became both a father, and a leader of a wide following which began to disperse his teachings in any number of avaricious, rebellious, and mystical directions. Luther then tasted fully the danger of this stage, which paradoxically is felt by creative people more deeply than by others, namely, a sense of *stagnation*, experienced by him in manic-depressive form. As he recovered, he proceeded with the building of the edifice of his theology; yet he responded to the needs of his parishioners and students, including his princes, to the very end. Only his occasional outbursts expressed that fury of repudiation which was mental hygiene to him, but which set a lasting bad example to his people.

We now come to the last, the integrity crisis which again leads man to the portals of nothingness, or at any rate to the station of *having been*. I have described it thus:

> *Only he who in some way has taken care of things and people and has adapted himself to the triumphs and disappointments adherent to being, by necessity, the originator of others and the generator of things and ideas—only he may gradually grow the fruit of these seven stages. I know no better word for it than ego integrity. Lacking a clear definition, I shall point to a few constituents of this state of mind. It is the ego's accrued assurance of its proclivity for order and meaning. It is a post-narcissistic love of the human ego—not of the self—as an experience which conveys some world order and some spiritual sense, no matter how dearly paid for. It is the acceptance of one's one and only life cycle as something that had to be and that, by necessity, permitted of no substitutions: it thus means a new, a different, love of one's parents. It is a comradeship with the ordering ways of distant times and different pursuits, as expressed in the simple products and sayings of such times and pursuits. Although aware of the relativity of all the various life styles which have given meaning to human striving, the possessor of integrity is ready to defend the dignity of his own life style against all physical and economic threats. For he knows that an individual life is the accidental coincidence of but one life cycle with but one segment of history; and*

that for him all human integrity stands or falls with the one style of integrity of which he partakes. The style of integrity developed by his culture or civilization thus becomes the "patrimony of his soul," the seal of his moral paternity of himself (". . . pero el honor/Es patrimonio del alma": Calderón). Before this final solution, death loses its sting.

The integrity crisis, last in the lives of ordinary men, is a lifelong and chronic crisis in a *homo religiosus.* He is always older, or in early years suddenly becomes older, than his playmates or even his parents and teachers, and focuses in a precocious way on what it takes others a lifetime to gain a mere inkling of: the questions of how to escape corruption in living and how in death to give meaning to life. Because he experiences a breakthrough to the last problems so early in his life maybe such a man had better become a martyr and seal his message with an early death; or else become a hermit in a solitude which anticipates the Beyond. We know little of Jesus of Nazareth as a young man, but we certainly cannot even begin to imagine him as middle-aged.

This short cut between the youthful crisis of identity and the mature one of integrity makes the religionist's problem of individual identity the same as the problem of existential identity. To some extent this problem is only an exaggeration of an abortive trait not uncommon in late adolescence. One may say that the religious leader becomes a professional in dealing with the kind of scruples which prove transitory in many all-too-serious postadolescents who later grow out of it, go to pieces over it, or find an intellectual or artistic medium which can stand between them and nothingness.

The late adolescent crisis, in addition to anticipating the more mature crises, can at the same time hark back to the very earliest crisis of life—trust or mistrust toward existence as such. This concentration in the cataclysm of the adolescent identity crisis of both first and last crises in the human life may well explain why religiously and artistically creative men often seem to be suffering from a barely compensated psychosis, and yet later prove superhumanly gifted in conveying a total meaning for man's life; while malignant disturbances in late adolescence often display precocious wisdom and usurped integrity. The chosen young man extends the problem of his identity to the borders of existence in the known universe; other human beings bend all their efforts to adopt and fulfill the departmentalized identities which they find prepared in their communities. He can permit himself to face as permanent the trust problem which drives others in whom it remains or becomes dominant into denial, despair, and psychosis. He acts as if mankind were starting all over with his own beginning as an individual, conscious of his singularity as well as his humanity; others hide in the folds of whatever tradition they are part of because of membership, occupation, or special interests. To him, history ends as well as starts with him; others must look to their memories, to legends, or to books to find models for the present and the future in what their predecessors have said and done. No wonder that he is something of an old man (a *philosophus,* and a sad one) when his age-mates are young, or that he remains something of a child when they age with finality. The name Lao-tse, I understand, means just that.

The danger of a reformer of the first order, however, lies in the nature of his influence on the masses. In our own day we have seen this in the life and influence of Gandhi. He, too, believed in the power of prayer; when he fasted and prayed, the masses and even the English held their breath. Because prayer gave them the power to say what would be heard by the lowliest and the highest, both Gandhi and Luther believed that they could count on the restraining as well as the arousing power of the Word. In such hope great religionists are supported—one could say they are seduced—by the fact that all people, because of their common undercurrent of existential anxiety, at cyclic intervals and during crises feel an intense need for a rejuvenation of trust which will give new meaning to their limited and perverted exercise of will, conscience, reason, and identity. But the best of them will fall asleep at Gethsemane; and the worst will accept the new faith only as a sanction for anarchic destructiveness or political guile. If faith can move mountains, let it move obstacles out of *their* way. But maybe the masses also sense that he who aspires to spiritual power, even though he speaks of renunciation, has an account to settle with an inner authority. He may disavow their rebellion, but he is a rebel. He may say in the deepest humility, as Luther said, that "his mouth is Christ's mouth"; his nerve is still the nerve of a usurper. So for a while the world may be worse for having had a vision of being better. From the oldest Zen poem to the most recent psychological formulation, it is clear that "the conflict between right and wrong is the sickness of the mind."

The great human question is to what extent early child training must or must not exploit man's early helplessness and moral sensitivity to the degree that a deep sense of evil and of guilt becomes unavoidable; for such a sense in the end can only result in clandestine commitment to evil in the name of higher values. Religionists, of course, assume that because a sense of evil dominated them even as they combated it, it belongs not only to man's "nature," but is God's plan, even God's gift to him. The answer to this assumption is that not only do child training systems differ in their exploitation of basic mistrust, shame, doubt, and guilt—so do religions. The trouble comes, first, from the mortal fear that instinctual forces would run wild if they were not dominated by a negative conscience; and second, from trying to formulate man's optimum as negative morality, to be reinforced by rigid institutions. In this formulation all man's erstwhile fears of the forces and demons of nature are reprojected onto his inner forces, and onto the child, whose dormant energies are alternatively vilified as potentially criminal, or romanticized as altogether angelic. Because man needs a disciplined conscience, he thinks he must have a bad one; and he assumes that he has a good conscience when, at times, he has an easy one. The answer to all this does not lie in attempts to avoid or to deny one or the other sense of badness in children altogether; the denial of the unavoidable can only deepen a sense of secret, unmanageable evil. The answer lies in man's capacity to create order which will give his children a disciplined as well as a tolerant conscience, and a world within which to act affirmatively.

Roland H. Bainton
LUTHER'S STRUGGLE FOR FAITH

Roland H. Bainton, who contributed the first selection in this volume on the interpretations of the Reformation, is the author of the best-selling biography of Martin Luther, Here I Stand!

Our interest in Luther's struggle for faith is not merely historical. We do not investigate this subject as we do Luther's views on monstrosities or the names for the gems in the Apocalypse, nor do we probe into his spiritual trials in order to collect additional specimens of abnormal psychology. If he was abnormal then the abnormal has become the normal. All of us today are engaged in a struggle for faith and our concern is not so much with the disease as with the cure. How was it that Luther, despite his travailing of spirit, could be so tremendous in his faith, so incredible in his courage, so astounding in his output? Luther's faith is our quest.

We must recognize—and we are glad to recognize, for it makes him closer to ourselves—that his groanings and travailings for the faith were lifelong. But this some scholars will not readily concede. They grant, of course, that Luther was subject to continual depressions, but insist that their character must have altered after the evangelical experience of 1513 when he came into the clear as to the faith. Boehmer claims that in the later years Luther was disturbed rather over his work, over the frivolities and turpitude of the rulers, over the ingratitude and sensuality of the masses, as well as over the more disconcerting thought that if he had been wrong he was taking so many souls to hell. A certain warrant for this distinction can be found in Luther's own statement that in the cloister he had been troubled concerning the graciousness of God but afterwards as to whether he had deceived others by his teaching. This difference, however, is only one of degree, with the latter torment the more intense. The question was still whether he had been correct in his insights as to the faith. But whereas formerly he had been involved only for himself, now he was responsible also for his converts.

From Roland H. Bainton, "Luther's Struggle for Faith," in *Church History* 17 (1948): 193–206, by permission of the editors of *Church History*. The article also appeared as a contribution to the *Festschrift für Gerhard Ritter* (Tübingen, 1950).

We cannot escape the plain fact that Luther's evangelical experience of 1513 did not clear up his religious difficulties for the remainder of his days. The understanding of the text, "The just shall live by faith," which had come to him as a flash on the Damascus road, left no tangible relic to which one could return at will. Rather it was like a sunset which would return, but no man could say where or when. The testimony of the later years makes abundantly evident that the ancient doubts recurred. In the 1530s Luther questioned the very existence of God. "The devil so assails me that I do not know whether there is any God or not." He questioned the justice of God. "Is it not against reason that all mankind should be subject to toil, sickness and death just because one man took a bite out of an apple?" He questioned the graciousness of God. "The worst temptation is when Satan says, 'God hates sinners. You are a sinner. God hates you.'"

"The devil can so beleaguer a heart, so terrify it that it will avoid God, become His enemy and blaspheme, for to a miserable conscience there is nothing other than that God, devil, death, sin, hell and all creatures are eternal unceasing enemies." The year 1527 was for Luther a time of depression as severe as any he had ever known. To a friend he wrote in August of that year, "For more than a week I was close to the gates of death and hell. I trembled in all my members. Christ was wholly lost. I was shaken by desperation and blasphemy of God." To lose Christ and blaspheme God, are not these the very assaults which plagued Luther in the cloister? Faith was no pearl to be mounted in a gold setting and gazed upon at will. Faith was ever the object of an agonizing search.

Who can read Luther's sermons in the later years on all the troubled spirits in the Bible without feeling that they are essentially autobiographical? With what feeling he portrays Adam when he crouches before the voice of God in the garden, the agony of Abraham when commanded to sacrifice the son through whom should have been fulfilled the promise to become a great people, the terror of Jonah as the monster which he did not yet know to be for his deliverance opened its cavernous jaws and the billows swept him into the belly of darkness, the desolation of Job before the mystery of the inscrutable providence of God, the anguish of the Virgin Mary when the child Jesus was lost and she believed herself to be rejected as his mother, the dismay of the Canaanite woman when Christ compared her to a dog, and supremely the agony of Christ in the garden and on the cross when he so identified himself with sinful humanity as to feel himself accursed and abandoned by God. Nowhere in all Christian literature will one find such poignant expositions of the words, "My God, my God, why hast Thou forsaken me?"

In the case of one whose emotional upheavals were so intense and so persistent, one cannot blithely dismiss the possibility of abnormal psychology. The intensity was on occasion so great that he could consider suicide and feared to pick up a carving knife for fear of what he might do to himself. As for persistence, we must recall that attacks of melancholia not only recurred after the evangelical experience but that they began before the entry into the cloister. Luther declared that after the receipt of his master's degree at Erfurt, and therefore during the six months prior to his entry into the monastery, he had been subject to continual melancholy. Also we must recognize that if at times Luther was depressed, on other occasions he was elated. In the cloister at times he had felt himself to be amid choirs of angels. And in later life when Katie, to bring him out of a fit of despondency, would take him for a drive in the woods, he would begin to sing lustily. He said himself that his moods were like April weather.

To a modern psychiatrist, such fluctuations suggest manic depressions, and if such a classification appears extreme for one whose working capacity was never impaired—witness the prodigious output despite melancholy at the Wartburg—at least one is prompted to inquire whether the times of despondency may not have been due to some glandular or gastric deficiency. Attempts have been made to trace a correlation between the moods and the maladies of Luther, but with very slight success. During the course of his life he suffered from constipation, insomnia, gout, hemorrhoids, stone, catarrh, and ringing in the ears—quite enough to depress anyone. But there is no record of any of these in the cloister days when he suffered such agonies of spirit that had they lasted a tenth of an hour he could not have survived. The attack of the stone in 1526 and the blood clot of January, 1527, had cleared before the great depression of the summer of that year. And this depression itself was not preceded but was followed by ringing in the ears and coma. The sense of spiritual desolation which came first was, according to Luther, vastly worse than the succeeding malady, though that brought him to the gates of death. At the Wartburg, again one wonders whether constipation and insomnia were the occasion or the aftermath of despondency coupled with superhuman industry.

Only slightly more successful is the attempt to link the emotional states to outward circumstances. However much prior depressions may have contributed, the decision to enter the monastery was precipitated by the terror of death in a thunderstorm. The upheavals in the cloister appear to have commenced with the terror of the Holy induced by the saying of the first mass. The great depression of 1527 was closely connected with the news of martyrdom among Luther's followers. He was distressed that his converts should suffer, while he, who was responsible for their faith, should be spared. Perhaps he was not worthy. Perhaps spiritual rather than physical torments were to be his portion. As Luther came out of the coma he remarked to Jonas, "I was not worthy to shed my blood for Christ as many of my fellow confessors of the Gospel have done. Yet this honor was denied to the beloved disciple, John the Evangelist, who wrote a much worse book against the papacy than I ever did."

Again Luther's tranquil periods have some relation to outward events. He remarked that during the first year in the monastery the devil is very quiet. Likewise he said that for some time after his marriage he was not troubled. From this, one would infer that a change in outward circumstances was able for a time to allay his sense of spiritual insecurity, but when the newness wore off the malady returned. But the correlation between outward and inward was never close. The very nature of the dark night of the soul is that it may be induced by nothing at all. Luther was very fond of a passage in the book of Leviticus (26:36) which describes how a host may be put to flight by the stirring of a wind-blown leaf.

The attempt to construct a cycle of Luther's ups-and-downs is equally futile. The Danish psychiatrist, Reiter, has made the attempt, but with how little success may be seen in that he places the years 1519–1521 on the curve of elevation. With regard to this, two comments are in order. The first is that during those years Luther was far from experiencing uniform exhilaration. After they were over, he was able in the retrospect of the Wartburg to recall how often during those very years he had been plagued by the taunt, "Are you alone wise?" The other comment is that if during that time Luther was highly elated the explanation is not to be found in any rhythm of his own but rather in the mood of an entire generation. Most of the leaders of Germany in that day were warbling with Hutten that it was a great time to be alive. Erasmus was exuberant because the sovereigns of Europe were embracing humanism and, he trusted, would unite their names and their hearts in loyalty to the Gospels and in the service of peace. The election of Charles V inspired the most sanguine expectation. The year 1521 brought disillusionment for everyone. The outbreak of war between Charles and Francis shattered the dream of European concord cherished by Erasmus; the fiasco of Sickingen wrecked the hopes and the life of Hutten; the Edict of Worms rendered nugatory Luther's *Appeal to the Nobility of the German Nation*. If Luther was at times cast down, we must bear in mind that Erasmus became a querulous old man. In neither case need we look for glandular or gastric deficiencies.

The source of Luther's depressions eludes us. Their form is more tangible. This is clear: they never assumed the shape of escape into a realm of illusion but only of an all too intense emotional reaction. He was always concerned with real problems, or at least they were real if his premises be granted. Anyone who considers the whole of religion to be unreal must, of course, say that he was concerned with unreality. Even so, it was not an unreality of his own constructing. He began with the religion and theology on which he had been reared and discovered there genuine difficulties to which others were not properly sensitive. His own emotional responses were too acute. He knew it, and when the assault was over, would say that the devil can turn a louse into a camel. Yet, he came to feel that even such excessive upheavals were necessary to the discovery of valid solutions. "If I live longer," he said, "I would like to write a book about *Anfechtungen,* for without them no man can understand Scripture, faith, the fear or the love of God. He does not know the meaning of hope who was never subject to temptations." "David must have been plagued by a very fearful devil. He could not have had such profound insights if he had not experienced great assaults." Luther verged on saying that an excessive emotional sensitivity is a mode of revelation. Those who are predisposed to fall into despondency as well as to rise into ecstasy may be able to view reality from a different angle than that of ordinary folk. Yet it is a true angle and when the problem or the religious object has been once so viewed, others less sensitive will be able to look from a new vantage point and testify that the insight is valid.

Luther felt that his depressions were necessary. At the same time they were dreadful and by all means and in every way to be avoided and overcome. His whole life was a struggle against them, a fight for faith. This is the point at which he interests us so acutely, for we too are cast down and we too would know how to assuage our despondency. Luther had two methods: the one was a head-on attack, the other an approach by way of indirection. Sometimes he would engage in direct encounter with the devil. This particular *mise en scène* may amuse the modern reader and incline him not to take Luther seriously; but it is noteworthy that what the devil says to Luther is only what one says to oneself in moments of introspection and, what is still more significant, only the minor difficulties were referred to the devil. In all of the major encounters, God Himself was the assailant. The devil was something of a relief. Luther relished, by comparison, the personification of his enemy in the form of a being whom he could bait without danger of blasphemy. He describes with gusto some of these bouts:

> When I go to bed the devil is always waiting for me. When he begins to plague me I give him this answer: "Devil, I must sleep. That's God's command, 'Work by day. Sleep by night.' So go away." If that doesn't work and he brings out a catalog of sins, I say, "Yes, old fellow, I know all about it. And I know some more you have overlooked. Here are a few extra. Put them down." If he still won't quit and presses me hard and accuses me as a sinner, I scorn him and say, "Saint Satan, pray for me. Of course you have never done anything wrong in your life. You alone are holy. Go to God and get grace for yourself. If you want to get me all straightened out, I say, 'Physician, heal thyself!'"

Sometimes Luther had the temerity to undertake also the greater encounter with God Himself. "I dispute much with God with great impatience," said he, "and I hold Him to His promises." The Canaanite woman was a source of unending wonder and comfort to Luther because she had the audacity to argue with Christ. When she asked him to come and cure her daughter, he answered that he was not sent but to the lost sheep of the house of Israel, and that it was

not meet to take the children's bread and give it to the dogs. She did
not dispute his judgment. She agreed that she was a dog. She asked
no more than that which befits a dog, to lick up the crumbs which
fall from the children's table. She took Christ in his own words. He
then treated her not as a dog but as a child of Israel.

> *All this is written for our comfort that we should see how deeply God
> hides His face and how we must not go by our feeling but only by His
> word. All Christ's answers sounded like no, but he did not mean no. He
> had not said that she was not of the house of Israel. He had not said that
> she was a dog. He had not said no. Yet all his answers were more like
> no than yes. This shows how our heart feels in despondency. It sees
> nothing but a plain no. Therefore it must turn to the deep hidden yes
> under the no and hold with a firm faith to God's word.*

At times, however, Luther advised against any attempt to wrestle
one's way through. "Don't argue with the devil," he said. "He has had
five thousand years of experience." "He has tried out all of his tricks
on Adam, Abraham, and David and he knows exactly the weak spots."
And he is persistent. If he does not get you down with the first assault, he will commence a siege of attrition until you give in from
sheer exhaustion. Better banish the whole subject. Seek company
and discuss some irrelevant matter as, for example, what is going on
in Venice. Shun solitude. "Eve got into trouble when she walked in
the garden alone. I have my worst temptations when I am by myself."
Seek out some Christian brother, some wise counselor. Undergird
yourself with the fellowship of the church. Then, too, seek convivial
company, feminine company, dine, dance, joke and sing. Make yourself eat and drink even though food may be very distasteful. Fasting
is the very worst expedient. Once Luther gave three rules for dis-
pelling despondency: the first is faith in Christ; the second is to get
downright angry; the third is the love of a woman. Music was especially commended. The devil hates it because it is never contentious.
Luther's physician relates that on one occasion he came with some
friends for a musical soirée only to find Luther in a swoon; but when
the others struck up the song, he was soon one of the party. Home
life was a comfort and a diversion. So also was the presence of his
wife, when the devil assaulted him in the night watches. "Then I turn
to my Katie and say, 'Forbid me to have such temptations and recall
me from such vain vexations.'" Manual labor was a relief. A good

way, counseled Luther, to exorcise the devil is to harness the horse and spread manure on the fields. In all of this advice to flee the fray Luther was in a way prescribing faith as a cure for the lack of faith. To give up the argument is of itself an act of faith akin to the *Gelassenheit* of the mystics, an expression of confidence in the restorative power of God who operates in the subconscious while man occupies himself with extraneous things.

This explains why Luther liked to watch those who take life blithely, such as birds and babies. When he saw his little Martin nursing, he remarked, "Child, your enemies are the pope, the bishops, Duke George, Ferdinand, and the devil. And there you are sucking unconcernedly." When Anastasia, then four years old, was prattling of Christ, angels, and heaven, Luther said, "My dear child, if only we could hold fast to this faith." "Why, papa," said she, "don't you believe it?" "Christ," commented Luther, "has made the children our teachers. I am chagrined that although I am ever so much a doctor, I still have to go to the same school with Hans and Magdalen, for who among men can understand the full meaning of this word of God, 'Our Father who art in heaven'? Anyone who genuinely believes these words will often say, 'I am the Lord of heaven and earth and all that is therein. The Angel Gabriel is my servant, Raphael is my guardian, and the angels in my every need are ministering spirits. My Father, who is in heaven, will give them charge over me lest I dash my foot against a stone.' And while I am affirming this faith, my Father suffers me to be thrown into prison, drowned, or beheaded. Then faith falters and in weakness I cry, 'Who knows whether it is true?' "

Merely watching children could not answer that question. The encounter had to be resumed on the direct level. If Luther were disturbed about the state of the world and the state of the church, he could gain reassurance only through the recognition that as a matter of plain fact the situation was not bad. Despite the many pessimistic judgments of his later years, Luther could say, "I entertain no sorry picture of our church, but rather that of the church flourishing through pure and uncorrupted teaching and one increasing with excellent ministers from day to day."

At other times, the depression was with regard to himself. Had he been presumptuous in assuming that he alone was right, or if, as a matter of fact, he alone was right had he then been sufficiently bold? At the Wartburg he would pass from one of these doubts to the other. Astounding as it may appear to us, he seemed to himself to have been almost craven at the Diet of Worms. For the future he was resolved to sound the trumpet with no uncertain tone and much of his vehemence was a sort of reassuring penance. But Luther was the last man to suppose that any penance could satisfy God. Man is and remains a sinner. When depressed on this score the only recourse is not to deny the sin but to be unconcerned about it. Sin blithely. That is the real sense of the famous *pecca fortiter.* We are real sinners. Very well. But God can forgive us and still use us. So then, no mithering, but up and on.

But how if God is not disposed to forgive us? Is He gracious? Is He good? Is He just? These deepest of all problems were forever recurring. Where lies the answer? One never knows where, but always somewhere. To inquire after the starting point of Luther's theology is futile. It begins where it can. Christ himself appears variable, sometimes as a good Shepherd and sometimes as the avenging Judge. If then Christ appeared hostile, Luther would turn to God and would recall the first commandment, "I am the Lord thy God." This very pronouncement is at the same time a promise, and God must be held to His promises. "In such a case we must say, 'Let go everything in which I have trusted. Lord, thou alone givest help and comfort. Thou hast said that thou wouldst help me. I believe thy word. Oh, my God and Lord, I have heard from Thee a joyful and comforting word. I hold to it. I know Thou wilt not lie to me. No matter how Thou mayest appear, Thou wilt keep what Thou hast promised, that and nothing else.'" On the other hand, if God hides himself in the stormclouds which brood over the brow of Sinai, then gather about the manger, look upon the infant Jesus as he leaps in the lap of his mother, and know that the hope of the world is here. Or again, if Christ and God alike are unapproachable, then look upon the firmament of the heavens and marvel at the work of God who sustains them without pillars. Or take the meanest flower and see in the smallest petal the handiwork of God.

All of the external aids of religion are to be prized. Luther attached great importance to his baptism. When the devil assailed him he would answer, "I am baptized." In his conflicts with the Catholics and the radicals he reassured himself similarly by making appeal to his doctorate. This gave him authority and the right to speak.

But always and above all else the one great objective aid for Luther was the Scriptures, because this is the written record of the revelation of God in Christ. "The true Christian pilgrimage is not to Rome or Compostella, but to the prophets, the Psalms, and the Gospels." The Scriptures assumed for Luther an overwhelming importance, not primarily as a source book for antipapal polemic but as the one ground of certainty. He had rejected the authority of popes and councils and could not make a beginning from within as did the prophets of the inward word. The core of his quarrels with them was that in moments of despondency he could find nothing within but utter blackness. He was completely lost unless he could find something without on which to lay hold. And this he found in the Scriptures.

He approached them uncritically, from our point of view, but not with credulity. Nothing so amazed him in all the biblical record as the faith of the participants: that Mary credited the annunciation of the Angel Gabriel; that Joseph gave credence to the dream which allayed his misgivings; that the shepherds believed the opening of the heavens and the angels' song; that the wise men were ready to go to Bethlehem at the word of the prophet. There were three miracles of the Nativity: that God became man, that a virgin conceived, and that Mary believed, and the greatest of these was the last. When the wise men relied upon their judgment and went straight to Jerusalem without consulting the star, God lifted it out of heaven and left them bewildered to make inquiry of Herod, who then called his wise men and they searched the Scriptures. And that is what we must do when we are bereft of the star.

But this is just the point where Luther's lead begins to elude us. We can follow him well enough in the description of his distress. It is when he offers us this way out that we are cast down. Must we leave him now like some Virgil in Purgatory and seek in another the Beatrice who may be able to conduct us to Paradise? Perhaps a word of Luther may help us, after all, for he declared that the Gospel is not so much a miracle as a marvel, *non miracula sed mirabilia*. There is no better way to feel the wonder than to take Luther as guide. Let him

portray for us, with all his power and poignancy, the spiritual de-
spondencies of the biblical characters and the way in which they
were able to find the hand of the Lord.

Take, for example, Luther's portrayal of the sacrifice of Isaac by
Abraham. Save for the initial assumption that God commanded the
sacrifice and that the angel intervened in the end, all else is the record of an inner struggle which is not hard to translate into the story
of an emerging insight or an unfolding revelation. Hear Luther as he
expounds the tale:

> *Abraham was told by God that he must sacrifice the son of his old age
> by a miracle, the seed through whom he was to become the father of
> kings and of a great nation. Abraham turned pale. Not only would he
> lose his son, but God appeared to be a liar. He had said, "In Isaac shall
> be thy seed," but now he said, "Kill Isaac." Who would not hate a God
> so cruel and contradictory? How Abraham longed to talk it over with
> someone! Could he not tell Sarah? But he well knew that if he mentioned
> it to anyone he would be dissuaded and prevented from carrying out the
> behest. The spot designated for the sacrifice, Mount Moriah, was some
> distance away; "and Abraham rose up early in the morning and saddled
> his ass and took two of his young men with him and Isaac his son. And
> he clave the wood for the burnt offering." Abraham did not leave the
> saddling of the ass to others. He himself laid on the beast the wood for
> the burnt offering. He was thinking all the time that these logs would
> consume his son, his hope of seed. With these very sticks that he was
> picking up the boy would be burned. In such a terrible case should he
> not take time to think it over? Could he not tell Sarah? With what inner
> tears he suffered. He girt the ass and was so absorbed he scarcely knew
> what he was doing.*
>
> *He took two servants and Isaac, his son. In that moment everything
> died in him: Sarah, his family, his home, Isaac. This is what it is to sit in
> sackcloth and ashes. If he had known that this was only a trial, he would
> not have been tried. Such is the nature of our trials that while they last
> we cannot see to the end. "And on the third day Abraham lifted up his
> eyes and saw the place afar off." What a battle he had endured in those
> three days! There Abraham left the servants and the ass and he laid the
> wood upon Isaac and himself took the torch and the sacrificial knife. All
> the time he was thinking "Isaac, if you knew, if your mother knew that
> you are to be sacrificed." "And they went both of them together." The
> whole world does not know what here took place. They two walked to-
> gether. Who? The father and the dearest son; the one not knowing what
> was in store but ready to obey, the other certain that he must leave his
> son in ashes. Then said Isaac, "My father." And he said, "Yes, my son."*

And Issac said, "Father, here is the fire and here the wood, but where is the lamb?" He called him father and was solicitous lest he had overlooked something, and Abraham said, "God will himself provide a lamb, my son."

When they were come to the Mount, Abraham built the altar and laid on the wood, and then he was forced to tell Isaac. The boy was stupefied. He must have protested, "Have you forgotten: I am the son of Sarah by a miracle in her age, that I was promised and that through me you are to be the father of a great nation?" And Abraham must have answered that God would fulfill his promise even out of ashes. Then Abraham bound him and laid him upon the wood. The father raised his knife. The boy bared his throat. If God had slept an instant the lad would have been dead. I could not have watched. I am not able in my thoughts to follow. The lad was as a sheep for the slaughter. Never in history was there such obedience save only in Christ. But God was watching and all the angels. The father raised his knife; the boy did not wince. The angel cried, "Abraham, Abraham!" See how divine majesty is at hand in the hour of death. We say, "In the midst of life we die." God answers, "Nay, in the midst of death we live."

Luther once read this story for family devotions. When he had finished, Katie, his wife, said, "I do not believe it. God would not have treated his son like that." "But Katie," answered Luther, "He did."

Hear Luther also as he describes the passion of Christ. The narrative is placed on a most human level. We are reminded that the death of Christ was of all the most terrible because it was an execution. This means death at a known moment for one who is fully aware of what is involved. In old age the angel of death often muffles his wings and permits us to slip peacefully away. Jesus went to his death in full possession of his faculties. He suffered even more than did the malefactors. A robber was simply crucified, not at the same time reviled. To Christ were spoken words of raillery, "If you are the Son of God, come down." As if to say, "God is just. He would not suffer an innocent man to die upon a cross." Christ at this point was simply a man and it was for him as it is for me when the devil comes and says, "You are mine." After the reviling of Christ, the sun was darkened and the earth trembled. If a troubled conscience shudders at the rustling of a wind-blown leaf, how much more terrible must it have been when the sun was blotted out and the earth was shaken. Christ was driven to a cry of desperation. The words are recorded in the original tongue that we may sense the stark desolation: *Eli, Eli, lama sabachthani?* My God, my God, why hast thou forsaken me? But note this, the prayer of the forsaken began, "My God." The cry of despair was a confession of faith.

What wonder then that Luther, in the year of his deepest depression, composed "A Mighty Fortress Is Our God."

Suggestions for Additional Reading

Martin Luther, prolific writer and man of action, once remarked: "Every great book is an action and every great action is a book." He and the Reformation movement, in turn, have been the subjects of an enormous literature. An American scholar has estimated that more books have been written about Luther than about any other person with the exception of Christ. As a reflection of the current renaissance of Reformation studies, Gordon Rupp, a well-known British historian, notes, more books on Luther have appeared in England since the World War II than in all the preceding centuries. From this mass of material a few titles, predominantly in English, may be selected to serve as a guide to further reading on the special problems discussed in this book.

The most recent general history of the Reformation is Lewis W. Spitz, *The Renaissance and Reformation Movements* (Chicago, 1971). Another new and thorough account is that of Hans J. Hillerbrand, *Christendom Divided: The Protestant Reformation* (New York, 1971). A fascinating "eye-witness" account is Hans J. Hillerbrand, *The Reformation: A Narrative History Related by Contemporary Observers and Participants* (New York, 1964). Hillerbrand's *Men and Ideas in the Sixteenth Century* (Chicago, 1969) offers a sprightly discussion of the intellectual turmoil of the times. An excellent comprehensive survey of the entire period is Harold J. Grimm, *The Reformation Era, 1500–1650,* 2nd ed. (New York, 1965). Owen Chadwick, *The Reformation* (Baltimore, 1964) writes primarily as a church historian. Oskar Thulin, *Illustrated History of the Reformation* (St. Louis, 1967) provides an interesting visual tour of Lutherland. *The New Cambridge Modern History,* II, *The Reformation* (London, 1958), while not escaping some of the pitfalls of multiple authorship, is in general a substantial and dependable work. Though outdated in some respects, as in the liberal attention given to mere by-products of the Reformation, Preserved Smith's old classic, *The Age of the Reformation* (New York, 1930), is still not without value. Three brief accounts which will serve as good introductions to the period are: Roland H. Bainton, *The Reformation of the Sixteenth Century* (Boston, 1952); George L. Mosse, *The Reformation* (New York, 1953); and E. Harris Harbison, *The Age* of the Reformation (Ithaca, 1955). Gerhard Ritter, Die Neugestaltung Europas im 16. Jahrhundert (Berlin, 1950), is an outstanding synthesis of the century. Myron P. Gilmore, The World of Humanism (New York, 1952), is a brilliant account of the period preceding the Reformation. Attention may be directed here to Hajo Holborn's excellent volume on Germany during the Reformation, A History of Modern Germany, I, The Reformation (New York, 1959). Lewis W. Spitz, ed., The Protestant Reformation (Englewood Cliffs, New Jersey, 1966) offers key writings of the reformers in English translation.

In the absence of a comprehensive study of the historiography of the Reformation comparable to Wallace K. Ferguson's The Renaissance in Historical Thought: Five Centuries of Interpretation (Boston, 1948), recourse must be had to a number of bibliographical articles and books for further useful titles. Among these the following are particularly helpful: Roland H. Bainton, Bibliography of the Continental Reformation (Chicago, 1935); Bainton, "Survey of Periodical Literature in the United States, 1945–1951," Archiv für Reformationsgeschichte 43 (1952); Wilhelm Pauck, "The Historiography of the German Reformation in the Past Twenty Years," Church History 9 (1940); John Dillenberger, "Major Volumes and Selected Periodical Literature in Luther Studies, 1950–1955," Church History 25 (1956); Harold J. Grimm, "Luther Research Since 1920," Journal of Modern History 32 (1960); Lewis W. Spitz, "Current Accents in Luther Study: 1960–1967," Theological Studies 28 (1967), 549–573; Vilmos Vajta, ed., Lutherforschung Heute (Berlin, 1958); John T. McNeill, "Thirty Years of Calvin Study," Church History 17 (1948); Bard Thompson, "Zwingli Study Since 1918," Church History 19 (1950). Of great value is the annotated bibliography in Erich Hassinger, Das Werden des neuzeitlichen Europa, 1300–1600 (Brunswick, 1959). The comprehensive bibliography of German history in the century of the Reformation has no equal: Karl Schottenloher, Bibliographie zur deutschen Geschichte im Zeitalter der Glaubensspaltung, 6 vols. (Leipzig, 1933–1940). The Bibliographie de la Réforme 1450–1648 (Leiden, 1958) covers works on Germany and the Lowlands appearing between 1940 and 1955.

The classic controversy between Dilthey and Troeltsch over the essential nature of the Reformation and its relationship to the Renaissance has reechoed through the halls of learning down to the present time. Troeltsch elaborated upon his thesis in a number of writings including *The Social Teachings of the Christian Churches* (London and New York, 1931; new ed., 1949) and *Protestantism and Progress* (London and New York, 1912; new ed., Boston, 1958), a misleading title for his essay of 1911 on the significance of Protestantism for the origin of the modern world. The leading scholar to attack the views of Troeltsch was Karl Holl, who showed how revolutionary Luther's new evangelical insights were for man's relationship to God and that Luther's conception of faith active in love had broad social and cultural implications. One essay from Holl's famous volume *Gesammelte Aufsätze*, I, *Luther* (Tübingen, 1928) has appeared in paperback, *The Cultural Significance of the Reformation* (New York, 1959). The same sharp difference of interpretation is evident on the part of two contemporary theologians, Reinhold Niebuhr, who seems to accept Troeltsch's conclusions on Luther's cultural defeatism uncritically and without benefit of modern Luther research, and Wilhelm Pauck, a student of Holl, who has been strongly influenced by the neoorthodox theologian Karl Barth. Niebuhr's views may be found in his *Nature and Destiny of Man,* 2 vols. (London, 1941, 1943) and in *The Self and the Dramas of History* (New York, 1955). Pauck's criticism of Niebuhr is articulated in his article "Luther and the Reformation," *Theology Today* 3 (1946). See also Pauck's penetrating essay in *The Heritage of the Reformation* (Boston, 1950). Relevant to the problem is the article by Herbert Weisinger, "English Attitudes toward the Relationships between the Renaissance and the Reformation," *Church History* 15 (1945), a survey through the early nineteenth century. On the general question of the relationship of the Reformation to modern culture the following merit mention: Preserved Smith, "The Reformation 1517–1917," *Bibliotheca Sacra* 75 (1918); Charles Beard, *The Reformation of the Sixteenth Century in its Relation to Modern Thought and Knowledge* (New York, 1927); Ernest Schwiebert, "The Reformation from a New Perspective," *Church History* 17 (1948); and Hanns Rückert, "Die geistesgeschichtliche Einordnung der Reformation," *Zeitschrift für Theologie und Kirche* 52 (1955), a notable overall article.

On the relation of Renaissance humanism and the Reformation, see Bernd Moeller, "Die deutschen Humanisten und die Anfänge der Reformation," *Zeitschrift für Kirchengeschichte* 70 (1959): 47–61. Lewis

W. Spitz, *The Religious Renaissance of the German Humanists* (Cambridge, Mass., 1963), analyzes the thought of the leading figures from Agricola to Erasmus and Luther. Lewis W. Spitz, ed., *The Northern Renaissance* (Englewood Cliffs, N.J., 1972) makes available in English key writings of the major northern humanists. For the positive stance of many reformers toward Renaissance humanist culture see the chapter by Lewis W. Spitz, "Humanism in the Reformation," in Anthony Molho and John Tedeschi, eds., *Renaissance Studies in Honor of Hans Baron* (Florence, 1971), pp. 643–662. To the bibliography on the generations problem which is to be found in the notes of the article "The Third Generation of German Renaissance Humanists," in Archibald R. Lewis, ed., *Aspects of the Renaissance* (Austin, Texas, 1967), pp. 105–121, may be added the chapter by Bruno Bettelheim, "The Problem of Generations," in Erik H. Erikson, ed., *Youth: Change and Challenge* (New York, 1963), pp. 64–92. Robert Schwoebel, ed., *Renaissance Men and Ideas* (New York, 1971), contains chapters on "Luther as Scholar and Thinker" and "Printing and the Spread of Humanism in Germany: the Example of Albrecht von Eyb," the latter by Rudolf Hirsch.

The importance of economic causation for the Reformation is related conversely to the Weber-Tawney hypothesis regarding religion and the rise of capitalism, a special problem with a very extensive literature of its own. The nature of the Reformation as an effect is related very naturally to its causes. Opinion today ranges from the economic determinism of the Marxian dialectical materialists to the spiritual-psychic emphasis of Western idealists. Thus in his *Deutschland vor der Reformation* (Berlin, 1955), M. M. Smirin of Moscow University, winner of the Stalin Prize (second class) for history and a hero of red labor, tailors known material to the ritual utterances of Marx, Engels, Lenin, and Stalin, an approach reflected in the work of Leo Stern and other communist historians. Of interest in this connection are Friedrich Engels, *The Peasants' War in Germany* (London, 1934), and Karl Kautsky, *Communism in Central Europe in the Time of the Reformation* (London, 1897). A more historical piece of work, though heavily Marxist in tone and not too carefully done, is Roy Pascal, *The Social Basis of the German Reformation* (London, 1933). See also Gordon Rupp, *Patterns of Reformation* (Philadelphia, 1969) and Hans J. Hillerbrand, *A Fellowship of Discontent* (New York, 1967).

On Thomas Müntzer, the excellent work of Eric W. Gritsch, *Reformer Without a Church* (Philadelphia, 1967), is to be recommended. For sober accounts of the economic history of the Reformation era, see Herbert Heaton, *Economic History of Europe,* rev. ed. (New York, 1948), and *The Cambridge Economic History,* II (Cambridge, 1952). Sound basic studies of the economic and social conditions of the time include R. Ehrenberg, *Capital and Finance in the Age of the Renaissance* (New York, 1928); T. A. Lacey, *The Reformation and the People* (London and New York, 1929); P. Boissonade, *Life and Work in Medieval Europe* (New York, 1927); G. Unwin, *Industrial Organization in the Sixteenth and Seventeenth Centuries* (Oxford, 1904); F. C. Palm, *The Middle Classes* (New York, 1936); and John Nef, "Industrial Europe at the Time of the Reformation," *Journal of Political Economy* 49 (1941). A pioneer investigation intended to present neglected economic aspects of the Protestant revolt was Jacob Schapiro, *Social Reform and the Reformation* (New York, 1909). O. A. Marti, *Economic Causes of the Reformation in England* (New York, 1929), and James Mackinnon, *The Origins of the Reformation* (London, 1939) are both useful studies. The following distinguished church historians hold the social and economic factors to have been secondary to religious considerations: John Faulkner, "Was There Need of a Reformation?" *Lutheran Quarterly* 47 (1917); David Schaff, "The Origin and Purpose of the Protestant Reformation," *Lutheran Quarterly* 48 (1918); and C. M. Jacobs, "The Economic Background of the Reformation," *Lutheran Church Review* (1922). In a volume very useful to the neophyte, Carl Gustavson, *A Preface to History* (New York, 1955), discusses common errors of the amateur historian in assessing the causes of the Reformation.

The question of the relative importance of political factors and religious forces in determining the origin and development of the Reformation is of major importance. The tendency of recent scholarship has been to reemphasize the centrality of theology and the religious impulses at work. G. Barraclough, *The Origins of Modern Germany* (Oxford, 1947), and Karl Brandi, *The Emperor Charles V* (London, 1949), provide a good insight into the political background and imperial structure at the time of the Reformation. A direct critique of Lea's analysis is H. Thurston, "Lea on the Causes of the Reformation," *American Catholic Quarterly Review* 28 (1903). Norman Sykes, *The Crisis of the Reformation* (London, 1950), in brief scope emphasizes as negative causation abuses which weakened the church, much in the manner of A. C. Flick, *The Decline of the Medieval Church,* 2 vols. (London, 1930). Wallace K. Ferguson, "The Church in a Changing World," *American Historical Review* 59 (1953), describes the difficulties of the church as a traditional institution in an age of transition in economics, politics, and culture. Willy Andreas, *Deutschland vor der Reformation,* 5th ed. (Stuttgart and Berlin, 1948), portrays religious and cultural conditions in the empire on the eve of the Reformation. Lucien Febvre explores the question of the indigenous or derivative nature of the French Reformation and the religious forces at work in his important article "Une question mal posée: les origines de la réforme française et le problème général des causes de la réforme," *Revue historique* 161 (1929), reprinted in his *Au Coeur Religieux du XVIe Siècle* (Paris, 1957). Joseph Lortz, a pioneer in the Catholic effort at impartiality and ecumenicity, has published an English translation of his pioneer ecumenical Catholic history *The Reformation in Germany,* 2 vols. (New York, 1969). There has also been an English translation of his essay, *How the Reformation Came* (New York, 1964). Of interest in this connection are: "Die Reformation und Luther in katholischer Sicht," *Una Sancta* 10 (1955), and *Die Reformation als religiöses Anliegen heute* (Trier, 1948). The new objectivity and irenical spirit evident in Roman Catholic scholarship is reflected also in the work of French Dominican Yves Congar, *Vraie et Fausse Réforme dans l'Église* (Paris, 1950), recognizing Luther's spiritual greatness and seeking to determine on the basis of the sources why he broke with the church. The same approach is to be seen in Henry Daniel-Rops, *Histoire de l'Église du Christ,* IV, *L'Église de la Renaissance et de la Réforme* (Paris, 1955). See also, Richard Stauffer, *Luther Seen by Catholics* (Richmond, 1967), and Albert Brandenburg, *Martin Luther Gegenwärtig. Katholische Lutherstudien* (Munich, 1969). Two excellent articles by Protestant scholars stressing the positive religious element at work are Gerhard Ritter, "Lutheranism, Catholicism, and the Humanistic View of Life," *Archiv für Reformationsgeschichte* 44 (1953), and Erich Roth, "Martin Luther and the Continental Reformation," *Church Quarterly Review* (1952). Ritter's biography of Luther, which has appeared in several revised editions, has also been translated into English, *Martin Luther: His Life and Work* (New York, 1963). A good summary article on intellectual currents of the century is Roland H. Bainton, "Changing Ideas and Ideals in the Sixteenth Century," *Journal of Modern History* 8 (1936).

In addition to the many volumes of Karl Barth's *Church Dogmatics* (Edinburgh, 1936–1969) which have been translated into English, many of his monographs and collections of essays have also been published in English. Among them are *Credo,* with a foreword by Robert McAfee Brown (New York, 1962); *God Here and Now* (New York, 1964); *A Shorter Commentary on Romans,* 2nd ed. (Richmond, Va., 1960); *The Word of God and the Word of Man* (New York, 1957); *The Knowledge of God and the Service of God According to the Teaching of the Reformation, Recalling the Scottish Confession of 1560* (London, 1960); *The Humanity of God* (Richmond, Va., 1960); *The Epistle to the Romans* (London, 1965); *How I Changed My Mind* (Richmond, Va., 1966), with an introduction and epilogue by John D. Godsey; *Evangelical Theology, an Introduction* (New York, 1963); *Protestant Thought: from Rousseau to Ritschl* (New York, 1959); *Anselm: Fides quaerens intellectum* (Richmond, Va., 1960). Among the growing number of books on Karl Barth and his theology those deserving of special mention are Hans Urs von Balthasar, *The Theology of Karl Barth* (New York, 1971); Gerrit Cornelis Berkouwer, *The Triumph of Grace in the Theology of Karl Barth* (Grand Rapids, Mich., 1956); Georges Casalis, *Portrait of Karl Barth,* translated with an introduction by Robert McAfee Brown (Garden City, N.Y., 1963); Thomas Forsyth Torrance, *Karl Barth, an Introduction to His Early Theology, 1910–1931* (London, 1962).

The literature on the "young Luther's" personal and theological development is very extensive indeed. The most perceptive and sprightly biography of Luther is Roland H. Bainton, *Here I Stand: a Life of Martin Luther* (Nashville, 1951), available in a paperback edition. Ernest G. Schwiebert, *Luther and His Times* (St. Louis, 1951), is a larger and more cumbersome work, which, however, seeks to place Luther in his university environment and general cultural milieu. Readable and brief in scope is the popular biography by the Dutch historian W. J. Kooiman, *By Faith Alone* (New York, 1955). A lively life of Luther emphasizing the heroic days and early career as reformer rather than the last three lustra is the popular book of Richard Friedenthal, *Luther His Life and Times* (New York, 1970).

William H. Langer, in his presidential address to the American Historical Association, called upon historians to make more extensive use of psychological and psychoanalytical insights in historical interpretation, "The Next Assignment," *American Historical Review* 63 (1958). Several decades before, Preserved Smith had written an exploratory article which is still of interest as a pioneer effort, "Luther's Early Development in the Light of Psychoanalysis," *American Journal of Psychology* 24 (1913). Since then a Danish Catholic psychiatrist, Paul J. Reiter, has written two volumes trying to demonstrate that Luther was a manic depressive, *Luthers Umwelt, Charakter und Psychose* (Copenhagen, 1937–1941). Reiter, however, has virtually no knowledge of theology and developed his tendential thesis on the basis of unreliable data and many unproven assumptions. The study by the American psychiatrist Erik H. Erikson, *Young Man Luther,* excerpted in this present book, is much more able, objective, and balanced. Roland H. Bainton, however, in a keen critical review of Erikson's volume, "Luther: A Psychiatric Portrait," *Yale Review* (Spring 1959), takes exception to the author's methodology, presuppositions, and insufficient knowledge of theology, as well as of the mature Luther. Roland H. Bainton, "Psychiatry and History. An Examination of Erikson's 'Young Man Luther,'" *Religion in Life* 40 (Winter 1971): 450–478, provides a more extensive criticism of Erikson's approach. Eric Fromm, *Escape from Freedom* (New York, 1941), in his opening chapters attempts crudely and with only indifferent success to apply psychological analysis to the Germany of the sixteenth century.

A classic and straightforward account of Luther's early life by a leading church historian is Heinrich Boehmer's *Road to Reformation* (Philadelphia, 1946). James Mackinnon, *Luther and the Reformation, I, Early Life and Religious Development to 1517* (London and New York, 1925), may still be read with profit, although it necessarily does not benefit from the intensive research on the young Luther of these past decades. Robert H. Fife, *The Revolt of Martin Luther* (New York, 1957), is a huge volume examining every biographical detail, but innocent of theological insight.

Three British Luther scholars have contributed studies of great value: Gordon Rupp, *Luther's Progress to the Diet of Worms, 1521* (London, 1951) and *The Righteousness of God* (London, 1953), a reconsideration of Luther's character and work; and Philip Watson, *Let God Be God!* (Philadelphia, 1948), particularly in this connection the first chapter on Luther's theological development. A. G. Dickens, *Luther and the Reformation* (London, 1967), provides a clear brief account. Wilhelm Pauck, "Martin Luther's Faith," *Religion in Life* 16 (1946–1947), discusses Luther's interpretation of faith as a result of being acted upon by God, religion as "a perpetual crisis and an unceasing battle," and the *tentationes* as the agonies of faith. Very excellent is the work by the noted Heidelberg historian Heinrich Bornkamm, available in English, *Luther's World of Thought* (St. Louis, 1958). The prominent churchman Hanns Lilje has written an appreciative analysis of Luther and his message with an eye for its relevance to the modern world, *Luther Now* (Philadelphia, 1952). Two articles in German especially valuable as a commentary on Luther's own moving account of his road to the Reformation, 1545, are Ernst Stracke, *Schriften des Vereins für Reformationsgeschichte* (Leipzig, 1926), vol. 44, no. 140: "Luthers groszes Selbstzeugnis 1545 über seine Entwicklung zum Reformator historisch-kritisch untersucht"; and Heinrich Bornkamm, "Luthers Bericht über seine Entdeckung der *iustitia dei*," *Archiv für Reformationsgeschichte* 37 (1940). Luther's own writings are now being made available in English in the excellent new fifty-six volume American edition, *Luther's Works*, Philadelphia: Fortress Press, and St. Louis: Concordia Publishing House.